# ATLAS OF WINE

For M.J. and P.J.

# $\mathcal{A}$TLAS
# OF $\mathcal{W}$INE

## ALICE KING

VISCOUNT

# CONTENTS

This edition published in 1990 by
Viscount Books, an imprint of
the Octopus Publishing Group,
Michelin House, 81 Fulham Road, London, SW3 6RB

© Text Alice King 1989
© Illustration and design Hennerwood Publications Limited 1989

ISBN 0 600 567 648

Produced by Mandarin Offset – printed in Hong Kong

# INTRODUCTION

**B**UYING WINE IS LIKE playing a fruit machine – there are so many permutations and it can be difficult to find the winning combination. This book will help you to hit the jackpot every time you buy a bottle of wine.

Wine has been around almost as long as mankind, but don't worry, this is not a history book. It will bring you up to date with what's happening *now* in the wine world; who's making the best wines, and which are the most exciting regions to watch. With the huge choice of quality wine available there has never been a better time to buy.

Wine has a lot more to offer than the uninspiring dictionary definition of 'fermented grape juice'. It's amazing

*BELOW: Wine enhances any occasion. These three generations of the same family are enjoying lunch together outside in the sunshine.*

to think of the vast array of flavours and styles of wine that are produced from just one fruit – the grape. Wine is much more versatile than any other drink, and one can be found to suit every palate and pocket.

This book deals with the many different aspects of wine, in three parts. In the first part you'll go from grape to glass, stopping at the winery on the way, and end up choosing a wine that you'll be sure to enjoy.

You'll be able to identify the different grape varieties and, at long last, decipher even the most complicated looking label. And to ensure that you always have good bottles to hand I'll tell you how to store wine, even if you don't have a cellar. I'll also explain the secrets of matching food and wine, demonstrating why you should ignore some of the conventional rules.

The second part will help you follow the grape trail across the world, examining each area and region, pinpointing the best wines and producers, the vintages to buy and those to avoid. And we don't just look at the traditional area of Europe – the exciting New World wine-producing countries are covered as well.

Finally there is a quick-reference question-and-answer session, exploding some of the wine myths and helping you expand your knowledge by answering many frequently asked wine-related questions.

The great thing about wine is that you can always keep on experimenting. Even the same wine will change with time, and every day yet more new and exciting wines are available. I hope you will enjoy reading this book as much as you would enjoy a good glass of wine. You could even try doing both at once!

*OPPOSITE: Traditional wicker harvesting baskets piled high with grapes at Pernand-Vergelesses in the Côte de Beaune.*

# FROM GRAPE TO GLASS

As all home winemakers will know, making wine is relatively easy – in principle. The great wine producers of the world invest a great deal of time and thought into perfecting this process.

### ∾ MAKING WINE – FROM VINE TO WINERY DOOR ∾

Winemaking is an entirely natural process – pick any fresh fruit (plums, apples, blackberries or grapes), leave them together in a bowl and after a few days (or sooner if any of the skins are broken) they will start to ferment. If you've ever left fresh fruit in the window in summer and forgotten about it, you'll be able to verify this!

The process of fermentation is the same in any fruit. The natural yeast cells present on the fruits' skins produce enzymes that devour the natural fruit sugar and transform it into alcohol and carbon dioxide. Putting it more crudely, the yeast gobbles up the sugar and, once finished, burps in satisfaction, thus creating the carbon dioxide. While this is a natural process, it is essential that the winemaker controls it. Before his grapes even get to the fermentation stage, care has been taken during the vine's growing cycle to ensure the grapes are of the best quality.

*Pruning Riesling vines by hand with a pair of pneumatic secateurs in Bad Durkheim.*

*Defoliating the vines with a tractor in Puligny-Montrachet in Burgundy.*

*Picking bunches of Jurancon grapes by hand near Mussidan in the Dordogne. The wearing of sun hats is almost a necessity here in order to protect pickers from the hot sun.*

Careful pruning throughout the year ensures that quality has not been sacrificed for the sake of quantity. Top producers now will crop-thin (a process known as éclaircissage), cutting off bunches of immature grapes in the summer in order that those remaining on the vine get more light and more nourishment, and achieve more concentrated flavour. Spraying the vines with Bordeaux mixture (copper sulphate) and sometimes other chemicals as well is generally necessary to avoid mildew and rot while the grapes are developing. The best producers will use as few chemicals as possible, especially towards the end of the growing season.

Once picked, the bunches of grapes are taken to the pressing house as quickly as possible to avoid any unnecessary contact of the juice with the air (oxidation). In the traditional wine regions the cellar or winery is generally fairly close to the vineyards, so that oxidation is not too much of a problem. But in some New World areas

*ABOVE: Waiting to unload the trailers full of Airéen grapes at Señorio de los Llanos Winery in Valdepeñas in La Mancha.*

*Good wines should be bright and clear, although older wines may contain sediment. You can check if your wine is clear by holding it up to the light.*

the winery can be some distance away. For example, in New Zealand some of the best wineries transport the grapes from the east to the west coast of the North Island, a distance of some 150 miles. Extra care has to be taken in these circumstances.

After this, the methods of making red and white wine differ markedly.

## ∽ THE PRODUCTION OF RED WINE ∽

After harvesting, the grapes are transported to the pressing houses, usually in large plastic crates on the back of a lorry. After being weighed and tested for sugar content and acidity they are then de-stemmed and crushed. The best winemakers will go through a process of *triage* (picking over the grapes by hand) as the grapes come in, to eliminate any rotten or unripe grapes. Traditionally grapes were fermented together with stalks and all, but the current thinking is that the stalks introduce an undesirable harsh element of tannin into the wine.

The grapes and juice are then pumped into a fermentation vat where they wait patiently until the first, or 'alcoholic', fermentation begins. This is a powerful fermentation, and people are often surprised by the violent bubbling in the fermentation vat, rather like a fiercely bubbling stew.

When the weather is warm the alcoholic fermentation will begin almost immediately, but if it's cool it may not start for several days. If the winemaker wants to speed up the reaction he can either heat the vat or add some cultured yeasts. Having said that, the best European winemakers steer clear of using cultured yeasts, because recent research indicates that the natural yeasts found in the vineyards can contribute up to 20 per cent of the wine's flavour and character.

As the wine ferments in the vat the carbon dioxide produced in the process forces the grapeskins up to the top of the vat forming a 'cap', known in France as *le châpeau*. This 'cap' will normally take up the top quarter of the space in the vat.

It is the grapeskins, rather than the juice, that give wine its colour. All black *Vitis vinifera* grapes (see chapter 2) have white juice that is only coloured by the pigments found in the black skins. So if a red wine is going to have a good colour it is essential that the skins are kept in contact with the juice while it is fermenting. One way to enhance this is to push the 'cap' down, or pump the juice over it, a process known in France as *remontage*.

Long, slow fermentations produce the most fruit, freshness and aroma in a wine, while faster, hotter fermentations can produce more colour although sometimes at the expense of the freshness of the fruit. Uncontrolled and over-hot fermentations in warm weather will produce wine that tastes jammy and stewed. The skill of the winemaker is essential in controlling the temperature so that he gets the best of both worlds – good colour, good aroma, the right amount of tannin, fresh fruit and enough acidity. For red wine production most winemakers agree that a fermentation temperature of around 29.5°C (86°F) produces the best results, and those that can afford it equip their vats with sophisticated temperature control devices.

After the fermentation has finished the juice is drawn off from the vats. This is referred to as the 'free-run juice', or *vin de goutte*, while the deep-coloured juice that is extracted from the remaining pips and skins is known as the press wine, or *vin de presse*. A percentage of this may be added back to the wine at a later stage to add colour and more body if required. The vats can be either large wooden ones (traditional but now disappearing), glass-lined cement vats, epoxy resin vats or large stainless steel vats. The advantage of the latter is that the temperature can be controlled very finely, although some Bordeaux proprietors maintain that it is just as easy to control in the old large wooden vats, and besides, they look prettier!

At this stage, if the producer has vinified various different grape varieties (and this applies to virtually all red Bordeaux and Sauternes, Champagne, and New World red wines), he will need to decide what proportions to include in the final blend. This process is known as the *assemblage* in France.

Before making this irreversible decision with large quantities of wine, the winemakers will take samples and make trial blends in glass flasks. An enormous amount of skill is involved in this process – the wines are still very young and it takes an expert to forecast how they will taste when mature. Once this is done the blended wine will be left to settle in vats or barrels for a while before the next stage in the process.

The wine is then transferred into stainless steel vats or wooden casks where it undergoes its malolactic fermentation. This is a process whereby the hard malic acid (like that found in a sharp, green apple) is transferred into lactic acid, which is softer.

*ABOVE: Pressing down the grapeskin 'cap' and pumping juice over it to extract more colour at Beaulieu Vineyard in the Napa Valley, California.*

*After being weighed and tested for sugar content and acidity the harvested grapes are de-stemmed and crushed in large presses.*

*After fermentation is complete the juice is drawn off the vats. This is called 'free-run' juice or vin de goutte.*

The choice of stainless steel or wooden vats depends on the style of wine required. Most everyday drinking wines are put into stainless steel vats and bottled fairly quickly.

But if the producer is making a wine for long-term keeping or of extra high quality, he will often age the wine in small wooden barrels with a 225 litre capacity (known as *barriques* in Bordeaux), which are normally made of oak. The oak helps the wine mature by gently oxidizing it, but also gives it added subtleties of taste and smell, the most noticeable being a nuance of vanilla and spices. New oak barrels give more flavour than ones that have been used for ageing wine in previous years, and they also give the wine a certain amount of soft tannin. Different types of oak have varying effects on a wine, and European oak gives a subtler, less aggressive flavour than American oak. In addition, the degree of 'toasting' (burning the insides of the barrels) makes a significant difference to the wine's eventual flavour.

All the top Bordeaux châteaux, Burgundy producers and New World winemakers age their wines in new oak barrels, representing a significant investment in new barrels. Using 100 per cent new oak barrels can add as much as 10 per cent to the production cost, and in addition to that, some 10 per cent of the wine is lost by evaporation, simply disappearing into thin air! In Cognac they call this 'The Angels' Share'.

While in barrel or vat, all wines are 'fined' (a natural filtration process which removes suspended particles in the wine) to make them clear. They are also 'racked' (transferred from vat to vat or barrel to barrel) leaving behind the natural sediment, or lees, so that the wine is free of sediment when bottled.

*ABOVE: Racking Nebbiolo wine at Monforte d'Alba in Piedmont.*

*Monitoring the fermentation process at Château Pétrus in Pomerol.*

---

## WINE PRODUCTION – RED WINES

### Macération carbonique

This is the fermentation technique used extensively throughout the Beaujolais region, and in some other regions that make wine for early drinking.

Whole grapes are placed in a *sealed* vat and the grapes at the bottom are crushed by the weight of those on top. The juice from those crushed at the bottom starts fermenting, releasing warm carbon dioxide. This then rises up inside the vat, heating the unbroken grapes and starting a fermentation *inside* their skins. These eventually explode, releasing their juice that then blends with the existing juice to continue the natural fermentation process within the tank. Today, many wine producers add carbonic gas to the vats to speed up the process.

Wines produced using this method are low in tannin, soft, rounded and fruity and have a distinct aroma of bubblegum – in fact many people mistake the aroma of wines produced in this way for the Beaujolais grape, Gamay.

Apart from Beaujolais, producers in the south of France in areas like the Ardèche use this method as well as some in California, Australia and Italy. Some wines are made in this method and then blended with wine that has undergone a traditional fermentation.

*In Beaujolais, a different vinification style is used called macération carbonique.*

## ∾ THE PRODUCTION OF SWEET WHITE WINE ∾

The undistinguished majority of sweet wines are sweetened artificially by the addition of sugar. Top-quality sweet wines like Sauternes and Barsac, sweet Vouvray, top German wines like Beerenauslese, and late-harvested New World wines, however, cannot be contrived. The main difference in winemaking techniques between the top sweet wines of the world and dry whites comes at harvest time. The grapes are left on the vines until they become shrivelled and infected by *Botrytis cinerea*, a fungus known as 'noble rot'. At this stage the grapes have an extremely high natural sugar content, so high that much of the natural sugar cannot be converted into alcohol during the alcoholic fermentation – the yeast cells die of gluttony before they can finish their work! The excess sugar is left in the wine, making a luscious, honeyed liquid that can be sensational.

*Sémillion grapes infected by Botrytis cinerea.*

## ∾ THE PRODUCTION OF ROSE WINE ∾

Having already explained how black grapes can make white wine, there are no prizes for guessing how black grapes can make rosé wine. Instead of removing the skins from the juice directly after the grapes have been crushed, they are left in contact with the juice for a certain length of time. This can vary from just a few hours to around twelve, depending on the producer's required colour. This is how rosé is produced all over the world. The main exception to this rule are the Champagne producers who once used this method, although now most Champagne houses have switched to a different technique because of the difficulty in controlling the exact colour. They simply add red juice made from grapes grown in the Champagne area to the white Champagne, and in this way can make a rosé wine of a consistent colour year after year.

Rosés vary from very pale pink, to salmon pink, through to a much deeper, almost orangey, light red. All colours are correct – it's up to the producer's taste in each case.

## ∾ THE PRODUCTION OF SPARKLING WINE ∾

### The méthode champenoise

This is the way Champagne is made, as well as most other decent sparkling wines worldwide. After the usual first fermentation in the vat the still wine is put into a bottle with some extra yeast and sugar. This causes a second fermentation in bottle and the resulting carbon dioxide (responsible for those wonderful bubbles) is trapped inside, and the end result is a bottle of sparkling wine. The majority of well-known sparkling wines are made in this method, including Saumur, sparkling Vouvray, Spanish Cava, and some Californian sparklers like Schramsberg and Domaine Chandon. The chapter on Champagne gives a more detailed explanation of Champagne-making.

### Cuve close

This method of producing sparkling wine is also known as the tank method, or *charmat*. The majority of the cheaper sparkling wines are made by this method, the initial process of which is not dissimilar to that of *méthode champenoise*. Instead of the second fermentation taking place inside the bottle, *cuve close* wines undergo their second fermentation inside a sealed vat. The wine is then bottled under pressure at cold temperatures. The major advantage of this method is the speed with which the wine can be made, and the large amounts of wine that can be vinified at one go. Because it is less time-consuming it is a far less costly way of producing a sparkling wine than *méthode champenoise*. However, as with most things relating to wine, a little extra time spent brings benefits, and *cuve close* never makes as good a wine as that made by the *méthode champenoise*.

### Carbonation (or 'The bicycle pump' method)

This method is even cheaper than *cuve close*, because the wine does not go through a second fermentation. It is exactly the same process as used in all fizzy drinks – carbon dioxide is bubbled through the juice.

## ∾ THE PRODUCTION OF FORTIFIED WINE ∾

The term 'fortified wine' refers to its method of production, and does not suggest that you might be fortified by drinking it (although many people might argue that it does this as well).

## ∾ THE PRODUCTION OF DRY WHITE WINE ∾

The basics of white winemaking are the same as for red, except for one fundamental difference – achieving the required colour. As explained earlier, the flesh of *Vitis vinifera* grapes is white, so it is possible to make white wine from both black and white grapes. Indeed, the world's favourite and most stylish sparkling wine, Champagne, is generally made from two-thirds black grapes.

So how does the winemaker ensure the skins do not stain the juice? He follows the same procedure as you would if washing a sweater with an unfixed colour. Rather than leaving it soaking, you wash it quickly and remove it

*RIGHT: Stainless steel fermentation tanks at Mussbach Winzergenossenshaft co-operative in the Rheinpfalz.*

*BELOW: Claude Ricard in his barrel room at Domaine de Chevalier in Graves.*

from the water. This is exactly what the winemaker does. He crushes his grapes and immediately draws off the free-run juice from the colour-producing skins.

The juice is then cleaned and pumped into fermentation vats. This entails leaving the wine to rest so that the fine particles in suspension fall to the bottom of the vat. Other, more advanced, methods include filtering the juice or cleaning it by using a centrifuging process.

In the past fermentation vats used to be wooden, but today most winemakers ferment their white wines in stainless steel or glass-lined cement vats. In this way the crucial fermentation temperature can be finely controlled. To ensure maximum extraction of fresh fruit flavours many white wines are today fermented at cool temperatures of around 10° to 18°C (50° to 64°F). This produces squeaky-clean wines, a far cry from the tired, yellow, often maderized (oxidized wine that becomes similar to Madeira) white wines of the past.

After the fermentation is complete the wine is then fined and racked and can then be put into vat and bottled for early drinking. If a heavier, more complex style of wine is required it will be aged in oak barrels, the same principles applying as for red wines (see page 11). Any wines that have the word *sur lie* on their label, for example Muscadet, are not racked but merely left on their lees (the dead yeast cells) until they are bottled.

There have been many improvements in white wine-making technology over the last decade. Many white wines are now 'cold stabilized'; that is, before bottling the wine is taken down to a very low temperature and the natural tartrate crystals (that look like sugar granules) fall out of solution. If you find a wine with tartrates in it (this could happen if the temperature dropped dramatically during shipment or if you had left it in the freezer) don't worry, as the taste of the wine will be unaffected.

Fortified wines are made in the same way as normal wines, the difference being that alcohol is added at some stage of the process. Generally a neutral spirit is used, and it is this that makes sherry, port and madeira much stronger than table wines. Many dessert wines are also fortified, like the popular Muscat de Beaumes de Venise. Standard table wine has an average alcohol content of around 11 per cent to 12 per cent by volume whereas fortified wines are in excess of 17 per cent, and can be as high as 24 per cent. The stage at which the alcohol is added varies according to the wine, and this will be discussed further in the section on fortified wines (see pages 178-187).

### ∾ BOTTLING THE MAGIC ∾

Today most major producers have very fast, efficient mechanical bottling lines. The bottles are filled, corked, labelled and packed into boxes automatically.

Glass bottles are not the only containers in use these days. We now have cans (just like those used for fizzy drinks), tetra packs (like orange juice or milk cartons), plastic bottles and bag-in-box wines. The latter phenomenon started in Australia, where they had the sense to put good wines in the boxes from the outset. It has taken a few years for the rest of the wine-producing world to follow suit – they started by putting only the cheapest in the boxes – a disaster.

*There are delicious wines produced all over the world.*

---

### SULPHUR IN WINEMAKING

Sulphur helps stop grapes and wine oxidizing and is used in winemaking almost from start to finish. When the grapes first arrive in the pressing house powdered sulphur is added, as it is at several stages of the winemaking process. E.E.C. laws regulate the amount of sulphur permitted, although many of the best producers think that existing permitted levels are too high. But very few wines are made without sulphur and those that are tend to be undrinkable. Unfortunately some of the more traditional European winemakers, especially those that make white wines, have a heavy hand with sulphur and their wines can reek of rotten eggs when the bottle is opened. This unpleasant characteristic will also be present in the wine. It is rare to find a New World wine with this kind of fault.

---

### ORGANIC WINE

The increased consumer awareness of additives and chemicals in foods in general has extended its influence to wine. Perhaps the excessive use of sulphur by some producers has speeded up this trend.

An ever-increasing army of producers has been encouraged to make organic wines. Unfortunately there is still no precise legal definition of the term 'organic', although most growers generally interpret it as meaning that no artificial fertilizers or pesticides are used on the vines. Instead, producers often keep cattle or horses and use their manure, or grow nitrogen-rich grasses between the rows of vines, later ploughing them back into the soil. Even so, the majority of wines that are sold with the description 'organic' still contain some sulphur, added during the process of vinification. Particularly good examples of organic wines are made by Listel in the Camargue region of France near Montpellier, where ungrafted vines are grown in the sand and the manure of the local Camargue horses is used as fertilizer.

---

Despite the convenience of the newer forms of packaging, wine lasts much longer in glass bottles with corks in them than it does in any of these alternatives. If you regularly buy wine in a can, bag-in-box or tetra pack, it's worth buying them from a shop with a fast turnover. Alternatively, make a note of the date that you purchased these products and make sure they are not kept for more than a few months.

---

# The Grape Trail

*T*HERE IS ONE VERY SIMPLE WAY of determining whether or not you will like a wine before even opening the bottle – discover the grape variety from which it is made.

### ∾ KNOW YOUR GRAPE ∾

If you know any wine's predominant grape variety (and there almost always is one) you can latch on to particular taste characteristics that will be consistent whichever country the wine comes from. The current thinking is that 60 per cent of a wine's flavour comes from the grape variety, and only 40 per cent from the soil, yeasts and the way in which it is made. The only major exception to this rule is Beaujolais, because of the *macération carbonique* technique that is used to produce it.

In France, Italy and Spain, it is still comparatively rare to see the grape variety listed on the label although many other countries invariably now show it. And in recent years more and more producers worldwide have realized its importance. When the New World countries like Australia, California, and New Zealand jumped on the modern wine-producing bandwagon they quickly saw the attraction in marketing terms of stating the grape variety on the label. Wines made from single grape varieties are known as 'varietal' wines. Thanks to them the different grape varieties are now marketed internationally and it's easier to work out which ones are to your taste (and those which are not), making wine buying safer, yet more enjoyable at the same time. Instead of simply sticking to the same old favourites, you can experiment with wines from around the world, secure in the knowledge that you like the general flavour of the grape. The only problem with this is that many of the more traditional European wines from France, Italy and Spain simply do not state on the label the grape variety from which they are made. For instance, virtually all white Burgundy is made from the Chardonnay grape, and all red Côte d'Or Burgundy is made from the Pinot Noir. On the other hand, red Bordeaux can be made from a mixture of any two, three, four or five of Cabernet Sauvignon, Merlot, Cabernet Franc, Petit Verdot and Malbec, although one grape variety (normally Cabernet Sauvignon or Merlot) will be the most important.

You can very easily overcome this problem as every region in Europe grows its own favourite grape variety, and I shall be telling you about these throughout this section as well as throughout the rest of the book. All you need do is remember that white Burgundy, for example, is made from the Chardonnay grape, meaning that if you like the character of Chardonnay you are likely to enjoy a good white Burgundy.

In the wine-producing world there are literally hundreds of different grape varieties, but here the characteristics of those most often found, and which countries and areas produce them successfully will be discussed. The description of each grape variety begins with a brief synopsis of its characteristics for quick reference.

Oak-ageing, whilst not a characteristic of the grape itself, has such a profound effect on the wine's character that it has to be included here.

With this varietal knowledge at your fingertips you, too, can follow the grape trail.

### ∾ WHITE GRAPES ∾

#### CHARDONNAY

STYLE: Dry; light to full; still and sparkling.
SUITABILITY FOR LONG-TERM KEEPING: Very good, especially the top wines.
OAK-AGED?: Normal for top Chardonnays.
WHERE GROWN SUCCESSFULLY: France (Burgundy, Champagne, Jura, Ardèche, Loire), North America (California, Oregon, New York State, Canada), South America (Chile), Australia, New Zealand, Italy (Sud-Tyrol), Spain (Penedés), Germany, Bulgaria, South Africa, India, China, Yugoslavia, Lebanon.

Chardonnay is today's most fashionable grape variety, in the eyes of both producers and consumers. Its claim to fame is in the great white wines of Burgundy – Chablis,

*CHARDONNAY*

Corton-Charlemagne, Meursault and Montrachet, for example. However, it's still unusual to find the word Chardonnay on the label of a bottle of white Burgundy.

Chardonnay is a relatively easy grape variety to grow and, because the world seems to love it, producers in virtually every wine-producing country have planted it. It is tremendously versatile, both in where it can be grown, and in the different styles of wine that it can produce. Chardonnay on its own, without being aged in oak barrels, has a flavour of white currants and makes dry, medium- to full-bodied wine, depending on where it is grown. But these characteristics change dramatically when the wine is aged in oak barrels. It takes on a much richer, deeper texture with buttery, toasted flavours and overtones of vanilla and spices. The best Chardonnays that have been aged in oak barrels can last for several decades.

This grape is not only responsible for some of the greatest still white wines in the world, it also produces the world's finest sparkling wine – Champagne. Chardonnay is one of only three permitted grape varieties (along with Pinot Noir and Pinot Meunier) grown in Champagne, and any Champagne called 'Blanc de Blancs' is made entirely from Chardonnay.

Chardonnay's popularity has something to do with its versatility of style. In its 'homeland' of Burgundy it produces almost every variation: relatively simple, straightforward wines in the Côte Chalonnaise (Rully, Mercurey); more elegant, sometimes powerful wines in Chablis.

It can produce light, undemanding wines like those from the Ardèche or light wines with a bit more body like those from Italy. Most of these wines are not oak-aged.

It is the New World producers who have done the most for Chardonnay in recent years. Their wines tend to be heavier than the traditional European Chardonnays, and are almost always aged in oak. The first Californian wines were very full, and often did not have enough acidity to balance them, but they have improved considerably and there are now some excellent wines. Australia seems to produce more high-quality Chardonnay than any other country, and now New Zealand is getting into the act with some stunning cooler-climate wines. There does not seem to be any stopping the rise and rise of Chardonnay.

### CHENIN BLANC

STYLE: Dry to sweet; light to full-bodied; sparkling and still.
SUITABILITY FOR LONG-TERM KEEPING: Can be good, but only for the top sweet or potentially sweet wines.
OAK-AGED?: Sometimes.
WHERE GROWN SUCCESSFULLY: The Loire (Vouvray, sparkling Saumur, Crémant de la Loire, Bonnezeaux, Savennières, Coteaux du Layon, Quarts de Chaume), South Africa, New Zealand, Australia, California, Chile.

Chenin Blanc can produce both dry and sweet wines, sometimes with considerable class, although when grown in cool climates it exhibits raspingly harsh acidity when young. Because of this factor it is often misunderstood, and most people do not realize that by keeping a bottle of decent Chenin for a few years they could have a wonderful wine in their glass.

It is difficult to describe Chenin Blanc's taste. The most noticeable characteristic is its high acidity, which can completely hide the ripe, sweet fruit lurking beneath it. But once you get behind the acidity the flavour is earthy, with honeyed, flowery overtones. And because Chenin Blanc is not as fashionable as Chardonnay it is generally very reasonably priced.

Early picked Chenin Blanc makes the crisp, dry, fairly simple white wines that we know so well from the Loire Valley in Northern France, from where it is supposed to have originated. Basic Anjou Blanc is made from Chenin, although now the tendency in the Loire Valley is to blend in a percentage of other grapes such as Sauvignon or Chardonnay to give it more character. These straightforward wines are designed for early drinking and are not oak-aged.

In my view the greatest wines made from the Chenin Blanc grape are the luscious, sweet wines from the Loire including Vouvray, Coteaux du Layon, Bonnezeaux and Quarts de Chaume. Wines like this can last for centuries, and I have enjoyed sensational wines well past their fiftieth birthday from some of Vouvray's top producers.

Chenin Blanc is grown very successfully throughout South Africa, where it is known as Steen, and modern cold fermentation techniques get rid of the earthiness it exhibits in the Loire. A few producers in South Africa are now making excellent sweet Chenins. Other countries successfully producing it include New Zealand, California and Australia, where it is often oak-aged.

The Chenin Blanc is one of the few grapes that actually seems to thrive in cold climates like the Loire and New Zealand – maybe English wine producers ought to try growing it too.

*CHENIN BLANC*

### GEWURZTRAMINER

STYLE: Off-dry to sweet; light to full-bodied; still.
SUITABILITY FOR LONG-TERM KEEPING: Good for the best qualities and sweet wines.
OAK-AGED?: Rarely.
WHERE GROWN SUCCESSFULLY: Alsace, Germany, Italy, New Zealand, Australia, California, Spain (Torres), Argentina. Gewürztraminer is probably the most flavourful white grape, and one which is difficult to disguise. The only

*GEWÜRZTRAMINER*

is much more aromatic and actually has some character. Italy produces some interesting wines from this variety, as does Austria and Switzerland. In England's first attempt at a wine-growing renaissance, it was planted widely but modern successful English growers prefer other, more individual grape varieties like Reichensteiner, Huxelrebe and Schönburger. Müller-Thurgau's naturally low acidity makes it a favourite with those who don't want their wines to make any bold statements.

*MULLER-THURGAU*

other grape that comes close to it in intensity is the Muscat. One whiff of a Gewürztraminer and you might think that you were smelling an exotic fruit salad. The bouquet is a mouth-watering blend of all sorts of tropical fruits – melons, mangoes and lychees are all there. And on top of all that, it has an added spiciness to it, almost a sweet pepperiness. Indeed, *Gewürz* means spice in German.

The skin of the Gewürztraminer grape is very tinted, giving a deep golden colour to many of is wines. Unlike Chardonnay, which has such popular appeal, Gewürztraminer is a grape that you will either love or hate. Because of its high degree of natural sugar it can make very sweet wines or off-dry wines. In France it is mainly grown in Alsace, where it is fermented dry, although the 'sweet' aroma and flavour still comes through. Other countries that grow Gewürztraminer successfully include Germany, Austria, and New Zealand.

If you see Gewürztraminer with *Sélection de Grains Nobles* on the label, expect the wine to be very sweet – it will have been made from grapes which were left on the vines until all the moisture in the grape has dried up, concentrating the natural sugar content to remarkable degrees. *Vendange Tardive* wines (literally 'late picked') will always be high in alcohol and often sweet. More recently there have been some sensational examples of lusciously sweet Gewürztraminer from New Zealand.

## MULLER-THURGAU

STYLE: Dry to sweet; light to full-bodied; still.
SUITABILITY FOR LONG-TERM KEEPING: Very poor.
OAK-AGED?: No.
WHERE GROWN SUCCESSFULLY: Germany, Italy, Austria, Switzerland, New Zealand.

Müller-Thurgau is the grape that most fans of ordinary German wine knock back all the time without realizing. The wines tend to be bland, dry and fairly innocuous. They don't have much flavour and wouldn't offend anyone, but they rarely titillate the wine-lover's palate. At one time it was thought that this grape was a cross of the Riesling and Silvaner grapes, but however many times viticulturists try to cross the two varieties they never come up with anything like the Müller-Thurgau of today.

Although very widely planted in Germany it is more successful in some other countries like New Zealand, where it

## MUSCADET

STYLE: Bone dry; light; still.
SUITABILITY FOR LONG-TERM KEEPING: Very poor.
OAK-AGED?: Not normally.
WHERE GROWN SUCCESSFULLY: Pays Nantais (France).

Muscadet is the name both of the grape and the wine which is made in the Loire Valley's Pays Nantais, surrounding Nantes. It is also known as the Melon de Bourgogne and is thought to have originated in the Burgundy area. Apart from the Loire valley in France this grape is hardly grown elsewhere, although recently the Californians have discovered that a grape they knew as Pinot Blanc was remarkably similar to the Muscadet grape, according to Jancis Robinson, MW. It is one of the few grape varieties that can survive the cold Atlantic weather conditions of the Pays Nantais and needs very little sunshine. It is a grape that is naturally high in acidity and produces crisp, dry, white wines that generally have little aroma. Muscadet is best drunk young.

*MUSCADET*

## MUSCAT

STYLE: Off-dry to sweet; light to full-bodied; still and sparkling.
SUITABILITY FOR LONG-TERM KEEPING: Good for the richer wines.
OAK-AGED?: No.
WHERE GROWN SUCCESSFULLY: Alsace, Rhône, South-West France, Australia, California, Madeira, Portugal, South Africa, Argentina, Chile, Spain.

*MUSCAT*

Muscat is the 'grapiest' grape of all. This might sound silly, but it is one of the few that really smells like the taste of a table grape. It is the only grape variety that can possibly be confused with Gewürztraminer because of its floral aroma, but it has a more grapey smell than the Gewürztraminer, and is somewhat richer.

Muscat flourishes all over the world, and in many different climates. It can be found in the cold depths of Germany and Alsace in France, as well as in much warmer climates such as Australia and California. There are hundreds of different varieties of Muscat, but they all exhibit the same type of distinctive grapey aroma and flavour. Muscat has become fashionable with the current popularity of Muscat de Beaumes de Venise, a fortified wine produced in the south of France; similar wines come from Rivesaltes and Frontignan.

Australians have been making the aromatic, heavy and sticky liqueur Muscats for many years – it is so rich that one bottle will serve about twenty people.

Muscat does not make only rich, sweet, cloying wine. Producers in both Portugal and Australia have produced fabulous off-duty Muscats, which are zippy and with enough acidity, but retain the up-front grapey fruitiness of the Muscat grape. Many people who assume that they just like medium-dry wines are delighted if you wean them on to a dry Muscat. Unlike many of the bland, anonymous, medium-sweet wines on the market, dry Muscats have plenty of character.

## PINOT BLANC

STYLE: Dry to medium-dry; light; still.
SUITABILITY FOR LONG-TERM KEEPING: Poor.
OAK-AGED?: Sometimes.
WHERE GROWN SUCCESSFULLY: Alsace, Germany, Italy (Alto Adige), California.

Pinot Blanc is grown mainly in France (Alsace) and Ger-

many, and is thought to have mutated from Pinot Noir, the red grape of Burgundy. It is also grown in Italy, where for some time producers confused it with Chardonnay. It produces wines without any particularly strong aromas and traditionally with a relatively bland taste, although the best modern examples have good acidity and fruit.

Recent experiments in both Germany and California have shown the Pinot Blanc more in its true light. Just like Chardonnay, it can improve dramatically if aged in oak barrels – the wine takes on a vanilla flavour that combines well with the acidity and fruit in the grape. And in Italy producers are making interesting wines with it in the Alto Adige region.

Pinot Blanc from Alsace can be delicious, particularly when you are not sure quite what to drink and do not want the overt grapiness of the Muscat or the spiciness of the Gewürztraminer.

Look out for the Pinot Blanc – in the past it has been unfairly overlooked and could well make a revival if and when the world becomes bored with its pet grape of the moment, the Chardonnay.

*PINOT BLANC*

## RIESLING

STYLE: Dry to sweet; light; still.
SUITABILITY FOR LONG-TERM KEEPING: Good for the best medium-sweet or sweet wines.
OAK-AGED?: Can be.
WHERE GROWN SUCCESSFULLY: Germany, Alsace, California, Italy (Alto Adige), Australia, Yugoslavia, Switzerland, Hungary, South Africa, New Zealand, Czechoslovakia, Chile, Argentina.

The first thing to establish about Riesling is how to pronounce it. It's *Reece-ling*, and not the commonly heard 'Rice-ling'. Riesling is so often blended with other bland German grape varieties that many people now associate it only with uninteresting wines;.but Riesling is the king of the German grape varieties and if more producers were to return to the tradition of producing pure, low-yield Riesling wines, German wines would be more interesting and perhaps regain the reputation they deserve.

Wine made from the Riesling is fairly oily, with a slightly musky/petrolly aroma, and a citrus tang of acidity on the palate. Both sweet and dry wines (and every stage between) are made, and the best (and sweetest) are those

*RIESLING*

which have been late-picked and affected by noble rot. For a classic mouthful, in every sense of the word, try a really good German Beerenauslese or Trockenbeerenauslese from a great vintage like 1976 or 1983.

The Riesling is grown extensively throughout Germany, and in many other parts of the world. It is a hardy grape variety and can survive great extremes of temperature.

Try some of the top German wines made from pure Riesling and you will see why it is such a shame that it does not enjoy the credit it deserves – perhaps it's due for a revival!

## SAUVIGNON BLANC

STYLE: Dry (but sweet in Sauternes); light to full-bodied; still.

SUITABILITY FOR LONG-TERM KEEPING: Poor apart from sweet wines.

OAK-AGED?: Not in Europe (apart from Sauternes) but often in the New World.

WHERE GROWN SUCCESSFULLY: France (Loire, Sancerre, Bordeaux, Duras), Italy, New Zealand, Australia, California, Oregon, Bulgaria, Chile, Argentina, South Africa.

Sauvignon Blanc is one of those grapes that, like Gewürztraminer, has a very distinctive aroma. It has been likened to all sorts of things, chiefly gooseberries and cat's pee being the most commonly heard. (And if you don't believe that, just smell a young, fresh Sancerre.)

When vinified by modern techniques Sauvignon Blanc produces crisp, dry wines that are green and grassy with a zippy flavour. It's the sort of unripe fruit flavour (though not unpleasant) you would find in a crisp, green, slightly sour apple such as a Granny Smith. It is the kind of wine that you have to be expecting when you drink it, otherwise its sharp acidity can come as something of a shock to the palate. Sauvignon Blanc can react well to oak-ageing, provided there is enough body to back it up, and many of the New World Sauvignons use this technique to good effect.

Most people know Sauvignon Blanc in the form of French Loire wines like Sancerre or Pouilly-Fumé – also from the same region are the less well-known Quincy, Reuilly, Sauvignon de Touraine and Menetou-Salon. It has many other facets, however, and is widely grown throughout the world.

Bordeaux producers have comparatively recently recognized the potential in Sauvignon to produce really good crisp, dry white wines made by the modern method of cold fermentation, particularly in the Entre-Deux-Mers region. And Sauvignon is essential to the great dry white wines of the Graves, as well as the stunning sweet wines of Sauternes and Barsac when it is affected by 'noble rot'.

California has been taking the Sauvignon grape very seriously, and Robert Mondavi and others have made great Fumé Blancs (the wine's name in North America). New Zealand Sauvignons are particularly fine, as are those from Torres in Chile. Most of the best ones are matured in new oak barrels.

But it's not all that easy to make good Sauvignon Blanc in warmer climates – the grapes need to be picked relatively early so that they retain their characteristic acidity. There's nothing worse than drinking a Sauvignon Blanc when the grapes have been allowed to ripen too much – the resultant wine is dull and flabby.

## SEMILLON

STYLE: Dry to sweet; medium to full-bodied; still.

SUITABILITY FOR LONG-TERM KEEPING: Excellent.

OAK-AGED?: Often.

WHERE GROWN SUCCESSFULLY: Bordeaux, Australia, Chile, South Africa, Romania, Argentina, New Zealand.

*SEMILLON*

*SAUVIGNON BLANC*

Although Sémillon does not enjoy the international superstar fame of its more high profile cousin Chardonnay, it can make comparable wines and is in fact the second most widely planted grape variety in the whole of France.

Sémillon produces full-bodied, flavourful wines when expertly vinified and, when aged in oak, can produce complex dry wines with a lanolin-like flavour and texture, balanced by zippy, limey, melony fruit.

In France Sémillon is grown in the Graves region, where it is blended with Sauvignon Blanc and produces some of the finest dry white wines in the world. Unfortunately, some of the most boring Sémillons in the world also come from the Graves, as still not enough producers are taking advantage of the grape's enormous potential. Sémillon is also blended with Sauvignon Blanc to make fabulous sweet Sauternes and Barsac. It is ideal for the latter because the grapes' thin, fragile skins are easily affected by 'noble rot', essential for the production of Sauternes.

Sémillon does particularly well in Australia where it is generally oak-aged and sold as a single varietal. And in California it is becoming more popular, especially when blended with the Sauvignon grape, as in the Graves. Sémillon deserves a climb up the popularity charts, and I feel it will be in the not too distant future.

### SILVANER

STYLE: Dry to medium sweet; light to medium-bodied; still.
SUITABILITY FOR LONG-TERM KEEPING: Poor.
OAK-AGED?: No.
WHERE GROWN SUCCESSFULLY: Alsace, Germany, England.

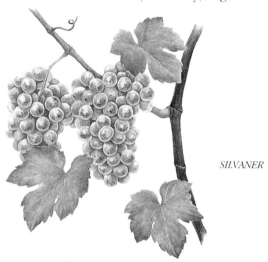

*SILVANER*

The Silvaner grape is grown mainly in Germany and unlike the Müller-Thurgau it has high acidity, but not much aroma. Its zippy aroma is not always backed up by a strong fruit flavour, although in Alsace in France (where it is known as Sylvaner) it tends to have a spicy fruit flavour that makes it a pleasant everyday drinking wine.

### TREBBIANO

STYLE: Dry; light; still.
SUITABILITY FOR LONG-TERM KEEPING: Poor.
OAK-AGED?: No.
WHERE GROWN SUCCESSFULLY: France (Cognac, Armagnac, Entre-Deux-Mers, the Midi), Italy.

Have you ever tasted wine or spirits made from Trebbiano? Most people would automatically answer no, but they would probably be wrong. Trebbiano produces more

wine than any other single grape variety in the world. Known in Italy as Trebbiano, it flourishes under a variety of other names, the most common being Ugni Blanc, found in the south of France and Cognac, where it is also known as the St Emilion.

*TREBBIANO*

It is Italy's most important grape variety, although it certainly does not produce the best wines. It appears in wines like Bianco di Custoza as Trebbiano Toscano and in Gambellara as Trebbiano di Soave. It's also used extensively in Central Western Italy in Frascati, Orvieto and Est!, Est!!, Est!!! It is even a permitted grape variety in the production of one of Italy's most popular red wines, Chianti.

Despite its prolific distribution Trebbiano is denied international stardom for the simplest reason – its unattractive taste. It is high in acidity, short on the palate and does not have any memorable or notable aroma and flavour. The French, particularly in the Cognac and Armagnac regions, have the right idea – they distil the vast majority of their production to make the well-known (and delicious) spirits of the same names.

### VIOGNIER

STYLE: Dry; medium to full-bodied; still.
SUITABILITY FOR LONG-TERM KEEPING: Very good.
OAK-AGED?: Yes.
WHERE GROWN SUCCESSFULLY: The Rhône.

*VIOGNIER*

Although not widely planted, the Viognier grape produces some of the rarest and most sought-after white wines of France. You will hardly ever see the name on the label, and it is mainly grown in France's Rhône Valley.

Viognier is a highly individual grape with a slightly peachy aroma which ranges from dry to sweet, but is always full-bodied. It is at its best in the wines of Condrieu and those of Château-Grillet. It is also allowed to be blended into the top red Rhône, Côte Rôtie.

## ∽ RED GRAPES ∽

### CABERNET FRANC

STYLE: Light to medium-bodied.
SUITABILITY FOR LONG-TERM KEEPING: Can be good.
OAK-AGED?: Sometimes (especially when blended in Bordeaux).
WHERE GROWN SUCCESSFULLY: Bordeaux, the Loire (Bourgeuil, Saumur-Champigny, Chinon), Italy, California, Hungary, Romania, Yugoslavia, Bulgaria.

*CABERNET FRANC*

Unfortunately the Cabernet Franc grape spends most of its life being overshadowed by the Cabernet Sauvignon. This is totally unfair, as it is an important component of any Bordeaux blend. Those who dismiss Cabernet Franc as being merely a poor relation of Cabernet Sauvignon should take into account the very high proportion of Cabernet Franc that goes into the blends that make up two of the greatest wines of St Emilion: Château Cheval-Blanc and Château Figeac.

Cabernet Franc has a much more earthy aroma and flavour than Cabernet Sauvignon, an almost herbaceous edge to it. I often think that if you taste Cabernet Franc with your eyes closed it smells quite similar to the white grape variety, Sauvignon Blanc, because of the grassy smell that the two grapes share. It has an aroma and flavour of red fruits, rather than the blackcurrants found in Cabernet Sauvignon, and a more earthy, raspberry-like aroma. Cabernet Franc is lower in acidity and tannin than its more highly revered brother and therefore produces wines that can be more appealing when young. It is a grape that blends well with others, and in particular with the Merlot in St Emilion and with Merlot and Cabernet Sauvignon in the Médoc and Graves.

Cabernet Franc comes into its own in the northerly region of the Loire Valley in France. Here it makes the best red wines in the Loire, Chinon, Bourgueil and Saumur Champigny, wines which can be enjoyed while young or which can mature well in bottle. As it develops with age, Cabernet Franc takes on more of the flavour of an old Cabernet Sauvignon-based wine. In the Loire Valley Cabernet Franc also makes some excellent rosé wines, simply known as Cabernet d'Anjou.

Outside France Cabernet Franc is widely planted in north-east Italy, where it produces soft, lightweight wines for everyday quaffing. Few sightings have been reported elsewhere, although the Californians are beginning to plant it to blend in with their Cabernet Sauvignon wines.

### CABERNET SAUVIGNON

STYLE: Medium to full-bodied.
SUITABILITY FOR LONG-TERM KEEPING: Outstanding, especially for the top wines.
OAK-AGED?: Often, especially the top wines.
WHERE GROWN SUCCESSFULLY: France (mainly Bordeaux, also Loire), California, Australia, Bulgaria, Spain, Portugal, Italy, Argentina, Chile, South Africa, Yugoslavia, Romania, Lebanon.

Cabernet Sauvignon is the red blood-brother of Chardonnay, the wine-drinker's favourite white grape. Like Chardonnay, Cabernet Sauvignon is easy to grow, so the producers like it as well.

Cabernet Sauvignon initially found fame as one of the three principal grape varieties that make red Bordeaux, or claret, as it is often known. However, its current fame in Britain is probably due to the delicious Cabernet Sauvignons from Bulgaria, bought in containerloads by the wine-drinking public.

Cabernet Sauvignon has a very distinctive aroma and taste of fresh, ripe blackcurrants. If you are given a wine to taste blind (i.e. not knowing what it is) and it smells like alcoholic blackcurrant juice, 90 per cent of the time you can safely bet that it is made from Cabernet Sauvignon. Top Cabernet Sauvignons can also take on eucalyptus, minty aromas and flavours (epitomized by Heitz Martha's Vineyard in California), adding to their complexity.

Cabernet Sauvignon, like many of the world's great grape varieties, demonstrates its greatest potential when it has been aged in oak barrels. It takes on cedary, spicy flavours with overtones of vanilla, cinnamon and cloves. All the best clarets go through this process, as do the top New World Cabernet Sauvignons.

Cabernet Sauvignon has the best potential of any grape for ageing in bottle, and most of those fabulous clarets from the 19th, and even 18th, centuries that fetch such mind-boggling prices at auction are made from it. Indeed, most claret is made to be kept for at least five years (or 15 to 20 in the case of the best ones) before it is drunk. As it matures, it becomes softer and less tannic, the blackcurrant flavour becoming less pronounced and more subtle, complex flavours taking over.

In Bordeaux the Cabernet Sauvignon is always blended with at least two other grapes, primarily the Merlot and Cabernet Franc. But many of the newer producers like

*CABERNET SAUVIGNON*

Cabernet Franc. But many of the newer producers like Australia, California and Bulgaria do not blend. One of the reasons is that in Bordeaux the Cabernet Sauvignon tends to produce less sweet wines than in the hotter climates of the New World.

Many other parts of the world are now planting Cabernet Sauvignon successfully, including Spain, Portugal, Italy (especially Sassicaia), as well as countries as far-flung as China and Japan, Chile, and South Africa. Even Lebanon has some plantings that go into the blend of Serge Hochar's remarkable Château Musar. It is a grape to follow if you like well-flavoured reds that are not too bitter and that have a very slight sweetness of fruit underneath the dry flavour.

## GAMAY

STYLE: Light to medium-bodied.
SUITABILITY FOR LONG-TERM KEEPING: Normally poor.
OAK-AGED?: No.
WHERE GROWN SUCCESSFULLY: France: Beaujolais, Loire, Ardèche.

Every year vast amounts of Gamay are knocked back unknowingly in the form of Beaujolais Nouveau. For this is the grape all Beaujolais, from Beaujolais Nouveau up to top quality single cru wines (like Fleurie or Juliénas), are made from. Gamay is the archetypal fruity grape, high in acidity and low in tannin – ideal for drinking when young. But more than any other grape variety, many of the characteristics attributed to Gamay are actually the result of the way in which the grapes are vinified. The technique known as *macération carbonique* (see page 11) is used for most Beaujolais production, and results in low tannin, masses of fruit and a distinctive bubblegum flavour.

*GAMAY*

The classic examples of Gamay at its best are the Beaujolais crus (see page 83), wines which can last and improve for a surprisingly long time, as much as 15 years in a good vintage.

Gamay is also produced in the Loire Valley (in wines like Gamay de Touraine) where it produces lighter wines than Beaujolais. It is also grown successfully in the south of France, where again the name appears on the label, being sold as Gamay de l'Ardèche.

Other supposed sightings of Gamay in the wine-producing world proved to be incorrect when the Californians realized that the grape they had been calling by that name was in fact a clone of the red Burgundy grape, the Pinot Noir.

## GRENACHE

STYLE: Medium-bodied
SUITABILITY FOR LONG-TERM KEEPING: Poor.
OAK-AGED?: Sometimes.
WHERE GROWN SUCCESSFULLY: France (Rhône, Provence), Spain, Australia, California.

*GRENACHE*

Grenache originated in Spain, where it is known as Garnacha, and is one of the most widely planted grape varieties in Spain's best known red wine-producing region, Rioja. It is also found extensively in the southern part of France's Rhône Valley.

The wines it produces are relatively light, low in tannin and certainly not suitable for lengthy keeping. It produces light rosé wines in the Rhône (Tavel and Lirac), and in Spain (*rosado*). Some of the better Grenache-based reds come from the Southern Rhône (like good Gigondas), but the best Châteauneuf-du-Papes normally contain a proportion of Syrah, which gives them real class. Even though Garnacha is widely planted in Rioja, it is mostly found in the lower-quality Rioja Baja, and the best Riojas contain more Tempranillo (see below) than Garnacha.

Grenache is Australia's second most widely planted grape, and flourishes in the Barossa Valley where it is mainly used in blends. Its capacity to survive in high temperatures has led to plantings in California's hot Central Valley where most of the blended jug wine is made. There are also some plantings in South Africa.

## MERLOT

STYLE: Medium to full-bodied.
SUITABILITY FOR LONG-TERM KEEPING: Very good, but only the very best.
OAK-AGED?: Often.
WHERE GROWN SUCCESSFULLY: France (Bordeaux [especially St Emilon and Pomerol], Languedoc-Roussillon), Bulgaria, California, Argentina, Portugal, Italy, Hungary, Yugoslavia, Romania, Chile, Australia.

Although not the world's best known red grape variety, Merlot produces one of the most expensive wines in the world, the famous Bordeaux, Château Pétrus, from Pomerol.

Merlot produces voluptuous wines that can exhibit the same kind of charm as those made from the Pinot Noir. It is traditionally used for blending with the harsher, harder Cabernet Sauvignon in Bordeaux because its up-front fruit and soft silky texture complement the Cabernet.

*MERLOT*

Pure Merlot has a slight sweetness that gives it an almost chocolatey edge – a character trait that contributes to the complexity of the wines of Bordeaux – and an aroma that always reminds me of Parma violet sweets. Although the Merlot is less well known than the Cabernet Sauvignon in Bordeaux, surprisingly almost twice as much of it is planted. Merlot is, however, much more difficult to grow than the hardy Cabernet Sauvignon grape and so many producers fight shy of it. It is lower in tannin than the Cabernet Sauvignon and can also be fairly low in acidity, particularly when grown in warmer climates like Italy, the south of France and California.

Merlot has not been as successful in New World wine-producing countries as its famous cousin, the Cabernet Sauvignon, although some reasonable wines have been produced in California and Australia.

## NEBBIOLO

STYLE: Medium-bodied.
SUITABILITY FOR LONG-TERM KEEPING: Can be good.
OAK-AGED?: Sometimes.
WHERE GROWN SUCCESSFULLY: Italy, Switzerland, California.

Nebbiolo is a grape that produces big, tannic, full-flavoured reds and is a favourite grape variety in north-west Italy. Its main characteristics are an abundance of tough tannin, acidity and dry fruit extract. The only grape it can

*NEBBIOLO*

possibly be likened to when young is the Syrah, found in the northern Rhône. Indeed, it has a similar tarry and slightly gamey aroma. Apart from Italy, the only other place that it is found in is Switzerland, and a tiny amount in California.

As lovers of Barolo and Barbaresco will know, the best wines made from Nebbiolo can last for decades.

## PINOT NOIR

STYLE: Light to medium-bodied.
SUITABILITY FOR LONG-TERM KEEPING: Can be good for the top wines.
OAK-AGED?: Often, especially for top wines.
WHERE GROWN SUCCESSFULLY: France (Burgundy, the Loire, Alsace, Champagne), Germany, North America (Oregon, California), Italy, Bulgaria, Romania, Chile.

The Pinot Noir is the grape of red Burgundy, but unlike Cabernet Sauvignon, it is difficult to grow successfully and few producers have mastered the technique. It is delicate, in terms both of its low resistance to inclement weather, and the style of wine it makes. It produces garnet-coloured wines that can range from deep garnet to a light red, almost rosé, a marked contrast to the deep, inky wines produced by the Cabernet Sauvignon. Its flavour is also much more difficult to describe than that of the forceful Cabernet Sauvignon, although good Pinot Noir has a distinct aroma and flavour of raspberries or strawberries, with an attractive 'sweetness' of fruit. When vinified correctly by Burgundy producers like Domaine de la Romanée Conti or Domaine Dujac, Pinot Noir produces some of the greatest, most seductive wines in the world.

Because Pinot Noir ripens early it is normally found in cooler climates like Burgundy and Champagne, where it is one of the three major grape varieties. This is also one of the reasons it is not suitable for growing in many of the warmer New World climates.

Also in France it flourishes in Alsace where it is the only black grape variety, making for somewhat more austere, quite light-coloured reds which are delicious when young. It is also the main red grape variety grown in Germany, where it is known as Spätburgunder. In Germany it

*PINOT NOIR*

has much less concentration of flavour than it does in Burgundy, and often has a slightly orangey colour.

Attempts have been made at growing Pinot Noir in California, but so far few have been successful, although there is the occasional triumph like Edna Valley Vineyard's Pinot and some of Mondavi's recent wines. It seems to flourish much better in the cooler climes of Oregon where it is now producing some quite stunning wines.

## SYRAH

STYLE: Full-bodied.
SUITABILITY FOR LONG-TERM KEEPING: Very good.
OAK-AGED?: Sometimes for the top wines.
WHERE GROWN SUCCESSFULLY: France (Northern Rhône, Midi, Vaucluse, Ardèche), Australia, South Africa, Argentina.

Syrah is the grape variety that produces the great wines of the northern Rhône like Hermitage and Côte Rôtie, the latter blended with a small amount of Viognier. It makes deep black, inky-coloured wines with a very strong, tarry or gamey aroma, high in tannin and ripe fruit flavour. The fruit flavour is very complex, like a mixture of blackcurrants and blackberries mixed together with loganberries and bilberries and an added dash of spice. When grown in hot areas, such as the Rhône and parts of Australia (where it is known as Shiraz), it takes on a rich, plummy, chocolatey flavour and aftertaste. Apart from the Rhône Valley, it is not found in many other areas of France except for some of the more southerly areas like the Ardèche and the Oc. The wines made here are much

lighter than those of the northern Rhône, and show how Syrah can be used to produce good everyday drinkable reds with lots of fruit.

In Australia, the grape becomes known as Shiraz and produces big, beefy full wines that are slightly sweet on the finish. The most famous is Penfold's Grange Hermitage, a legend in its own lunchtime! Indeed, 'Hermitage' has often been interchangeable with 'Syrah' in the past – in pre-phylloxera Bordeaux a surprisingly high number of the top châteaux grew Syrah in their vineyards. They also blended in Syrah from the Rhône making wines that rejoiced in names like Lafite-Hermitagé.

Today Syrah is blended with Cabernet Sauvignon in Australia, their answer to the Bordeaux practice of blending Cabernet and Merlot, and they seem to work together.

## ∾ OTHER GRAPE VARIETIES ∾

The grape varieties described in the previous pages are the most important in the world of wine but there are many others, sometimes of great importance but in a very localized way. The following are mentioned in the various sections in the rest of the book.

### RED GRAPES

| Grape variety | See section on |
| --- | --- |
| Bastardo | Port |
| Malbec | Bordeaux |
| Montepulciano | Italy |
| Periquita | Portugal |
| Petit Verdot | Bordeaux |
| Pinotage | South Africa |
| Pinot Meunier | Champagne |
| Mouvedre | Rhône |
| Tempranillo | Rioja |
| Touriga Nacional | Port |
| Zinfandel | North America |

### WHITE GRAPES

| Grape variety | See section on |
| --- | --- |
| Aligoté | Burgundy |
| Bual | Madeira |
| Colombard | North America |
| Furmint | Hungary |
| Huxelrebe | Germany/England |
| Kerner | Germany/England |
| Madeleine Angevine | England |
| Ortega | Germany/England |
| Pedro Ximenez | Sherry |
| Reichensteiner | Germany/England |
| Scheurebe | Germany/England |
| Schönburger | Germany/England |
| Sercial | Madeira |
| Seyval Blanc | England |
| Tocai Friulana | Italy |
| Tokay/Pinot Gris | Alsace |
| Verdelho | Madeira |
| Verdicchio | Italy |
| Viura (Macabeo) | Rioja |

*SYRAH*

# READING BETWEEN THE WINES

**I**F YOU KNOW HOW TO read a wine label in several languages, you'll save yourself a fortune in ▓▓▓▓▓▓ unnecessary wine purchases and make your wine-drinking days much more enjoyable. Many wine labels look confusing (and some of them are, even if you know how to read them!) but knowing just a few of the basic terms will help you enormously.

## ∞ DECIPHERING THE LABEL ∞

First, identify the legal quality category (listed below under each country) to give you an indication of the wine's supposed quality status. Try to find out which grape variety it's made from (see pages 15-24), and then look for other hints like the producer's name, whether the wine is dry or sweet, whether it's oak-aged and so on. All these will provide valuable hints to the wine's character without even having to buy a bottle!

You will find here two tables – the first an international glossary of some of the more common words found on labels from every country, the second a country-by-country guide to legal quality terms and specific words or phrases relating to the style of the wine.

## ∞ SPECIALIST WINE TERMS BY COUNTRY ∞

The following terms are split into two types:

**1 Legal quality definitions**
These are the statutory quality terms as designated by each individual country and only apply to European countries. The New World countries (America, Australia, *et al.*) have not yet formulated consistent enough rules to be included here. They are still in the experimental stages as far as legislation is concerned, and they do not have the same (sometimes self-destructive) traditional regional concepts as Europe.

The terms within Europe are a matter of law, and the wines have to conform to certain standards to be allowed to state as much on the label. While most of the legislation is well intentioned and the result of attempts at improving and maintaining high quality, sadly much of it is a waste of time. Here are a couple of examples to prove the point:

**a)** Buying a French *Appellation Controlée* (AC) wine does not guarantee quality. There are thousands of examples of AC wines not living up to their name. It is much better (although more confusing!) to follow a producer, rather

---

## GLOSSARY

### How to find your way around a wine label in six different languages

| English | French | German | Italian | Spanish | Portuguese |
|---|---|---|---|---|---|
| Bottle | Bouteille | Flasche | Bottiglia | Botella | Garrafa |
| Estate-bottled | Mis en bouteille au château/domaine | Erzeugerabfüllung | Imbottigliato nel'origine | Embotellado de Origen | Engarrafado na origem |
| Dry | Sec/Brut | Trocken | Secco/Brut | Seco | Seco/Bruto |
| Medium-dry | Demi-sec | Halbtrocken | Semi-secco/Amabile/ Abboccato | Semi-seco/Abocado | Meio Seco |
| Red | Rouge | Rot | Nero Rosso/Nero | Tinto | Tinto |
| Rosé | Rosé | Rosé/Weissherbst | Rosato | Rosado | Rosado |
| Sparkling | Mousseux/méthode champenoise | Sekt | Spumante metodo classico/ spumante classico | Espumoso/Cava | Espumante |
| Sweet | Doux/Moelleux | Süss | Dolce | Dulce | Doce/Adamado |
| Table wine | Vin de Table | Tafelwein | Vino da Tavola | Vino de Mesa | Vinho de Mesa |
| Vintage | Millésime | Jahrgang/Weinlese | Vendemmia | Cosecha | Colheita |
| White | Blanc | Weiss | Bianco | Blanco | Branco |

than to purchase on the basis of the wine's AC, although the latter will give you an indication of its style. I have drunk wines with the lowly appellation of Bourgogne Rouge which have been much better than the supposedly superior (and more expensive) appellation of Volnay or Pommard.

b) Italy's most basic (and cheapest) wine is supposed to be *Vino da Tavola* (VT). However, many of Italy's best wines (much better than most DOCs), like Antinori's Tignalello, are only VT because they are not made from legally recognized grape varieties.

## 2 Other wine terms

There are various words and phrases found on wine labels which often apply only to the specific country under which they are listed.

### 1 FRANCE

#### France – Legal quality definitions

*Vin de Table*   Basic table wine that can come from any region of France. No quality controls.

*Vin de Pays*   Wine from a designated region of France, with quality controls that are less strict than those for AC wines (see below). Over 130 regions currently. Also says 'Vin de Table' on the label.

*Vin Délimité de Qualité Supérieur* (VDQS)   In between *Vin de Pays* and AC wines in quality. Designated regions.

*Appellation d'Origine Controlée* (AC)   The highest quality of all French wines. Designated regions with strictly limited production and quantity that vary according to the appellation. Many larger ACs (e.g. AC Bordeaux or AC Bourgogne) can include many other smaller (and higher quality) ACs.

#### France – Other wine terms

*Barriques neuves*   New oak barrels.

*Blanc de Blancs*   White wine made from white grapes.

*Blanc de Noirs*   White wine made from black grapes.

*Clos*   Walled vineyard.

*Crémant*   Sparkling but not as frothy as champagne.

*Cru*   A vineyard classification.

*Cru Classé*   Classified wine.

*Cuve*   A vat or barrel – sometimes indicates a better wine.

*Cuve Close*   Sparkling wine made in tanks (not as good as méthode champenoise).

*Cuvée*   Contents of a barrel or vat – usually a better wine if included in the wine name.

*Deuxième Vin*   Second wine (see *Bordeaux*).

*Doux*   Sweet.

*Fûts de Chêne*   Oak barrels.

*Grand Vin*   Literally 'great wine' – often the main wine if a property makes a second wine as well – but can mean anything – not a guarantee of quality!

*Grand Cru*   In Burgundy, a specific legal/geographical definition. Elsewhere, it can mean anything.

*Grand Cru Classé*   Specific châteaux in Bordeaux.

*Méthode Champenoise*   Sparkling wine made in the same way as Champagne.

*Millésime*   Vintage.

*Mis en bouteille dans nos caves*   Meaning bottled in our cellars; generally bottled by a large company or blender.

*Moelleux*   Sweet.

*Mousseux*   Sparkling or frothy.

*Négociant*   A merchant who buys wine, and generally bottles it himself before selling it on.

*Nouveau*   New.

*Perlé*   Lightly sparkling.

*Pétillant*   Sparkling but less so than Champagne.

*Premier Cru*   A legal/geographical definition in Burgundy, usually indicating high quality. The same in Bordeaux when suffixed by 'Classé'.

*Société*   Company.

*Sur lie (or Tiré sur Lie)*   Wine bottled off its lees (the natural sediment).

*Vendange tardive*   Wine made from grapes that are picked late in the season, often making sweet wines.

*Vin ordinaire*   Table wine.

*Vin tranquille*   Still wine.

*Vignoble*   Vineyard.

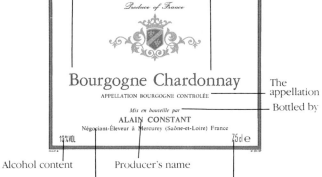

Part of the name of the wine refers to its appellation

The grape variety

The appellation

Bottled by

Alcohol content

Producer's name

Description of producer and address – in this case a *Négociant-Éleveur*, or 'blender and wine-ager'

Bottle contents

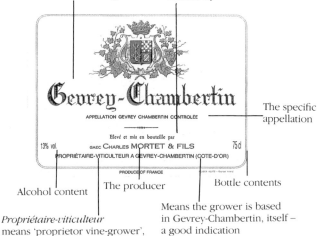

The name of the wine – in this case named after the village

Literally 'brought up and bottled by'

The specific appellation

Alcohol content

The producer

Bottle contents

*Propriétaire-viticulteur* means 'proprietor vine-grower', an indication of a potentially more interesting wine than one from a *négociant*

Means the grower is based in Gevrey-Chambertin, itself – a good indication

## 2 GERMANY

### Germany – Legal quality definitions
*Tafelwein*   Table wine – the most basic. Wine from anywhere in Germany. But watch out for E.C.C. Tafelwein – it normally does not come from Germany at all, but is a blend of various E.E.C. wines.

*Landwein*   Like French *Vin de Pays*. A Tafelwein that can come from any one of 15 different areas.

*Qualitätswein bestimmter Anbaugebeite* (QbA)   Quality wine from one of 11 demarcated regions.

*Qualitätswein mit Prädikat* (QmP)   Higher in quality than QbA wine, with a minimum natural sugar level. QmP wines are found in the following categories (in ascending order of natural sugar content): Kabinett, Spätlese, Auslese, Beerenauslese, Eiswein and Trockenbeerenauslese.

### Germany – Other wine terms
*Abfueller*   Bottler.

*Aus eigenen lesegut*   Producer's estate wine.

*Bereich*   Wine district, containing a number of Grosslagen.

*Eiswein*   Very rare, very sweet wine made from grapes picked when they are frozen, normally in December or January.

*Erzeuger*   Producer.

*Grosslage*   Smaller area than a Bereich.

*Halbtroken*   Between dry and medium-dry.

*Perlwein*   Lightly sparkling.

*Spritzig*   Semi-sparkling.

*Weinkellerei*   Winery.

*Weinzergenossenschaft*   Growers' co-operative.

## 3 SPAIN

### Spain – Legal quality definitions
*Vino de Mesa*   Table wine – the most basic.

*Vino de Tierra*   Similar to German *Landwein* or French *Vin de Pays*.

*Denominación de Origen* (DO)   Demarcated region with certain quality requirements. Like France's AC.

*Sin Crianza*   Not aged in oak barrels – young wine.

*Crianza (or Con Crianza)*   Aged in wood (minimum one year).

*Reserva*   Wine at least three years old with one year ageing in barrel.

*Gran reserva*   Wine at least three years old with at least two years ageing in barrel.

### Spain – Other wine terms
*Bodega*   Wine cellar or name of wine company.

*Clarete*   Light red.

*Consejo Regulador*   Wine governing body.

*Cosecha*   Vintage.

*Embotellado por*   Bottled by.

*Vendimia*   Vintage/harvest.

*Viña/vinedo*   Vineyard.

*Vine de l'anne/cosechero/nuevo*   New.

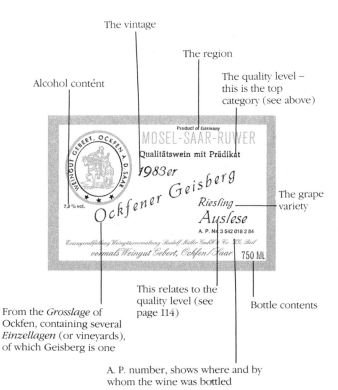

The vintage

The region

Alcohol content

The quality level – this is the top category (see above)

MOSEL-SAAR-RUWER

Product of Germany

Qualitätswein mit Prädikat

1983er

*Ockfener Geisberg*

Riesling

Auslese

A. P. Nr 3 542 018 2 84

The grape variety

From the *Grosslage* of Ockfen, containing several *Einzellagen* (or vineyards), of which Geisberg is one

This relates to the quality level (see page 114)

Bottle contents

A. P. number, shows where and by whom the wine was bottled

The brand name

Indicates a certain age (see above)

RIOJA-RESERVA
Prado Enea
Muga®

The contents   75 cl e

COSECHA   1981

Desde 1932

BODEGAS MUGA, S.A.   HARO·Rioja Alta·ESPAÑA

CONSTA DE 178.805 BOTELLAS NUMERADAS PROCEDENTES DE LA CRIANZA EN 600 BORDELESAS DE ROBLE AMERICANO.

The name of the bodegas (i.e. the winemakers)

Vintage 1981

The Rioja denomination official seal

Literally 'since 1932' (refers to the winemaker, not the wine)

The town and region where bottled

An unusually precise description. In this case it says that 178,805 bottles were made and that 600 barrels of American oak were used for ageing

## 4 PORTUGAL

### Portugal – Legal quality definitions
*Vinho de Mesa*　Table wine. But like Italy, many of Portugal's good wines come into this category, due to the lack of formal legal structure for wine quality control.
*Região demarcada* (RD)　Similar to Spain's DO – demarcated region.

### Portugal – Other wine terms
*Adega*　Large cellars where the wine is bottled.
*Carvalho*　Oak.
*Clarete*　Light red.
*Engarrafado na origem*　Estate-bottled.
*Espumante*　Sparkling.
*Garrafeira*　Vintage wine (at least three years old for reds).
*Quinta*　Farm/estate.
*Reserva*　Vintage wine (at least five years old for reds).
*Velho*　Old.
*Vinho Verde*　'Green wine' – white or red wine from a specific region.

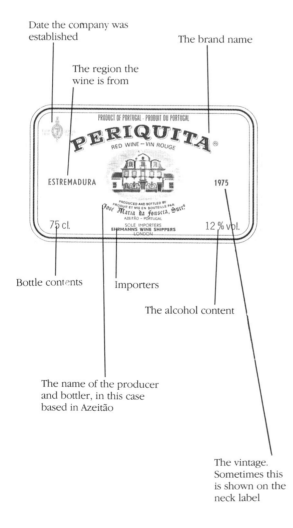

Date the company was established

The brand name

The region the wine is from

ESTREMADURA　　1975

75 cl.　　12 % vol.

Bottle contents　　Importers

The alcohol content

The name of the producer and bottler, in this case based in Azeitão

The vintage. Sometimes this is shown on the neck label

## 5 ITALY

### Italy – Legal quality definitions
*Vino da Tavola* (VT)　Table wine, but includes some of Italy's best wines which are made from unorthodox grape varieties.
*Denominazione die Origine Controllata* (DOC)　Similar to the French *Appellation Controlée* system. There are over 500 DOCs.
*Superiore DOC*　More alcoholic or higher quality than DOC.
*Denominazione di Origine Controllata e Garantita* (DOCG)　Higher classification – six wines only.

### Italy – Other wine terms
*Abboccato*　Slightly sweet.
*Amabile*　Semi-sweet.
*Amaro*　Bitter.
*Asciutto*　Bone dry.
*Auslese*　(*Alto Adige* only) – sweet.
*Botte*　Barrel.
*Cantina*　Winery.
*Casa vinicola*　Wine company.
*Chiaretto*　Deep rosé.
*Consorzio*　Promotional group of producers.
*Frizzante*　Semi-sparkling.
*Imbottigliato da*　Bottled by.
*Liquoroso*　Very high in alcohol (can be sweet).
*Nero*　Dark red.
*Recioto*　Alcoholic sweet wine made from *passito* (sun-dried) grapes.
*Riserva*　Wines with specific ageing.
*Riserva speciale*　More age than straight Riserva.
*Vecchio*　Old.
*Vino novello*　New.

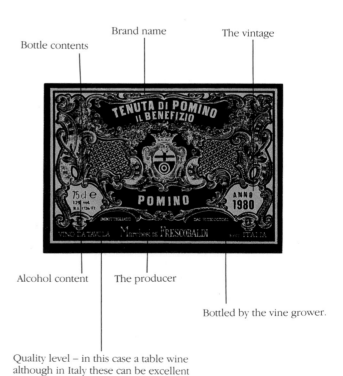

Bottle contents

Brand name

The vintage

Alcohol content

The producer

Bottled by the vine grower.

Quality level – in this case a table wine although in Italy these can be excellent

# $\mathcal{A}$CQUIRING $\mathcal{A}$ $\mathcal{T}$ASTE

HERE IS ONE SIMPLE WAY of determining whether or not you like a wine – taste it! Everyone has eyes, a mouth and a nose so don't be put off just because you think wine-tasting is something only for élite wine-tasters of the world – you do it every time you drink a glass of wine. It's like eating: every time you take a bite of food you make a judgement as to whether or not you like it. Does it appear sweet or sour, and what kind of texture does it have? All you need do is apply the same type of questions when tasting a wine. The main point in wine-tasting is not to try to guess which country or region the wine has come from (as the 'experts' do in 'blind tastings'), but to assess the actual quality of the wine and, more importantly, to decide whether or not you like it.

### ∾ HOW TO TASTE WINE ∾

Tasting wine is easier than people imagine. Prove this by experimenting with a glass each of two different wines of the same colour – you will be amazed at the obvious differences. They are far more pronounced than if you were to try the same two wines on different occasions.

Start off by finding a glass you are comfortable tasting from. I prefer fine, thin glass that is easier to handle and does not get in the way of looking at the wine as cut glass does. The shape of the glass can help your tasting enormously. It is best not to have one that's too closed in at the top, otherwise the aroma of the wine cannot escape. On the other hand a shallow glass (like champagne saucers) allows the delicious smells to escape too quickly. My favourite glasses are tulip-shaped, with a bulbous bottom, tapering towards the top.

Once you have opened the bottle pour some of the wine into the glass until it is about one third full. This is not because I think wine should be served in stingy measures (far from it!), but so that you can have a really good look at the wine. Tilt the glass without spilling it, and let all those lovely aromas fill the space inside the glass.

### ∾ YOU CAN TELL A LOT FROM THE COLOUR ∾

Before even taking a mouthful of wine, have a good look at it. Tilt the glass away from you and observe the wine against a well-lit white background (a sheet of white paper will do). The colour of a wine can tell you many things about it before you even taste it.

First, make sure that the wine is bright and clear, not murky or hazy. If it is hazy there is almost always a problem and the wine should be returned to its place of purchase. But if it has bits floating in it this will normally mean that the wine has thrown a sediment (an entirely natural process) and should have been decanted before being poured into the glass (see chapter 5). If, especially with white wines, there are small crystals lurking in the bottom of the glass there's no cause for worry – they are only tartrates thrown out of solution by extremes of temperature and are entirely harmless.

Next, look at the colour itself. Once the wine is in a glass, the colour will always appear to change the closer the wine is to the glass itself. Many wine experts use the phrase 'fading towards the rim (of the wine)' which, although apparently true, is not physically accurate. What actually happens is that more light gets through the wine the nearer it is to the glass, because there is less depth of wine to block it. This can change the perceived colour, making the wine appear browner (in the case of a red wine) as it nears the glass. But it's a useful technique to use – you'll be able to see more detail in the colour by tilting the glass and examining the rim of the wine. You can see how concentrated a wine is (and generally speaking, the more concentrated the better) by how close to the glass the wine starts to lighten: the closer the better!

### Looking at red wines
The younger the wine the more purple the colour. Indeed, many young wines are so intensely coloured that they appear to be almost black and opaque. This is particularly true of deep-coloured black grapes such as the Cabernet Sauvignon or the Syrah. As the wine becomes older and more mature the colour becomes lighter, turning to brick red and then, eventually, to a tawny colour. It depends on the quality of the wine how long this process takes, but a basic table wine can mature completely in only two months, whereas the best clarets can take 30 or 40 years to reach full maturity.

### Looking at white wines
Whites can vary in colour from a pale, almost colourless liquid like Soave, to a deep golden orange colour like a good Sauternes. When very young, white wines often have a greeny hue and, as the wine matures and oxidizes in bottle, this colour will become a deeper yellow. Certain grape varieties have much more depth of colour than others. For instance, Muscat and Gewürztraminer grapes

can produce wines which have great depth of colour and are golden and even slightly pinky, in contrast to the Muscadet grape that produces colourless wines with a slightly green tinge when young. Often, the sweeter a wine the deeper its colour will be.

### Looking at rosé wines

The colours of different types of rosé wines are more varied than reds or whites, even when they have just been made. They range from very pale rose-petal pink to deep salmony pink, from pale orange to dark onion-skin pink. As there is no definitive pink all these are correct, and it's up to the winemaker to decide. The colour is affected by the type of grape used, and how long the grapeskins have been left in contact with the juice. The more pronounced colour the winemaker desires, the longer he leaves the skins in with the wine.

### Looking at sparkling wines

When looking at sparkling wines the comments above about general colour also apply, but there is an additional factor which is very important: the bubbles! In Champagne, the king of sparkling wines, the bubbles should be lively, and there should be plenty of them. They should also carry on fizzing for some time after opening the bottle. If you have a glass of flat Champagne there is something wrong with it and cause for complaint – the most common reason is that your glass has not been rinsed properly, as detergent kills the fizz. However, the older the Champagne becomes, the less bubbles there will be. Any Champagne past its fifteenth birthday will have considerably less bubbles than a youngster, and really old Champagne often has virtually no bubbles at all. *Cuve close* wines or *vins mousseux* will have less bubbles and they will not last for as long in the glass.

### ∾ GETTING TO THE SMELLS! ∾

Once you've finished your visual inspection of the wines (which won't take nearly as long as reading how to do it!), give the wine a really good swirl around in the glass. This is not just an affectation but a very effective way of releasing the delicious aromas. Now's the time to use your nose – the bigger the better! Because our taste and smell organs are so closely linked physically inside our heads, the smell of anything will give you a very accurate indication of what it's going to taste like. You've probably used the technique before with food that you are not sure about. You smell it before eating it, to make sure it's not off! So take a really good sniff of the wine.

Try to think what the wine reminds you of – does it have a floral, spicy aroma, or does it smell of wet dogs or farmyards? Does it remind you of the smell of some kind of food, spice, fruit, or even something inedible like polish? A musty smell often indicates that the wine is corked, although this can only be confirmed by tasting it. And always watch out for the first glass poured from the bottle – it can smell of 'bottle stink'. This is normal because the first glass of every bottle poured will contain the small amount of air that has been cooped up between the cork and the bottle, sometimes for decades. You'd probably be fairly

*Look at the difference in colour of these two white wines. The one on the left is an Italian Soave, and the darker coloured one on the right, a rich, sweet Sauternes.*

*The wine on the right which shows more browning in its colour is much older than the wine on the left.*

smelly if you'd spent several years in a confined space with no fresh air! To avoid the problem, either pour a small amount of the first bit of wine into a glass and throw it away or, if you have already poured the wine, swirl it in the glass and blow into it vigorously, taking care not to blow it right out of the glass!

## ✎ GETTING YOUR TEETH INTO IT! ✎

Now at last you can taste the wine. Take a moderate sized sip and try to swirl it around between your tongue and the roof of your mouth, giving your palate the maximum possible exposure to the wine. It is important to ascertain whether the wine is sweet or dry, how much acidity it has, whether it is fruity, or sweet and sticky without any acidity. Also consider the weight of the wine: is it light bodied and elegant or full bodied and powerful? Is it bitter and tannic (i.e. young), or smooth and rounded (mature). If you are tasting lots of wines it's essential to spit them out if you want to remain standing after tasting a few of them. You can practise your spitting technique in the bath – it's less messy. And don't worry too much about the formalities – it is not necessary to have a proper spittoon, just use whatever is handy; the kitchen sink, or an ice bucket or jug. But remember to make sure that the opening is large enough if you have yet to perfect the art of straight spitting. Once you have spat out your wine make a note of the wine's aftertaste – the flavour left in your mouth. Does the wine leave a clean, fruity flavour? Or does it leave a nasty, bitter or acidic flavour? Ask yourself whether the wine is long or short, that is to say whether the aftertaste stays for a long time or disappears immediately.

It's always well worth making a note of your observations so that you can compare one wine tasted to another, or look back after a few weeks or even years and remind yourself of its taste. Don't be worried if your descriptions are different to other people's – wine-tasting is very subjective. Indeed, it can be great fun to taste in a group with other people, as their comments can add new dimensions to a wine.

## ✎ TASTING TERMS ✎

You will come across tasting terms wherever you read about or whenever you discuss wine. Don't be put off by other people's comments, even if they are very experienced wine-tasters. Your comments are just as valid as theirs, and as you become more experienced you will discover immediately identifiable traits that several wines might have in common. Any adjective or noun that reminds you of the taste or smell is valid, even if it sounds bizarre. Remember that tasting is subjective and you might pick out nuances that are not obvious to other people. Even a very obvious smell, like sulphur, is not immediately apparent to everyone, and some people are more sensitive to it than others. The following list is intended to give you some pointers in the right direction, and includes some of the more commonly found flavours, smells and terms. And don't forget, if a wine reminds you of something that does *not* appear on this list, never be afraid to use that term.

*The Director of Oenology at Mondavi's Winery in the Napa Valley, California, tasting a vast selection of wines.*

*When tasting wine, first look at the colour. Make sure you have good light to do this. Tilt the glass away from you. To see the colour clearly it helps to hold a white sheet of paper behind the glass. The wine should be clear. Murkiness generally indicates a fault in the wine. The younger a wine is, the more purple it will be.*

*As long as the glass is only about one-third full, you can swirl the wine around in the glass without spilling it. This helps release the wine's aromas and gives the wine a chance to breathe after being closed up in the bottle.*

*Then take a really good sniff of the wine. Try to think what the smell reminds you of – wine-tasters use all sorts of strange adjectives to describe taste. A faulty wine can often be detected by its aroma, particularly when it is 'corked'.*

*Finally, take a gulp of wine and try to swirl it around your mouth. Again, think what the taste reminds you of. Is the wine dry or sweet, soft or acidic, light or full-bodied? When you have swallowed the wine (or spat it out), note whether the wine's flavour lingers on.*

## TASTING TERMS

*aftertaste*   The taste remaining in the mouth after swallowing or spitting out the wine.

*aggressive*   Sometimes sharp, assaults the taste buds!

*aroma*   The smell of a wine.

*aromatic*   Has a lot of smell.

*astringent*   Bitter (as in tannic).

*austere*   Not very forthcoming, lacking fruit.

*backward*   Slow in maturing.

*backbone*   Underlying structure of the wine. Means it has potential to age well.

*balance*   The balance between the different elements (e.g. fruit, acidity, tannin) in the wine.

*big wine*   Full-bodied and powerful.

*bite*   Sharp, high acidity.

*bitter*   Dries out the mouth.

*blind tasting*   Tasting a wine (or several) without knowing its identity.

*blowsy*   Very obvious flavour, without much complexity.

*body*   Apparent weight of the wine in the mouth, related to texture.

*bottle age*   How long the wine has been in bottle.

*bouquet*   Smell.

*burnt*   Smells/tastes as though the grapes have been subjected to too much heat.

*charm*   Has charm: is attractive in an elegant way.

*chewy*   Full-bodied wine, fleshy.

*classic*   Typical of the grape variety or region.

*clean*   Without any unpleasant or untypical odours or flavours, fresh.

*closed*   Unforthcoming smell and/or taste.

*cloudy*   A hazy wine, not clear.

*cloying*   Over-sweet, sickly, unclean sweetness.

*coarse*   Obvious, rough.

*complete*   All the elements in the wine are present, in the correct balance and at the right levels. Also displays more subtle nuances than a wine that is simply 'correct'.

*complexity*   Many facets of smell and/or taste.

*concentrated*   Intense aroma/flavour.

*cooked*   The smell/taste of overheated grape juice (similar to jammy).

*corked*   A musty smell/taste, similar to mouldy cork or rotten wood, that makes a wine undrinkable. *Not* bits of cork in the wine.

*correct*   Like complete, but with less complexity.

*creamy*   Texture and taste combined, normally found in white wines.

*crisp*   Fresh, noticeable acidity.

*declining*   Past its peak of maturity and will get worse.

*delicate*   Not obvious, lightweight, subtle.

*depth*   Depth of flavour.

*dilute*   Watery, made from over-produced grapes.

*dirty*   Unclean, unpleasant smells/flavours.

*drying out*   Well past its peak of maturity and losing its fruit rapidly.

*elegant*   Similar to delicate.

*fading*   Similar to declining.

*fat*   Full-bodied.

*finesse*   The difference between good and outstanding.

*finish*   The flavour just before the aftertaste.

*flabby*   Similar to blowsy, lacks acidity and/or tannin.

*flat*   Unexciting (still wines) or has lost its fizz (sparkling wines).

*fleshy*   Full-bodied.

*floral*   Smells like fresh flowers.

*fresh*   Lively, youthful flavours. Not stale.

*fruit*   As in a 'fruity' wine. Ripeness, should balance with acidity and tannin.

*full*   Either plenty of flavour or a weighty texture.

*generous*   The opposite to austere.

*green*   Unripe fruit, seems to have been made from unripe grapes.

*gutsy*   Plenty of oooomph!

*hard*   Tannic, unyielding, needs time to mature or soften out.

*hollow*   Lacking depth of flavour.

*hot*   Can refer to the climate in which the grapes were grown.

*inky*   Refers to colour – very deep purple/opaque, young wines.

*jammy*   Smells like jam being made, sometimes an indication that the temperature of fermentation has not been properly controlled.

*length*   The length of time one can still savour the aftertaste of a wine. The better the wine, the longer the length (unless the flavour is revolting!).

*light*   Light colour, or lightweight (opposite of full-bodied).

*lingering*   Flavour and/or aroma that lingers.

*lively*   Normally refers to sparkling wine, lively bubbles are active ones.

*luscious*   Rich, full-bodied.

*maderized*   Tastes like Madeira, normally a white wine that is too old.

*mature*   A wine in which the various elements (tannin, acidity and fruit) have softened over a period of time and will not improve further.

*mean*   Lacking fruit and flavour.

*meaty*   Like chewy, full-bodied.

*mellow*   Mature and soft.

*musty*   Unpleasant mouldy smell/taste.

*nose*   Smell or bouquet.

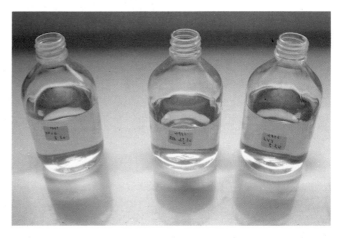

*Wine samples, such as those shown above, are taken from the vats at regular intervals, in order for tests to be carried out by the wineries' oenologist.*

*A mobile bottling line at Cantina Silvio Jermann in Villanova di Farra di Friuli.*

*oily*   Can refer to texture, or the smell/taste of the Riesling grape.

*opaque*   Refers to colour – light cannot pass through. The opposite to translucent.

*opulent*   Upfront, full, obvious flavour/smell.

*overtone*   Nuance found over and above the more obvious tastes/smells.

*oxidized*   Wine that has reacted with the oxygen in the air, like a wine that has been left open for several days, turning it to vinegar.

*palate (on the)*   The part of the mouth that identifies a wine's flavour (or the flavour of the wine).

*peak*   At its peak – a fully mature wine.

*pear-drops*   Smell of acetone, often found on *macération carbonique* wines like Beaujolais Nouveau. Also found on some white wines.

*perfume*   Smell.

*pétillant*   Lightly sparkling.

*piquant*   A slight edge to any flavour.

*prickly*   A wine with carbon dioxide trapped in it – not noticeably fizzy, but prickles on the tongue.

*racy*   Liveliness.

*rich*   Very ripe, concentrated fruit.

*ripe*   As in ripe grapes.

*robust*   Full-bodied, powerful flavours, often tannic.

*rounded*   Soft, easy-going wine, not much tannin or acidity.

*sharp*   High acidity.

*short*   Not much length.

*smooth*   Smooth on the tongue, texture.

*soft*   Low tannin and acidity.

*spritz*   Like *pétillant*.

*stalky*   Smells/tastes as though the grape stems have been left in the wine.

*subtle*   Not obvious, with delicate flavours/smells.

*sulphur*   Smells of rotten eggs – some producers overdose their wines with sulphur (NB: 99 per cent of wines contain sulphur).

*sumptuous*   Richness and opulence combined.

*tannic*   A wine with a high level of tannin, a bitter substance also found in tea, coffee and leather. Tannin comes from the grapeskins and oak barrels.

*tangy*   Fresh, lively fruit flavour.

*tart*   Acidic, sharp.

*thin*   Light-bodied, watery.

*toasted*   Flavour/smell of toast, generally comes from the insides of the oak barrels that are charred and transmit that flavour to the wine.

*translucent*   Wine that lets-light through – the opposite to opaque.

*undertone*   Subtle flavours underlying the main ones.

*ungenerous*   Unforthcoming, mean, lacking fruit and flavour.

*unripe*   Smells and tastes of unripe grapes.

*upfront*   Obvious, immediate.

*varietal*   Varietal character – tastes/smells of the grape variety from which it is made.

*vegetal*   Smells/tastes of boiled green leaf vegetables.

*velvety*   Silky-smooth texture.

*voluptuous*   Full-bodied, sumptuous.

*watery*   Dilute, thin.

*weighty*   Full-bodied, plenty of depth of flavour.

*yeasty*   Wines bottled off their lees often have a yeasty taste (not unpleasant).

*zingy*   Lively, fresh, crisp, youthful.

*zippy*   Similar to zingy.

Opposite is a list of the fruits and flavours often found in wines and the wines that taste of them. This is not a comprehensive lift, but an indication of the types of flavours to look for, and where to find them.

## ∽ THE FRUIT MACHINE ∽

| Fruit/flavour | Grape varieties or wines exhibiting these flavours | Well-known wines made from these grapes |
| --- | --- | --- |
| Gooseberries | Sauvignon Blanc | Sancerre, Pouilly-Fumé, Fumé Blanc |
| Apples | – | Comes from malic acid – can be found in any white wine |
| Biscuity | – | Older or oak-aged white wines, normally Chardonnay (e.g. white Burgundy) and Champagne |
| Blackberries/blackcurrants | Cabernet Sauvignon, Syrah, Merlot | Claret, Hermitage, New World reds |
| Bubblegum | – | Any wine made by *macération carbonique*, particularly Gamay (as in Beaujolais) |
| Buttery | Chardonnay | White Burgundy, oak-aged white wines |
| Cassis | See 'blackcurrant' | – |
| Cedarwood | Oak-aged red wines | Claret, Rioja |
| Chocolatey | Merlot, Cabernet Sauvignon, Syrah, Grenache | Mature Clarets, lesser St Emilions, mature Rhônes |
| Cigar box | Mature oak-aged red wines | Claret, Rioja |
| Cinnamon | Any oak-aged red wine | Claret, Burgundy, Hermitage |
| Citrus | Crisp young white wines | Soave, Muscadet, Frascati |
| Cloves | Any oak-aged red wine | Claret, Burgundy, Hermitage |
| Earthy | Cabernet Franc, Chenin Blanc | Loire reds and whites |
| Elderflower | Spicy white wines | Asti, Alsace whites |
| Eucalyptus | Cabernet Sauvignon | Mostly New World heavy reds |
| Farmyardy | Pinot Noir | Red Burgundy |
| Foxy | Zinfandel | Californian Zinfandel |
| Grapey | Muscat | Muscats worldwide |
| Grassy | Sauvignon Blanc, Cabernet Franc | Sancerre and Loire reds |
| Lemony | See 'citrus' | – |
| Liquorice | Cabernet Sauvignon, Syrah, Grenache | Young clarets and Rhônes, heavy New World reds |
| Lychee | Gewürztraminer, Muscat | Alsace whites |
| Mango | See 'Lychee' | – |
| Nutty | Oak-aged Chardonnay, Sémillon, Chenin Blanc | White Burgundy, New World heavy whites |
| Oak | Any oak-aged wine, red or white | – |
| Peppery | Syrah, Grenache, Cabernet Sauvignon | Rhône reds, Clarets, New World heavy reds, mostly when young |
| Petrol | Riesling | German whites |
| Plummy | Any ripe red | – |
| Raisins | Madeira, Setúbal, Sémillon | Any wine that has been late harvested when the grapes have shrivelled |
| Raspberries | Pinot Noir | Red Burgundy |
| Spicy | Gewürztraminer, Muscat, Pinot Blanc | Alsace wines and any oak-aged wine, red or white |
| Strawberries | Pinot Noir, Muscat | Red Burgundy, light Muscat |
| Tobacco | Mature oak-aged reds | Claret, Rioja |
| Vanilla | Any oak-aged wine, red or white | – |

# Tools Of The Trade

$O$nce you've bought all your bottles and got them safely home (or have taken them out of your wine cellar), what's the next thing to do? Drink them of course! But first you've got to open the bottle.

### ∾ OPENING THE BOTTLE ∾

Before even reaching for the corkscrew, you should cut the plastic or metal capsule off below the lip of the bottle, so that when you pour the wine it does not come into contact with the capsule. This can be done with a knife (sometimes there is one attached to the corkscrew), but the best device on the market today is the Foil Cutter (designed and manufactured by Screwpull), which effortlessly removes the capsule in a few seconds, leaving a good clean cut. Whether you remove the entire capsule or cut it just below the rim is a matter of personal preference.

The range of corkscrews available seems to get bigger every year. You can select real Heath Robinson-type contraptions, or simple, well-designed, utilitarian models, but always avoid cheaply made ones – they will normally break after extracting only a few corks.

The choice of corkscrew is really up to you – use whichever type you find easiest, or whichever is handy! But one point to remember if you do not want the cork to break is that the screw itself should be a hollow spiral.

The 'Waiter's Friend' is probably the most common variety around, a corkscrew that works by lever action: once you've inserted the screw into the cork, you wedge a metal lever on to the rim of the bottle and then lever the cork out. The two main disadvantages are that it requires some strength and that it can sometimes chip the glass round the rim of the bottle. Two other popular corkscrews that are relatively foolproof are the wooden double helix, and the metal double lever, a contraption with arms that rise up as you insert the screw into the cork and which are then pushed down to extract the cork.

But my favourite corkscrew is the Screwpull, an ingenious device that does not require superhuman strength and very rarely breaks a cork. Having placed it on the bottle you simply turn the screw and when it reaches the bottom of the cork you keep turning it the same way and the cork magically rides all the way up the screw. I have opened up to 100 bottles at a time with this and can vouch for its durability. It is coated with a type of Teflon, developed by NASA for use in the American space programme, which creates minimal friction with the cork.

For very fragile corks – and if you've had lots of practice

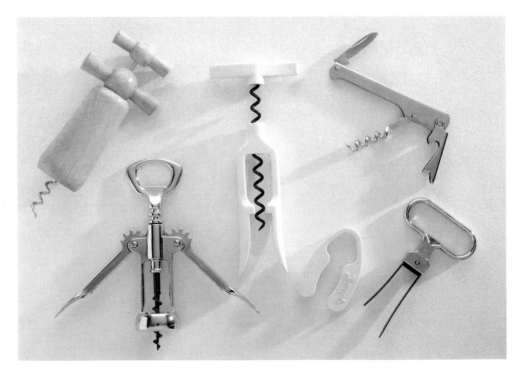

*A selection of the most common varieties of corkscrew available. Clockwise from left: wooden double helix, 'screwpull', 'waiter's friend', 'butler's friend', foil cutter (for removing the capsule) and the metal double lever.*

*A selection of different sized and shaped glasses. From the left: Champagne flute, red wine glass, white wine glass, port glass and sherry glass. You can of course use any ones you prefer. A glass that is bulbous at the bottom, becoming slightly narrower at the top is best as the aromas are then concentrated.*

– you can use the 'Butler's Friend', a two-pronged metal affair, that when inserted down either side of the cork, pulls it out intact.

To open Champagne or sparkling wine, undo the foil and, keeping your thumb on top of the cork, unwind the wire. Then, grasping the cork in one hand, use the other hand and turn the bottle round the cork – it should come out with a gentle sigh. If the cork is a little stiff, a pair of Champagne pincers that grip the cork firmly can come in handy (or a monkey wrench will do, although it's not as elegant!). Never point a bottle of Champagne at anyone while opening it – a cork can come out at the speed of a bullet and can seriously damage anyone in its path.

Once you have removed the cork from any wine wipe the top of the bottle with a cloth to remove any dirt or bits of cork.

## CHOOSING THE RIGHT GLASS

Once you've opened the bottle what kind of glass should you use? There is a vast range of different types on sale, although often this has more to do with the manufacturers' wish to sell more glasses than a need to put different wines into glasses of different sizes or shapes. Choosing the right glass is very easy, however; all you need do is remember a few basics, and after that the choice of style is up to you.

Clear, rather than coloured or cut, glass is best – you can appreciate the wine's colour better, and the size *is* important. Wines should never be poured right up to the top of the glass – one third full is about right – and so a bigger glass is desirable. By only filling the glass up this much you'll have a chance to savour all those delicious aromas. How big a glass you use is up to you and although the enormous fish-bowl glasses (that will hold the contents of an entire bottle when full) might seem absurd, they really can add to your enjoyment of the wine.

The shape of the glass is also important – one that is bulbous at the bottom, becoming slightly narrower towards the top, is best. This will concentrate the aromas that dissipate too quickly if you use a wide-mouthed glass. Every glass should have a decent length stem, so that you can swirl the wine around in it more easily and not leave finger prints all over the bowl of the glass. Champagne retains its fabulous fizz for longer when served in tall thin flute-shaped glasses rather than the flat saucer shape. And the latter tend to spill Champagne very easily, especially at a party when everyone is walking around.

While it is traditional to serve white wine in a smaller glass and red in a larger one, this is not a hard-and-fast rule, and you can use whatever size you want.

## DECANTERS & DECANTING

Decanters aren't just for show, no matter how attractively decorated they might be – they are genuinely useful. If a wine is old (often only more than eight years old) and has thrown a sediment it is essential to decant it, otherwise you will have glasses full of murky, muddy wine. Not only does this look unpleasant, but you taste all the sediment which, although not harmful, will detract from the wine's flavour. It's like the difference between a glass of pure water and one which has a fine suspension of mud in it. I know which I would prefer to drink!

The older the wine, the more necessary it will be to decant it. Most mature clarets, Rhônes, Burgundies and vintage ports will need decanting because of sediment.

Decanting also does something else – it aerates or oxygenates the wine. If you have a young claret (for example a bottle of Château Margaux 1978) that you want to drink, it's worth decanting it. In this example, although 1978 is old for some wines, for a wine of Château Margaux's quality it is still young, and the wine will still be hard and tannic. Decanting it a couple of hours before you drink it will mix it with the air, softening the tannins, removing any harshness and bringing out the fruit. But, by the same reasoning, if you have a very old bottle, it's best to decant it a very

*A selection of different decanters; these really are useful, especially if the wine is old and has thrown a sediment.*

short time before you intend to drink it – because it is mature, too much oxygen could damage it beyond repair.

You can also have fun with decanters by asking your friends to guess what the wine is in the decanter. Tasting a wine 'blind' (not seeing the label) can be amusing as well as educational – it helps you focus on the different tastes and aromas without being influenced by the label. There is a saying among wine professionals – 'one glance at the label is worth a hundred years' tasting experience when blind tasting'!

Don't worry if you don't possess a decanter – a jug will do, or even an empty wine bottle (provided it's clean).

**How to decant a wine with sediment**
Old wines that have thrown a sediment should always be decanted. And before decanting, make sure the bottle has not been shaken about, otherwise the sediment will be mixed in with the wine. Stand the bottle up for a few days before decanting or, if it has been in a wine rack, put it into a decanting basket (label uppermost if that is how the bottle has been stored). This will help keep the bottle at the same angle and leave the sediment resting along the side of the bottle.

Pull the cork carefully. Then using a candle (or more practically a bicycle lamp) gently tilt the bottle and start pouring it into the decanter. With the light shining from underneath the bottle, stop decanting when you see the sediment reaching the neck of the bottle. The trick is to decant as much clear wine as you can, leaving all the sedi-

ment and as little wine as possible in the bottle.

If you want to open a impromptu bottle or your decanting efforts have not been entirely successful, don't despair. You can pour the wine or port either through fine muslin or through a clean coffee filter, and the quality won't be significantly affected.

### ∾ SERVING WINE AT THE RIGHT TEMPERATURE ∾

The right temperature is that at which you enjoy your wine. If you really want to boil the wine by leaving the bottle in front of the fire that's fine by me, although it's a shame to stew it when the winemaker has taken so much trouble not to!

The phrase *chambré* was invented long before central heating, and the ambient room temperature was considerably lower than it is today. So serve your wines cooler rather than warmer – you can always cup the glass in your hand and warm the wine up that way!

White wines (and some light reds like Beaujolais) are best served chilled, though not freezing, and normal refrigerator temperature is fine. If you need to cool a bottle quickly, immerse it in cold water with lots of ice in it – this is much better than a bucket full of ice only, and will cool it a lot more quickly. There are some excellent ice buckets available nowadays containing removable packs that are kept in the freezer. Their main advantage is that the bottle does not have to be immersed in water, and so does not drip everywhere.

# BEST CELLARS

YOU MAY NOT KNOW IT, but you need to store your wine and, what's more, you probably do anyway. If you are a regular wine drinker (and most medical sources indicate that wine is good for us *in moderation*) you will always have some wine knocking about the house, mansion, estate or castle. This might be just a few bottles, or caseloads if you have the money and aim to have a 'serious' cellar. What's more, even if you are in the 'small' league at the moment, you can often save money (and extra shopping trips) by buying by the case.

## ∽ STORING WINE & PLANNING A CELLAR ∽

Here are the essential rules that apply to every cellar, or collection of wine, big or small, assuming you want to enjoy your wine in its best condition.

1. *It's important where you keep them.* By all means keep a few bottles in the kitchen or drinks cupboard, provided you intend to drink them after only a couple of weeks. Don't keep them for any longer because they will be subjected to extremes of temperature which will damage the majority of wines.

2. *Lay them flat.* All wine bottles to be stored for more than a couple of weeks (or days if the wine is very old) should be kept lying on their sides. You don't even have to possess a wine rack for this – lie them on the floor and stack them on top of each other. A wine rack is best, though, because it will enable you to get at the bottles at the bottom more easily. The reason for keeping bottles on their sides is that the cork expands when it is wet and if the bottle is kept upright the cork will shrink, letting in air which will turn your precious wine into vinegar. And always keep your bottles with the labels uppermost. This is how they are kept in every good cellar and it means that, when you come to decant them, the sediment will always have fallen on to the side of the bottle opposite the label.

3. *Create a good environment.* Much is discussed about temperature, plenty of it hot air! Although temperature *is* important, it's better to have a constant temperature than an occasionally cold temperature. Lots of vibration can damage a wine, particularly if kept for a long period. And light is certainly to be avoided – wine likes darkness.

A traditional underground cellar is the best environment – it is cool, dark, the temperature fluctuates minimally, and, unless it is next to an Underground line, it has

little vibration. But unless you are lucky enough to own an old country mansion, most basements nowadays are inhabited by people or central heating boilers and rodents! *Never* store your wine close to a boiler – the heat and temperature fluctuation will damage it beyond repair.

In today's thin-walled houses a different solution needs to be found. The traditional cupboard under the stairs is often the answer – it's dark, is unlikely to contain a heat source, and can be relatively vibration free. Or, if you have enough rooms, a spare bedroom can be converted into a wine cellar without too much problem. Garden sheds have been known to be used, but you'll have to insulate most of them, and then there's the additional problem of security.

But if you have a number of cases to store, and your house simply isn't big enough, most good wine merchants can offer storage facilities for a small fee.

## ∽ PLANNING A CELLAR ∽

Planning a cellar, or a wine collection, and maintaining it, takes a lifetime because wine and winemaking is constantly changing. You could go out today and buy the top 100 wines of the world, but in 5 or 10 years' time your cellar would be out of date. More winemakers would have emerged, techniques would have changed, probably radically, and 5 or 10 new vintages would have been put on the market. The secret is to add to your collection gradually. Whether this is by the caseload or by the bottle depends on your budget!

It's great news having a wine collection, however small, at home. It will give you more variety when you want to drink a wine or when you have some friends round for a meal – without having to go out to the nearest shop to buy a bottle.

A good cellar should be balanced between wines for drinking now, or over the next year, and wines for drinking in the future. You can choose the former purely by buying what you like now, but the latter require a little more skill in choosing, and it's best to seek the advice of your wine supplier. You'll find details of the best producers and wines in each region in the relevant chapters later on in this book, but here is some broad advice to help you on your way. Always remember that a wine called after an area (e.g. Rhône or Chianti) is likely to be made by many different producers. Don't just go out and buy any bottle with the name of the area on it – make sure you also identify the right producer.

*RIGHT: A large, traditional, well stocked, underground cellar. This is the best environment in which to store wine as it is cool, dark, has minimal fluctuation of temperature and little vibration.*
*BELOW: A cupboard under the stairs can easily be converted to a wine cellar. It is ideal and space saving as well as being dark and practical as long as it doesn't contain a heat source.*

### Wines for drinking now – Reds

Always go for the best vintages (although there can be exceptions that your wine supplier should tell you about) and you can buy any of the best vintage from the most recent to the rarest and most expensive. The following is not a comprehensive list of wines to buy for current drinking, but my personal favourites: red Loires, fruity Beaujolais, mature red Bordeaux (especially Pomerol and St Emilion) and Burgundy, mature Rioja, Navarra, Ribera del Duero, soft Californian Merlot, Bulgarian Cabernet Sauvignon and Merlot, Portuguese reds, Chilean reds.

### Wines for drinking now – Whites

The same comment applies as to the reds for drinking now, but again here are some personal favourites. White Burgundies (provided they don't have too much sulphur), fresh Loires, rich New World whites from Australia, California and New Zealand, Bulgarian Chardonnay, Alto-Adige and Friuli whites, Champagne, Cava, good Muscadet, new-style Spanish whites, Alsace, Provence rosés.

### Wines to lay down medium term – Reds

Good vintages from two to eight years' old of the following: Bordeaux *crus bourgeois* (like Chasse-Spleen or Potensac), Côte d'Or Burgundy, Rioja, Beaujolais from good vintages, good Californian and Australian Cabernet and Shiraz, lesser northern Rhônes (like Crozes-Hermitage).

**Wines to lay down medium term – Whites**

Good vintages from one to three years' old of the following wines: Graves, German Kabinett to Beerenauslese, New World Chardonnay and Sauvignon, sweet Loires, lesser Sauternes, Burgundy, Champagne.

**Wines to lay down long term – Reds**

Any good vintage up to 15 years old of the following wines: top red Bordeaux, Côte d'Or Burgundy, Rhône (especially northern), top California and Australian Cabernet Sauvignons and Shiraz, top Italians like Sassicaia or Barolo, good Riojas, Vega Sicilia, vintage ports.

**Wines to lay down long term – Whites**

Any good vintage up to 10 years' old of the following wines: the best Graves, German Auslese to Beerenauslese, sweet Loires, top Sauternes, the best Côte d'Or Burgundy (like Corton-Charlemagne or Puligny-Montrachet), vintage Champagne.

### ∾ WHEN TO BUY THE BOTTLES ∾

This might seem like rather a silly heading, but it isn't! While many young wines can be bought directly from your local wine supplier, you'll have to think a bit more carefully if you want to enjoy stocks of older wines. You'll see what I mean if you go into any good wine outlet, and look at the vintages of the wines on the shelves. If you find any at all over 10 years old, you'll be lucky, and the majority are likely to be five years old or less.

There's a very simple reason for this situation. Most wine suppliers cannot finance stocks for long periods of time – they would just not get their money back. Because, while certain wines have in the past increased considerably in value over several years as they matured, the majority do not appreciate in value. This means that most wines get drunk for too young and then cannot be bought when they are mature. The only way to ensure that you have mature wines to drink is to buy them young and then lay them down yourself.

When you are buying wines to keep, you need to look for certain traits in the wine if you cannot obtain expert advice. Is there enough tannin (red wines only), is there enough acidity, and is there enough concentrated fruit? And, most important, are these three elements well-balanced and does the wine have good length? (see *'Getting Your Teeth Into It!'*, page 31).

The traditional wines to lay down are claret, Burgundy and vintage port, but there are many others worth experimenting with like Rioja, some Italian reds, Rhône, white Graves, white Burgundy and even some New World reds and whites. When you buy them depends on when you can find stocks of the right wines. If you are buying them from a typical shop that stores its bottles upright, make sure you ask for fresh stock that has been kept lying down. By doing this you can ensure that the corks will not have shrunk, and that the wines will keep well.

Claret, Rhône and vintage port can be bought from specialist merchants *en primeur*, a unique type of wine-buying. While there is no guarantee that this will always be the case, it has been one of the cheapest ways of buying fine wine in the past. It involves paying for the wine when it is first released on to the market (*en primeur*), often several years before it is bottled. In return, the château owner will release it at a price that is likely to be lower than when it is eventually available in bottle.

*A very old cellar in which wine has been left to mature in oak barrels.*

# MIX AND MATCH

IGNORE ALL THE RULES – they were made to be broken. After all, it's your palate and you can decide whatever combination of flavours to inflict on it, so mix and match as *you* like!

### ∾ WINE & FOOD ∾

To help you start, and avoid unnecessary pitfalls (you can try really wild experiments once you've had more practice!), here's some guidance on the theory behind matching food and wine. I'll follow that with a list of suggested combinations for you to try.

The skill in achieving the right result is to ensure that the wine and the food balance each other. A subtle, complex wine needs delicate, bland food to set it off. And likewise if you are eating delicately flavoured food, don't overpower it with the wine unless the wine is more important to you. Fully flavoured dishes need full-bodied, powerful wines or, if spicy, a spicy wine can often match up well. The choice also depends on whether you place more importance on the food or on the wine – whichever is the most important should take precedence.

Ignore the 'red with meat, white with fish' rule and experiment – that's what makes food and wine so much fun. Oily fish (like mullet or mackerel), whether grilled or fried often demand a light red rather than a white. And a full-bodied white can go extremely well with red meat.

But there are some basic rules that should *not* be ignored. It is best to serve young wines before old ones, as a young, acidic wine can taste unpleasant after the palate has become used to the velvetiness of a mature wine. The highest quality wine of the same colour should always come last, otherwise the lesser wine will be disappointing after the better one.

Here are some suggestions for what to drink with what food. But remember, they are only suggestions and it's up to you to make the final choice!

### ∾ APERITIFS ∾

An aperitif should stimulate the appetite before the meal. Avoid spirits, especially if you are drinking good wine – they will anaesthetize your taste buds.

Light white wines are ideal aperitifs – Alsace whites like Riesling or Pinot Blanc, or a lower-alcohol German wine. Add a bit more colour by serving a rosé or blush wine – Alsace Pinot Noir, Lirac or Provence rosé if you like dry wines, or a Californian blush wine if you want something sweeter.

Champagne is always stylish and few people will refuse a glass (either white or rosé) but if your budget won't stretch to that, try a good quality *méthode champenoise*

*A glass of red wine is a good accompaniment to any type of lunch, in this case goat's cheese salad.*

*Chilled sweet white wine will complement this first course dish of asparagus with Hollandaise sauce.*

wine like sparkling Saumur, Crémant de Bourgogne or a good Spanish Cava. Add a dash of Crème de Cassis (black-currant liqueur) or Crème de Mûre (blackberry liqueur) to make Kir Royal, transforming a glass of ordinary fizz into something much more exciting.

In Portugal chilled white port is all the rage, on the rocks or mixed with tonic, and in Spain what else would one drink but a chilled fino sherry, so much more refreshing than tired old cream sherry. The French don't save the port until the end of the meal, but drink both tawny and ruby port as an aperitif. Chilled Sauternes is also popular both before the meal and with the first course.

*A fine port is the ideal accompaniment to this wedge of Stilton, at the end of a meal.*

## WINES FOR THE MEAL

Plainly cooked fish or white meat needs something fairly delicate, and dry whites seem to be the best suited. Try light whites from the Loire, Burgundy, Friuli, Alsace, German Trocken, new-style white Rioja, Muscadet, Champagne, Cava, California French Colombard, Australian Rhine Rieslings.

If the fish or meat has a flavourful sauce or is cooked in herbs, light reds, rosés or heavier whites will match well – try Beaujolais, Gamay de l'Ardèche, Loire reds, Gewürztraminer, Sauternes, sweet Vouvray, California and Australian Chardonnay, Sauvignon, Chenin Blanc, top white Burgundy, good German wines up to Auslese quality, Provence white and rosé, Lirac and Tavel rosé, Alsace Pinot Noir, Champagne.

Red meat courses without too much flavouring or spice can take just about anything – it depends on the overall flavour of the dish. Try Beaujolais *crus*, rosé, claret, Burgundy, Rhône, Rioja, lighter California and Australian Cabernet Sauvignon, Zinfandel or Shiraz, Italian reds, and just about anything else red you can think of. Big, full-flavoured Chardonnays and Sémillons from Europe and the New World can also be a good match.

Highly spiced or well-flavoured red meats need something a bit stronger, often youthful. Try youngish claret, top quality Rhône, heavy Rioja, heavy Italian reds like Tignanello, gutsy California and Australian Cabernet Sauvignon, Zinfandel and Shiraz, Provence red, Fitou, Corbières and Cahors.

Spicy oriental cooking (Chinese, Thai, Malay, or Indian) makes special demands on a wine, and most wines are not suitable unless the flavouring of the food is *very* delicate. Try the following reds and whites: Alsace (especially

Gewürztraminer, Muscat or Sylvaner), more powerful dry white Loires or Sauvignon-based wines (good Sancerre, Pouilly-Fumé), Chianti, Barolo, good dry rosé, Provence red, heavy Rhônes, Australian Shiraz, Zinfandel. If all else fails, drink lager.

With the desserts there is one rule to follow: ensure that the wine is sweeter than the pudding, otherwise after just one taste of the pudding a wine that normally seems sweet will appear to be dry. Try any of the fortified Muscat wines like Muscat de Beaumes de Venise or Muscat de Rivesaltes, or one of the classic dessert wines like Sauternes, Barsac, Loupiac, sweet Vouvray, Asti, demi-sec Cava, or German wines from Kabinett to Trockenbeerenauslese. Chocolate puddings require a different treatment. Believe it or not they go best with red wines like Australian Shiraz, soft chocolatey flavoured Californian Merlot or St Emilions and, strangely enough, chilled Beaujolais – the acidity seems to balance well with the sweetness of the chocolate. And one of my favourites with *any* dessert is chilled Champagne – the fine bubbles and biscuity flavour of a good Champagne balance the sweetness of any pudding very well indeed.

### THE RESTAURANT WINE LIST

On the whole, wine waiters are among my least favourite people. That is not to say there aren't some good professional ones around, and maybe I have been particularly unfortunate, but in my years as a wine writer I have met many pompous and unhelpful wine waiters.

The trick is not to let them worry you or hustle you; after all, you are the customer and you are paying the bill. Always ask for the wine list if it is not given to you. The waiter will normally give it to the male in the party but, if you are female (and are choosing the wine), make sure he/she is put in his/her place by telling him/her that you would like to see it as you are choosing the wine. Don't let an

*ABOVE: This French family are enjoying an informal lunch outdoors, where they have an abundance of wine. RIGHT: Chilled flutes of Champagne accompany this wickedly sweet raspberry flan and mint chocolate ice cream, the fine bubbles and biscuity flavour of the Champagne balances the sweetness of the desserts.*

*This Californian Chardonnay goes really well with both the fresh tuna salad and the rhubarb ice cream.*

In theory the wine waiter should offer the host (male or female) a taste of the wine. He will simply pour a little bit of wine into your glass. Tilt the glass slightly away from you and have a good look at the colour which should be clear and not hazy. Then take a good sniff: it should smell fresh and clean. Then taste it. Few restaurateurs would be amused if you were to spit out the wine all over their carpet, so swallow it! Now is *not* the time to practise your wine-tasting techniques, but it *is* the time to say if the wine is not in good condition or if you think it is corked – don't wait until three-quarters of the bottle has gone or you will find the wine waiter is justifiably unsympathetic. Any decent restaurant will replace a wine that is corked immediately, although many waiters do not know what a corked wine tastes like!

If your wine is too warm, don't be afraid to say so. Many restaurants think that *chambré* (see page 38) means very warm and interpret 'room temperature' to mean almost boiling. However ritzy the restaurant, don't be afraid of asking for an ice-bucket, even for the red wine. If your wine is too cold, the quickest remedy is to pour it into the glass and simply cup the glass with your hands – it will soon warm up.

*A light red Beaujolais is perfect with dishes as diverse as roast lamb or even ice cream.*

enormous wine list worry you – take your time. Nor should you think that big always means good – it is the selection that is more important.

A good indicator of the quality of the wines in any restaurant is the house wine. If the person in the restaurant buying the wine is worth their salt they will have worked hard to ensure that the quality of their house wine is top rate. So if you are not sure what to have or whether many of the wines on the list are worth the money, why not start off with a glass of the house red or white. If this is terrible there is a fair chance that the rest of the wines on the wine list will have been badly chosen. At least by choosing the house wine you haven't wasted lots of money.

Choose whichever wine you think will go best with your food – ignore any raised eyebrows from the waiter if your choice is unconventional. Don't take any notice of the 'Is Sir/Madam sure they really want this wine?' comment.

Once you have chosen your wine, the waiter should bring you the bottle and show you the label before he has opened it. This is the time to check that the vintage is the same as it is on the wine list, often worth doing because many restaurants will substitute a less good vintage without telling you. Also ensure that they have given you the correct wine from the grower or producer mentioned on the wine list.

# FRANCE

RANCE IS NOT JUST HOME to most of the world's great classic wines, it's also the most exciting and varied wine-producing country in the world.

The range of wines made is staggering – there are big, beefy reds from the Rhône, light, fragrant whites from the Loire, sensational sweet whites from the Loire and Sauternes, massive, blockbuster dry whites from Burgundy and Graves, the world's best sparkling wine from Champagne, delicious fortified dessert wines from the Rhône and elsewhere, classic, powerful long-lived reds from Bordeaux, light, zesty reds from Beaujolais . . . and so it goes on. And this is just scratching the surface.

Since the climate varies from cold and northerly (Alsace and Champagne), to marginal Atlantic (Bordeaux), to blisteringly hot (the south), every type of grape can be grown successfully.

France has inspired many imitators, and many of the New World wine producers called their wines after the classic areas (Burgundy, Chablis, Sauternes, Champagne) before more recently developing their own idiosyncratic styles. Despite the fact that imitation is the sincerest form of flattery, the French have had to pull their socks up in recent years because of the superb technical know-how of their New World competitors.

The French as a race tend to be chauvinistic and can be parochial, especially as far as wine is concerned. It is more difficult to find a good Burgundy on the wine list of a restaurant in Bordeaux than it is in New York or London. The attitude towards wine has too often been 'we know we make the most expensive wine in the world and so we will ignore what anyone else is producing'. It is only in recent years, for instance, that many of the top winemakers of Bordeaux have stopped resting on their laurels and are again producing wines worthy of their price. This has been helped enormously by the far-sightedness of a few winemakers, in particular the late and great Baron Philippe de Rothschild who teamed up with California's Robert Mondavi to produce Opus One from Napa. Sadly other regions, like Burgundy, still have much to learn and until they real-ize that other country's winemakers are just as good, if not better, than they are, indifferent wines will continue to be produced.

Despite the innate chauvinism, there are still hundreds, indeed thousands, of fabulous wines coming out of France. It is Europe's leading quality producer (by a long way), and the country as a whole merits serious attention.

*You don't have to stray far from any route in France to discover rows and rows of vines – it's the most exciting and varied wine-producing country in the world.*

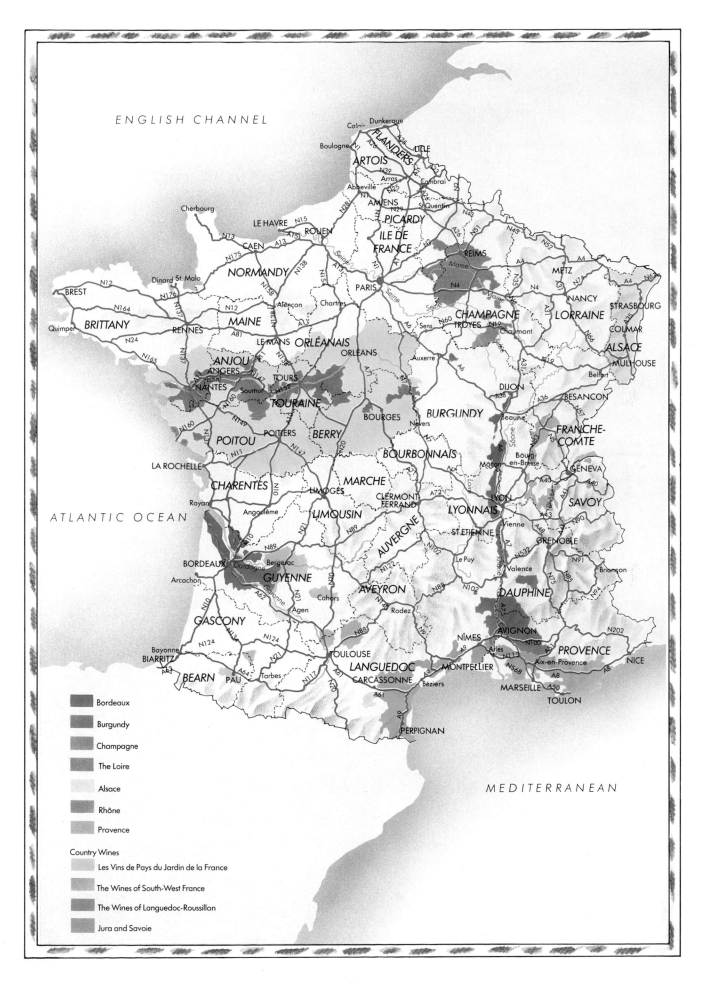

**ENGLISH CHANNEL**

Dunkerque
Calais
Boulogne
FLANDERS
LILLE
ARTOIS
N39
Arras
Cambrai
Abbeville
St Quentin
AMIENS
Cherbourg
PICARDY
LE HAVRE
ROUEN
ILE DE
FRANCE
REIMS
METZ
CAEN
Seine
PARIS
NANCY
STRASBOURG
NORMANDY
Chartres
CHAMPAGNE
LORRAINE
COLMAR
BREST
Dinard St. Malo
Alençon
MAINE
Sens
TROYES
ALSACE
MULHOUSE
BRITTANY
RENNES
LE MANS
ORLÉANAIS
Auxerre
Belfort
Quimper
ANJOU
TOURS
ORLEANS
DIJON
BESANCON
ANGERS
NANTES
Saumur
TOURAINE
BOURGES
BURGUNDY
FRANCHE-
COMTE
Nevers
Beaune
POITOU
POITIERS
BERRY
Bourg-
en-Bresse
GENEVA
LA ROCHELLE
CHARENTES
MARCHE
BOURBONNAIS
Mâcon
SAVOY
Limoges
CLERMONT
FERRAND
LYON
LYONNAIS
**ATLANTIC OCEAN**
LIMOUSIN
ST ETIENNE
Vienne
GRENOBLE
Royan
Angoulême
AUVERGNE
Le Puy
Valence
Briançon
BORDEAUX
Bergerac
Dordogne
GUYENNE
AVEYRON
DAUPHINE
Arcachon
Garonne
Cahors
Rodez
Agen
GASCONY
Bayonne
NÎMES
AVIGNON
PROVENCE
BIARRITZ
TOULOUSE
Arles
Aix-en-Provence
NICE
BEARN
PAU
Tarbes
LANGUEDOC
CARCASSONNE
MONTPELLIER
Béziers
MARSEILLE
TOULON
PERPIGNAN

**MEDITERRANEAN**

Bordeaux

Burgundy

Champagne

The Loire

Alsace

Rhône

Provence

Country Wines

Les Vins de Pays du Jardin de la France

The Wines of South-West France

The Wines of Languedoc-Roussillon

Jura and Savoie

# BORDEAUX

Ask anyone to name a French red wine and the chances are they'll say claret, the English name for red Bordeaux. This fabulous wine has long been a favourite – there's something about the rich, velvety flavour of an old claret that is seductive!

It's not just the British, however, who have a taste for claret, even though they were one of the first to discover its magic – wine-lovers (and producers) around the world bow to the superiority of great claret.

Bordeaux is one of France's most important wine regions. It is home to some of the world's greatest and most famous wines – names like Châteaux Latour, Lafite-Rothschild and Margaux spring to mind – as well as producing a remarkably wide range of styles of wine. You can

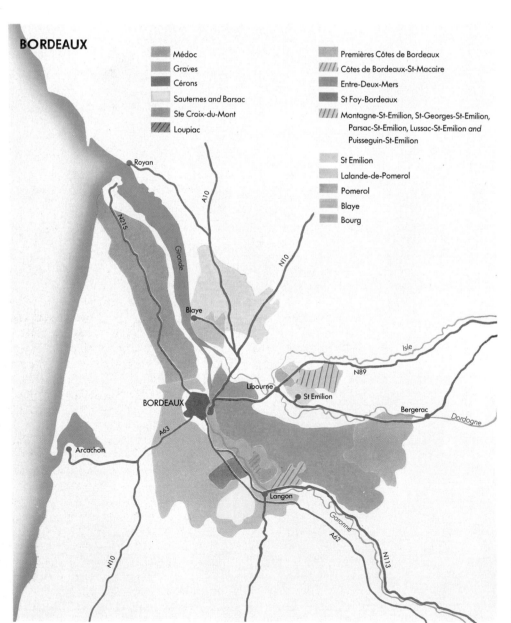

**BORDEAUX**

| | |
|---|---|
| Médoc | Premières Côtes de Bordeaux |
| Graves | Côtes de Bordeaux-St-Macaire |
| Cérons | Entre-Deux-Mers |
| Sauternes *and* Barsac | St Foy-Bordeaux |
| Ste Croix-du-Mont | Montagne-St-Emilion, St-Georges-St-Emilion, |
| Loupiac | Parsac-St-Emilion, Lussac-St-Emilion *and* |
| | Puisseguin-St-Emilion |
| | St Emilion |
| | Lalande-de-Pomerol |
| | Pomerol |
| | Blaye |
| | Bourg |

*Bordeaux is not just about famous châteaux, the co-operatives can produce good wines too.*

find light or heavy reds, both for drinking young or for laying down; dry whites, from light wines that will hardly last one year to full, classic wines that will last for decades; light, softly sweet whites, to massively intense ultra-sweet wines that will last for centuries. Even rosé (known as *clairet*) is produced, although it is rarely found outside the region today.

## ∾ THE GEOGRAPHY OF BORDEAUX ∾

The town of Bordeaux sits on the left bank of the river Garonne which then flows into the Gironde estuary, at the same place as the river Dordogne. This busy commercial centre (one of France's biggest cities) is like the hub of a wheel, with the different wine regions radiating from its centre like spokes. It is, admittedly, rather an elliptical wheel as the rim is stretched, echoing the course of the river Garonne which flows roughly south-east to north-west, defining the path of the vineyards that line its banks.

There are six classic regions in Bordeaux, producing mainly red wine, but also a small quantity of top quality dry and sweet white. All the white wines are produced to the south of town, and the reds can be split between the west (dominated by Cabernet Sauvignon), the east (dominated by Merlot), and the south (a bit of both). Those of the west and south lie on mainly gravel soils (especially the Médoc), and those to the east (St Emilion and Pomerol) are normally clay and/or sandy soils, with some outbreaks of gravel, on a limestone base.

| THE CLASSIC WINE REGIONS OF THE BORDEAUX AREA | | |
|---|---|---|
| *Region* | *Principal styles* | *Direction from town of Bordeaux* |
| Médoc | very dry reds | NNW to WNW |
| Graves | dry reds dry whites | SW to SSE |
| Sauternes | sweet whites | SSE |
| St Emilion (Libournais) | soft reds | ENE |
| Pomerol (Libournais) | meaty reds | ENE |

To the east of Bordeaux there are four lesser regions which are still important in size. They produce dry white and red wines, mostly for drinking young. The soil is normally clay, although there are some gravel areas and, like St Emilion and Pomerol, this lies on a limestone base.

| THE LESSER WINE REGIONS OF THE BORDEAUX AREA | | |
|---|---|---|
| *Region* | *Principal styles* | *Direction from town of Bordeaux* |
| Entre Deux Mers | soft reds dry whites | N to SE |
| Libournais | soft reds | ENE |
| Bourg | soft reds dry whites | N |
| Blaye | soft reds dry whites | N |

## ∾ THE HISTORY OF BORDEAUX ∾

Bordeaux, like many of the now-defunct ports that used to line the Gironde estuary, was once a very important seaport. In the vast docks, now seldom used because most of the wine is taken by road to Calais and other Channel ports, the massive old U-boat base left over from the Second World War can still be seen.

Many of the famous *négociants* (the merchants of Bordeaux) still have their offices overlooking the port, on the Quais des Chartrons and Bacalan. And behind the impressive old stone fascias are extensive cellars filled with cases and vats of Bordeaux wine.

The vineyards and the châteaux date back centuries, those in St Emilion to the Romans, and those in the Médoc to the Middle Ages. The difference between the Libournais (i.e. Saint Emilion and Pomerol) and the Médoc is pronounced in every respect, from the main grape varieties grown, to the types of soil, to the size of the properties. The Médoc properties are often ten times the size of those in the Libournais, and many are the legacy of feudal estates for whom vine-growing was very much a secondary occupation. Those of the Libournais, with a very few exceptions, have never been part of such large estates.

## THE APPELLATIONS AND CLASSIFICATIONS OF BORDEAUX

Wine at all levels of quality is made in Bordeaux, bad and indifferent, good and great, and it is important not to assume that anything with Bordeaux on the label will be of good quality. Of course, any wine with the name of Bordeaux on the label will come under the jurisdiction of the laws of *Appellation Controlée* but this is not necessarily the guarantee of quality it should be, neither here nor in the rest of France.

There are two types of Bordeaux wine that can be bought: single-property wines or generic wines. The former come from specific châteaux, and will have the château name on the label; the latter are just known simply by the name of their appellation and are a mixture of wines from all over the relevant region. Single-property wines (of which there are over 7,000 in the region) are normally better, with more individuality, than the generics.

The quality assessment of Bordeaux wines starts with the appellation (Bordeaux and Bordeaux Supérieur at the bottom, going up to appellations like Pomerol or Pauillac), and then the individual châteaux in certain areas are graded by classifications. The appellations with these classifications are Médoc, Graves, St Emilion and Sauternes, the only major area without a classification is Pomerol.

The Médoc's classification starts at the top with the *Premiers Crus* (or First Growths), going down through to *Cinquièmes Crus* (or Fifth Growths), beneath which are the *Crus Bourgeois*. In the Graves there is just one First Growth, Haut Brion, then several châteaux which are classed both for their red and their white wines. St Emilion has two 'A' First Growths, followed by nine 'B' First Growths, then numerous *Grands Crus Classés* and finally hundreds of *Grands Crus*.

The classification in Bordeaux is made by château, and the château is allowed to change its vineyard area provided it stays within the same appellation. The most important classification, that of the Médoc, was made in 1855, and so much has changed since then (including the winemakers of course!) that it is debatable whether one should still use it. Some supposedly lowly Fifth Growths (like Lynch-Bages) make wine of a higher quality than some Second Growths, and even some of the *Crus Bourgeois* (like Chasse-Spleen or d'Angludet) make wine that is better than some Third Growths!

## THE MAIN GRAPE VARIETIES OF BORDEAUX

Bordeaux is one of the few classic regions of France (with the exception of Châteauneuf-du-Pape and Champagne) that traditionally make their wines from a blend of grape varieties. The reds are made from five different varieties, Cabernet Sauvignon, Cabernet Franc, Merlot, Petit Verdot and Malbec. Of these the first three are by far the most important. The Cabernet Sauvignon is the main grape of the Médoc and Graves, the Merlot and Cabernet Franc the main grapes of the Libournais and the lesser regions. The Petit Verdot, although rarely accounting for more than 10 per cent of the vines in a particular vineyard, is said by many producers to be an important part of the mixture.

Merlot and Cabernet Sauvignon produce wine with very different styles – the former's wines are softer and more voluptuous than the latter's. Some producers, however, like Peter Sichel, say that the only reason they grow more than one grape variety is as an insurance policy against there being bad weather, since the Merlot ripens long before the Cabernet Sauvignon.

The classic flavour of red Bordeaux is of *cassis* (blackcurrants), laced with hints of vanilla and spices if the wine has been aged in new oak barrels. When young, a good Bordeaux will be tannic and astringent, and will soften out with age.

For white wines there are only two main grape varieties, Sauvignon Blanc and Sémillon. And nobody can say that either is grown only as a hedge against bad weather – they produce totally different styles of wine. Sauvignon wines are fresh, fruity, full of zip, whereas the Sémillons are more rounded and fuller bodied. Both varieties are used for making both dry and sweet white wines.

## TRENDS IN WINEMAKING IN BORDEAUX

There has been a revolution in winemaking techniques in Bordeaux in recent years. Most of the dreary, old-style red wines have thankfully disappeared, and there are a significant number of exciting whites, vinified by credit of the new-style methods.

Professor Emile Peynaud must take much of the praise for what has happened to the great red wines – he has encouraged proprietors to invest in their cellars and in new technology, as well as looking after the vineyards and using modern vinification techniques. And while the Bordelais would be loath to admit it, the increased competition from producers in California and Australia must have made them pull their socks up. They still dislike being reminded of the seminal tastings in the early 1970s organized by the likes of Stephen Spurrier, when

*Château Latour is one of only five 'Premiers Crus' of the Médoc, this position being within a classification which was created in 1855, but which still stands today. The wines produced at this top château are capable of ageing for decades.*

California wines trounced Bordeaux First Growths in New York blind tastings!

Red wines are vinified in the traditional way, and are aged in new (or a proportion of new) oak barrels for up to two years after the fermentation. This is the same technique used in Rioja, whose producers imported it from Bordeaux. Because of the techniques used and the quality of the grapes, the best Bordeaux reds can last for decades, and even centuries, becoming more and more interesting as they mature.

The best white Bordeaux wines are made either using cold fermentation techniques (see page 13) or new oak barrel fermentation. The latter technique is only used for the most expensive wines, but can produce sensational results. Oak barrels are also used for maturing the top sweet wines of the area, from Sauternes and Barsac, wines made from botrytized grapes (see page 12).

Comprehensive tastings of the top wines from recent vintages confirm that there is now more really good wine coming out of Bordeaux than ever before.

## ∾ HOW THE BORDEAUX MARKET WORKS ∾

Few of the top classified châteaux sell directly to foreign wine merchants. Instead they sell to *négociants* (through the medium of courtiers) who then sell their wine on. Many firms of *négociants* also buy in standard Bordeaux and Bordeaux Supérieur wines from smaller growers, which they bottle and sell under their own brand. More recently, many of the co-operatives in Bordeaux have started to make really excellent wines and are equipped with the latest technology.

## ∾ THE IMPORTANCE OF THE WINEMAKER ∾

Although the soil and the location is very important, it is the winemaker himself (or herself) who finally dictates whether the wine will be exceptional, great, average or poor. Bordeaux has more than its fair share of great winemakers (and proprietors who support them), and it's interesting to see how their influence extends.

The following is a roll of honour of some of the winemakers, oenologists and proprietors who have been most instrumental in establishing and influencing today's high standard of winemaking in Bordeaux:

| WHO'S WHO IN BORDEAUX | |
| --- | --- |
| Professor Emile Peynaud | Most of the best non-Libournais châteaux, including Margaux and Haut-Brion |
| The Moueix family | Many of the best Libournais châteaux, including Pétrus and Lafleur |
| Michel Rolland | Pomerol guru who owns le Bon Pasteur |
| Alexis Lichine | Prieuré-Lichine & Lascombes |
| Bruno Prats | Cos d'Estournel and Petit-Village |
| Peter Sichel | Palmer and d'Angludet |
| Bernadette Villars | Chasse-Spleen, Haut-Bages-Libéral and la Gurgue |
| Michel Delon | Léoville-Lascases, Pichon-Lalande, Lagrange and Potensac |
| Jean-Michel Cazes | Lynch-Bages, Pichon-Baron and others |
| The Borie family | Ducru-Beaucaillou, Grand-Puy-Lacoste, Haut-Batailley and others |
| The Vialard family | Cissac and others |
| The Cordier group | Gruaud-Larose, Talbot, Meyney and others |
| Baron Philippe de Rothschild | Mouton-Rothschild and others |
| The Mentzenopoulos family | Margaux |
| Madame de Lencquesaing | Pichon-Lalande |
| Anthony Barton | Léoville- and Langoa-Barton |
| The Thienpont family | Vieux Château Certan, le Pin, Labégorce-Zédé, and others |
| Claude Ricard | Domaine de Chevalier |
| Pascal Delbeck | Ausone and Belair |
| Gérard Gribelin | de Fieuzal |
| Peter Vinding-Diers | Rahoul and others |

# THE MÉDOC

Serious wine-lovers get very excited about the Médoc – not only do they start jumping up and down but they lick their lips in anticipation! For this is the region that is known for some of the world's most expensive and most fabulous wines like Châteaux Mouton-Rothschild, Margaux and Latour. The top wines are produced in a small area of the higher quality Haut-Médoc, more specifically in three areas of gravel banks centred around (from north to south): St Estèphe, Pauillac and St Julien, Listrac and Moulis, and Margaux. In this chapter I will concentrate on looking at these areas in detail.

The Médoc is essentially a large peninsula, bordered by the Atlantic on one side, and the river Garonne and the Gironde estuary on the other. It produces a large quantity of wine, of many varying qualities.

The wines of the Médoc were classified in 1855, and this classification is still widely used (see the table on page 54), but many of the parameters have changed since 1855: the winemakers, the owners and even the vineyard areas themselves. So the classification is only a guideline – supposedly lowly Fifth Growths (*Cinquièmes Crus*) like Châteaux Grand-Puy-Lacoste or Lynch-Bages can be better than many Second Growths (*Deuxièmes Crus*). You will find my personal recommendations of the best châteaux in the following pages, regardless of classification.

The style of Médoc wines is full, heavy and tannic when young, but capable of maturing, often over long periods of time, into something which is delicious, complex and rounded, often with rich, peppery fruit and spicy/cigar box overtones. The vast majority are red, although there are a few exceptions like Château Loudenne and Pavillon Blanc de Château Margaux.

A recent phenomenon in the Médoc is the incredible increase in the number of so-called Second Wines (see table). These are made from wine not considered to be quite good enough for the *Grand Vin* (the wine sold under the main château name), and are made from the same grapes grown in the same vineyards. Normally the wine comes from younger vines or particular vats not considered to be up to scratch for the *Grand Vin*. But provided the *Grand Vin* itself is good, they can be remarkable value – often selling at a third of the price. Drinking Second Wines gives you a good indication of the characteristics of the *Grand Vin*, and there is an added bonus in that they tend to mature earlier.

Apart from the well-known Classed Growths there are many excellent *Crus Bourgeois* included in the recommended list of producers from the Médoc on page 55.

## VINTAGE CHART – MEDOC AND GRAVES (RED)

Vintages of clarets come up for sale at auction frequently.

| | |
|---|---|
| 1988 Very good | 1975 Very inconsistent – |
| 1987 Average, but some | be careful |
| good early-maturing | 1974 Poor |
| wines made | 1973 Average |
| 1986 Very good/outstanding | 1972 Poor |
| 1985 Outstanding | 1971 Excellent |
| 1984 Poor | 1970 Outstanding |
| 1983 Very good | 1969 Poor |
| 1982 Exceptional, but | 1968 Abysmal |
| beware 'hot' wines | 1967 Average: drink up |
| 1981 Very good, great value | 1966 Very good |
| 1980 Poor, with a few | 1965 Abysmal |
| exceptions | 1964 Can be very good |
| 1979 Good, but not great | 1963 Abysmal |
| 1978 Great potential | 1962 Very good but drink |
| 1977 Dreadful | up |
| 1976 Some very good wines | 1961 Outstanding |

Other exceptional older vintages that are still drinking well:
1953, 1952, 1949, 1947, 1945, 1929, 1928.

*LEFT: The majority of châteaux in Bordeaux still harvest their grapes by hand.*
*BELOW: Although St Julien boasts no Premiers Crus at all, the overall quality of its wines is high.*

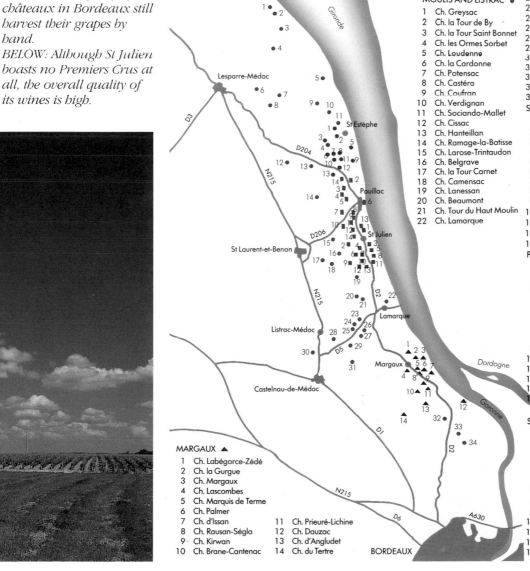

**MÉDOC**

MÉDOC, HAUT MÉDOC, MOULIS AND LISTRAC ●
1 Ch. Greysac
2 Ch. la Tour de By
3 Ch. la Tour Saint Bonnet
4 Ch. les Ormes Sorbet
5 Ch. Loudenne
6 Ch. la Cardonne
7 Ch. Potensac
8 Ch. Castéra
9 Ch. Coufran
10 Ch. Verdignan
11 Ch. Sociando-Mallet
12 Ch. Cissac
13 Ch. Hanteillan
14 Ch. Ramage-la-Batisse
15 Ch. Larose-Trintaudon
16 Ch. Belgrave
17 Ch. la Tour Carnet
18 Ch. Camensac
19 Ch. Lanessan
20 Ch. Beaumont
21 Ch. Tour du Haut Moulin
22 Ch. Lamarque
23 Ch. Maucaillou
24 Ch. Poujeaux
25 Ch. Dutruch-Grand-Poujeaux
26 Ch. Grossior Grand Poujeaux
27 Ch. Chasse-Spleen
28 Ch. Clarke
29 Ch. Brillette
30 Ch. Moulin-à-Vent
31 Ch. Citran
32 Ch. Cantemerle
33 Ch. la Lagune
34 Ch. d'Agassac

ST ESTÈPHE ●
1 Ch. le Boscq
2 Ch. Calon-Ségur
3 Ch. les Ormes de Pez
4 Ch. de Pez
5 Ch. Meyney
6 Ch. Pomys
7 Ch. le Crock
8 Ch. Haut Marbuzet
9 Ch. Montrose
10 Ch. Chambert Marbuzet
11 Ch. de Marbuzet
12 Ch. Cos d'Estournel
13 Ch. Cos Labory

PAUILLAC ■
1 Ch. Lafite-Rothschild
2 Ch. Clerc-Milon-Rothschild
3 Ch. Mouton-Rothschild
4 Ch. Mouton-Baron-Philippe
5 Ch. Pontet-Canet
6 Ch. Grand-Puy-Ducasse
7 Ch. Grand-Puy-Lacoste
8 Ch. Haut-Bages-Libéral
9 Ch. Lynch-Bages
10 Ch. Haut-Batailley
11 Ch. Fonbadet
12 Ch. Pichon-Longueville-Baron
13 Ch. Latour
14 Ch. Pichon-Longueville, Comtesse-de-Lalande

ST JULIEN ■
1 Ch. Léoville-Lascases
2 Ch. Talbot
3 Ch. Léoville-Poyferré
4 Ch. Langoa-Barton
5 Ch. Léoville-Barton
6 Ch. Lalande-Borie
7 Ch. Terrey-Gros-Caillou
8 Ch. Ducru-Beaucaillou
9 Ch. Lagrange
10 Ch. Hortevie
11 Ch. Beychevelle
12 Ch. Gruaud-Larose
13 Ch. St Pierre

MARGAUX ▲
1 Ch. Labégorce-Zédé
2 Ch. la Gurgue
3 Ch. Margaux
4 Ch. Lascombes
5 Ch. Marquis de Terme
6 Ch. Palmer
7 Ch. d'Issan
8 Ch. Rausan-Ségla
9 Ch. Kirwan
10 Ch. Brane-Cantenac
11 Ch. Prieuré-Lichine
12 Ch. Dauzac
13 Ch. d'Angludet
14 Ch. du Tertre

BORDEAUX

# THE 1855 CLASSIFICATION OF THE RED WINES OF THE GIRONDE
## SHOWING SECOND WINES

Châteaux no longer in existence are not listed, and the modern names are shown where appropriate.

| PREMIERS CRUS (First Growths) | SECOND WINES |
|---|---|
| Château Lafite-Rothschild, Pauillac | Moulin des Carruades |
| Château Margaux, Margaux | Pavillon Rouge de Château Margaux |
| Château Latour, Pauillac | Les Forts de Latour |
| Château Haut-Brion, Pessac (Graves) | Bahans Haut Brion |
| Château Mouton-Rothschild, Pauillac (First Growth since 1973) | NONE |

| DEUXIEMES CRUS (Second Growths) | SECOND WINES |
|---|---|
| Château Rausan-Ségla, Margaux | Château Lamouroux |
| Château Rauzan-Gassies, Margaux | NONE |
| Château Léoville-Lascases, St Julien | Clos du Marquis |
| Château Léoville-Poyferré, St Julien | Château Moulin Riche |
| Château Léoville-Barton, St Julien | A C St Julien |
| Château Durfort-Vivens, Margaux | NONE |
| Château Gruaud-Larose, St Julien | Sarget de Gruaud Larose |
| Château Lascombes, Margaux | Château Segonnes |
| Château Brane-Cantenac, Cantenac | Château Notton |
| Château Pichon-Longueville-Baron, Pauillac | Les Tourelles de Longueville |
| Château Pichon-Longueville, Comtesse-de-Lalande, Pauillac | Réserve de la Comtesse |
| Château Ducru-Beaucaillou, St Julien | Château la Croix |
| Château Cos d'Estournel, St Estèphe | Château de Marbuzet |
| Château Montrose, St Estèphe | La Dame de Montrose |

| TROISIEMES CRUS (Third Growths) | SECOND WINES |
|---|---|
| Château Kirwan, Cantenac | A C Margaux |
| Château d'Issan, Cantenac | NONE |
| Château Ferrière, Margaux | NONE |
| Château Lagrange, St Julien | Les Fiefs de Lagrange |
| Château Langoa-Barton, St Julien | NONE |
| Château Giscours, Labarde | NONE |
| Château Malescot-St Exupéry, Margaux | NONE |
| Château Boyd-Cantenac, Cantenac | NONE |
| Château Cantenac-Brown, Cantenac | NONE |
| Château Palmer, Cantenac | Réserve du Général |
| Château la Lagune, Ludon | Ludon-Pomiés-Agassac |
| Château Desmirail, Margaux | Domaine de Fontarney |
| Château Calon-Ségur, St Estèphe | Marquis de Ségur |
| Château Marquis d'Alesme-Becker, Margaux | NONE |

| QUATRIEMES CRUS (Fourth Growths) | SECOND WINES |
|---|---|
| Château St-Pierre, St Julien | Château Saint Louis le Boscq |
| Château Talbot, St Julien | Connetable de Talbot |
| Château Branaire-Ducru, St Julien | NONE |
| Château Duhart-Milon-Rothschild, Pauillac | Moulin de Duhart |
| Château Pouget, Cantenac | NONE |
| Château la Tour-Carnet, St Laurent | NONE |
| Château Lafon-Rochet, St Estéphe | NONE |
| Château Beychevelle, St Julien | Réserve de l'Amiral |
| Château Prieuré-Lichine, Cantenac | Château de Clairefont |
| Château Marquis de Terme, Margaux | Domaine des Gondats |

| CINQUIEMES CRUS (Fifth Growths) | SECOND WINES |
|---|---|
| Château Pontet-Canet, Pauillac | NONE |
| Château Batailley, Pauillac | NONE |
| Château Haut-Batailley, Pauillac | Château la Tour l'Aspic |
| Château Grand-Puy-Lacoste, Pauillac | Lacoste-Borie |
| Château Grand-Puy-Ducasse, Pauillac | NONE |
| Château Lynch-Bages, Pauillac | Château Haut-Bages-Averous |
| Château Lynch-Moussas, Pauillac | NONE |
| Château Dauzac, Labarde | Château Labarde |
| Château Mouton-Baronne-Philippe, Pauillac | NONE |
| Château du Tertre, Arsac | NONE |
| Château Haut-Bages-Libéral, Pauillac | NONE |
| Château Pédesclaux, Pauillac | NONE |
| Château Belgrave, St Laurent | NONE |
| Château Camensac, St Laurent | NONE |
| Château Cos Labory, St Estèphe | NONE |
| Château Clerc-Milon-Rothschild, Pauillac | NONE |
| Château Croizet-Bages, Pauillac | NONE |
| Château Cantemerle, Macau | Baron Villeneuve de Cantemerle |

| UNCLASSIFIED CHATEAUX (including Crus Bourgeois) | SECOND WINES |
|---|---|
| Château Chasse-Spleen, Moulis | l'Ermitage de Chasse-Spleen |
| Château Cissac, Haut-Médoc | Château Abiet |
| Château d'Angludet, Margaux | Château Bory |
| Château Meyney, St Estèphe | Le Prieuré de Meyney |
| Château Beaumont, Haut-Médoc | Château Moulin d'Arvigny |
| Château Coufran, Haut-Médoc | Domaine de la Rose-Maréchal |
| Château Clarke, Listrac | Château Malmaison |
| Château Fonbadet, Pauillac | Château Tour du Roc Moulin |
| Château Hanteillan, Haut-Médoc | Château Larrivaux-Hanteillan |
| Château Labégorce-Zédé, Margaux | Domaine Zédé |
| Château Moulin-à-Vent, Moulis | Moulin de St Vincent |
| Château Monbrison, Margaux | Château Cordet |
| Château Potensac, Médoc | Château Lassalle |
| Château Ramage-la-Batisse, Haut-Médoc | Château Tourteran |
| Château Poujeaux, Moulis | Château la Salle de Poujeaux |
| Château Sociando-Mallet, Haut-Médoc | Château Lartigue de Brochon |
| Château la Tour de By, Médoc | La Roque de By |

## ∞ MEDOC, HAUT-MEDOC, MOULIS AND LISTRAC ∞

These four appellations cover a very large area between them, especially Médoc and Haut-Médoc, and there are many châteaux and generic wines produced. The latter are generally best avoided altogether, as one is only paying for the name Médoc (or whatever) on the label, and they mature very quickly. And regrettably many of the smaller châteaux are not really worth considering.

It's not all bad news, however – the top wines of these four appellations (see the table below) represent some of the best value to be had in the entire Bordeaux area! There are only five classed growths, of which Château la Lagune is the star. It is a wine of Second Growth quality, consistently out-performing many other supposedly better wines from the more famous appellations of the Haut-Médoc. Other wines from these areas that deserve to be singled out for their consistently high quality and remarkable value for money are Châteaux Chasse-Spleen, Cissac, Gressier-Grand-Poujeaux, Hanteillan, Lanessan, Potensac, Poujeaux, Ramage-la-Batisse, Sociando-Mallet and Tour du Haut Moulin.

The best wines (almost all red) normally need to be

### RECOMMENDED CHATEAUX
#### MEDOC, HAUT-MEDOC, MOULIS AND LISTRAC
#### (not including Second Wines)

Château Beaumont, A C Haut-Médoc
Château Belgrave, A C Haut-Médoc (*5ème Cru Classé*)
Château Brillette, A C Moulis
Château Camensac, A C Haut-Médoc (*5ème Cru Classé*)
Château Cantemerle, A C Haut-Médoc (*5ème Cru Classé*)
Château Castéra, A C Médoc
Château Chasse-Spleen, A C Moulis
Château Cissac, A C Haut-Médoc
Château Citran, A C Haut-Médoc
Château Clarke, A C Listrac
Château Coufran, A C Haut-Médoc
Château d'Agassac, A C Haut-Médoc
Château de Malleret, A C Haut-Médoc
Château Dutruch-Grand-Poujeaux, A C Moulis
Château Gressier-Grand-Poujeaux, A C Moulis
Château Greysac, A C Médoc
Château Hanteillan, A C Haut-Médoc
Château la Cardonne, A C Médoc
Château la Lagune, A C Haut-Médoc (*3ème Cru Classé*)
Château Lamarque, A C Haut-Médoc
Château Lanessan, A C Haut-Médoc
Château Larose-Trintaudon, A C Haut-Médoc
Château la Tour Carnet, A C Haut-Médoc (*4ème Cru Classé*)
Château la Tour de By, A C Médoc
Château la Tour Saint Bonnet, A C Médoc
Château les Ormes Sorbet, A C Médoc
Château Loudenne, A C Médoc
Château Maucaillou, A C Moulis
Château Moulin-à-Vent, A C Moulis
Château Plagnac, A C Médoc
Château Potensac, A C Médoc
Château Poujeaux, A C Moulis
Château Ramage-la-Batisse, A C Haut-Médoc
Château Sociando-Mallet, A C Haut-Médoc
Château Tour du Haut Moulin, A C Haut-Médoc
Château Verdignan, A C Haut-Médoc

kept from 5 to 20 years before they are ready to drink, but they can last for a really long time. In December 1988 I tasted a 1928 Château Chasse-Spleen which was still very enjoyable!

## ∞ MARGAUX ∞

Margaux is probably the most famous commune and appellation of the entire Bordeaux region – the name is easy to pronounce (even for the English-speaker), and its magnificent (in terms of both its architecture and its wine) First-Growth Château shares the same name.

It is the most southerly of all the Médoc communes, and generally produces softer, more easily accessible wines than the more northerly Pauillac or St Estèphe. Indeed, so significant is the geography, that the grapes in Margaux can ripen as much as a week before those in St Estèphe. This gives it a distinct advantage in difficult years when the autumn is not that hot, although it can produce stewed wines in very hot years if the winemaker is not careful. The wines of Margaux are made to be laid down, and the best will last for many decades, even centuries. However, they can often be drunk sooner than the more tannic, austere wines from further north.

Margaux is home to two very famous names (Châteaux Margaux and Palmer), and in the 1855 Classification it boasts no less than 21 (or over 30 per cent) of all the classified growths. But this just goes to show that the 1855 Classification should be taken with a pinch of salt, because many of the châteaux in Margaux have produced only indifferent wines in the past. Quality is improving dramatically, however, and the main thrust has come over the last decade or so, led by just a few notable personalities in Margaux – the Mentzenopoulos family aided by Professor Emile Peynaud (Château Margaux), Peter Sichel (Châteaux Palmer and d'Angludet) and Lionel Cruse (Château d'Issan). And it's important not to forget the redoubtable Alexis Lichine (of Château Prieuré-Lichine) whose efforts in the 1960s and early 1970s were visionary.

More recently properties like Châteaux Rausan-Ségla and Lascombes have made enormous investments to (successfully) improve their quality. The former is particularly impressive, with its ultra modern temperature-controlled stainless steel fermentation vats and computer controlled pumping equipment. And Rausan-Ségla is the only Classed Growth Médoc château to have a tank that can hold the whole production in one go. The advantage of this is that bottle variation (a too-frequent Bordeaux problem) should be totally eliminated.

As well as the Classed Growths, Margaux boasts three remarkable *Crus Bourgeois*. All produce wines of outstanding quality (better than many Classed Growths) which are fantastic value for money. They are Châteaux d'Angludet (owned by Peter Sichel of Château Palmer), Labégorce-Zédé (Luc Thienpont, the same family as Vieux Château Certan) and Monbrison (the Vonderheyden family).

The great châteaux of Margaux prove that, when well made, the appellation can produce stunning, world-beating wines. If the recent trends to improve quality continue, any Classed Growth or *Cru Bourgeois* from Margaux should be well worth buying.

RECOMMENDED CHATEAUX
MARGAUX
(not including Second Wines)

| | |
|---|---|
| Château Brane-Cantenac | Château Lascombes |
| Château d'Angludet | Château Margaux |
| Château Dauzac | Château Marquis de Terme |
| Château la Gurgue | Château Monbrison |
| Château d'Issan | Château Palmer |
| Château du Tertre | Château Prieuré-Lichine |
| Château Kirwan | Château Rausan-Ségla |
| Château Labégorce-Zédé | |

## ∽ ST JULIEN ∽

Three of the 'Big Four' Médoc appellations (St Julien, Pauillac and St Estèphe) adjoin each other towards the north of the Haut-Médoc, separated from Margaux (to the south) by a stretch of alluvial soil. The appellations are essentially large, gently undulating gravel banks, only separated by small streams, and St Julien is the most southerly of these three. Indeed, the names of some of the châteaux echo the importance of the gravelly soil to the wine – *beaucaillou* means 'beautiful pebble' (as in Château Ducru-Beaucaillou) and *gros-caillou* means 'large pebble' (as in Château Terrey-Gros-Caillou).

The difference between the appellations is sometimes so blurred, however, that the wines in the north of St Julien (in particular the three Léovilles) have much in common stylistically with the more southerly of the Pauillacs, immediately to their north.

Although St Julien is relatively small, and boasts no *Premiers Crus* at all, the overall quality of is wines is astonishingly high. Even though (or perhaps because) the estates are comparatively large, it is very rare to find a poor quality St Julien in recent vintages, and some of its wines can be as good as, if not better than, *Premiers Crus*. As is so often the case in Bordeaux, today's greatest St Juliens are produced by winemakers who are totally dedicated to their task. These include Jean-Eugène Borie and his son Xavier (Château Ducru-Beaucaillou), Michel Delon (Leóville-Lascases and Lagrange), Didier Cuvelier (Léoville-Poyferré), Anthony Barton (Léoville- and Langoa-Barton), and the Cordier group (Gruaud-Larose and Talbot). Some of the best 'Second Wines' come from St Julien, too, Clos du Marquis and Sarget de Gruaud Larose being excellent examples.

The wines of St Julien are characterized by their elegance and finesse, often showing a more pronounced *cassis* flavour than other Médoc wines. But the elegance when young is deceptive – great St Juliens can last for decades, sometimes centuries. A 1928 Château Gruaud-Larose tasted in 1988 was still vigorous and youthful, with time on its side!

If you want to try a really classic claret of exceptional quality, try one of the wines listed in the chart on the opposite page – it's highly unlikely that you will be disappointed!

*Château Lagrange, one of the most exciting properties in St Julien, bought by the Japanese firm Suntory in the 1980s. Under the management of Michel Delon of Château Léoville-Lascases.*

## ∾ PAUILLAC ∾

Pauillac must be potentially the greatest of all the Médoc appellations, containing no less than three First Growths: Château Mouton-Rothschild, Château Lafite-Rothschild and Château Latour. But in total its 18 classed growths cannot compete with the high average quality of St Julien, for example, with only 11 classed growths. There has been much resting on laurels in Pauillac, and it would be good to see quality overall improving. But there are indications that this *is* beginning to happen, with châteaux like Clerc-Milon-Rothschild, Mouton-Baron-Philippe and Pontet-Canet now producing radically improved wines.

Having said that, the best wines are outstanding. Among the First Growths I would place Mouton-Rothschild as one of Bordeaux's top three wines, and would also single out for their exceptional quality Châteaux Latour, Pichon-Lalande and Lynch-Bages, although the latter two are not First Growths. The other top wines of Pauillac are Châteaux Pichon-Baron (under the new direction of Jean-Michel Cazes of Lynch-Bages), Clerc-Milon-Rothschild, Mouton-Baron-Philippe and Grand-Puy-Lacoste.

Pauillac's great winemakers include the late Baron Philippe de Rothschild (Mouton-Rothschild, Clerc-Milon-Rothschild and Mouton-Baron-Philippe), Madame de Lencquesaing (Pichon-Lalande), Jean-Michel Cazes (Lynch-Bages and Pichon-Baron) and the Borie family (Grand-Puy-Lacoste and Haut-Batailley).

Pauillac gets more publicity than any other area of Bordeaux. The appellation has produced some of the region's most famous wines and it is often old vintages of Château Lafite-Rothschild that hit the headlines, being auctioned at unbelievably high prices. And the policy of château-bottling, now mandatory for all Classed Growths, was initiated by Baron Philippe de Rothschild with the 1924 vintage of Château Mouton-Rothschild.

Pauillac's wines are massive, very full-bodied, very tannic with a marked blackcurrant (*cassis*) flavour that shouts out Cabernet. The best wines need to be laid down for 10 to 20 years before they are ready to drink. At their best they achieve enormous complexity, subtlety and richness, typifying all the qualities that maintain the reputation of Bordeaux as one of the world's finest red wine areas.

There are some very good value Second Wines from Pauillac, including Les Forts de Latour, Lacoste-Borie, Carruades de Lafite, Haut-Bages-Averous and Réserve de la Comtesse. These can be drunk when around five years old, although will last a good decade if from a good vintage. Look carefully at the label of some generic Pauillacs which are the 'third' wines from well-known châteaux. Often the tell-tale words that will reveal the wine's origin are in the small print indicating where the wine has been bottled. With just a little bit of detective work you can find some excellent value-for-money wines.

## ∾ ST ESTEPHE ∾

St Estèphe is the most northerly of the Médoc's Classed Growth appellations. Its wines are tough, tannic and astringent when young, but have the ability to soften out beautifully with maturity. They need to be kept for longer than any other Bordeaux region, and the best will take decades to be ready for drinking. This style is reflected in the neighbouring commune of Cissac, where the well-known château of the same name is to be found. Lesser wines can be drunk between two and five years old, but will still exhibit the fairly full-bodied characteristics of this commune.

There are no First Growths at all in St Estèphe, and indeed very few Classed Growths, but one of its châteaux is among the most magnificent in Bordeaux, and also produces one of the Médoc's top wines. This is Château Cos d'Estournel, owned by Bruno Prats, and famous for its chinoiserie architecture complete with pagodas. Every visitor to the region should at least pass by it, and preferably stop for a longer look. The wine produced at Cos (pronounced koss), as it is commonly known, often beats Médoc First Growths in blind tastings, and is also very reasonably priced when sold *en primeur*.

St Estèphe's other great wine is Montrose, located up behind Cos d'Estournel, although Calon-Ségur is improving its quality every year.

There are some very interesting *Crus Bourgeois* in St Estèphe, notably Châteaux Chambert-Marbuzet, de Marbuzet, de Pez, Domeyne, le Boscq, le Crock, les Ormes de Pez, Haut Marbuzet, Meyney and Pomys. They are often sensational value for money.

# GRAVES

*T*he Graves region, stretching to the south of Bordeaux, produces red and dry white wines. It is often said that the reds have a *goût de terroir*, that's to say a taste of the soil! And, in fact, the wines do have a nuance of the taste of the dry, gravelly soil on which many of the vines are grown. If you think about it, it's not all that unlikely – the dust settles on the grapes, and is still there when they are picked. It's inevitable that there will be some (not unpleasant) flavour that is transmitted to the wine.

It's important to be choosy with Graves – it's a big region geographically, with over 500 different châteaux, most producing very indifferent wines. Many wines which bear the name 'Graves' on the label are no better than table wine, but four times the price, so only go for the best châteaux. Apart from those mentioned below, châteaux producing good wines include Bouscaut, Cabannieux, Carbonnieux, de Chantegrive, Chicane, Couhins-Lurton, Ferrande, de la Grave, La Louvière, Magence, Millet, Rahoul, Respide-Médéville, Roquetaillade-la-Grange, Smith-Haut-Lafitte, and La Tour Martillac.

The region has recently been split into two: Graves, and the smaller, more prestigious Pessac-Léognan. The latter contains the most famous châteaux, generally those making the best wines. The best châteaux are Domaine de Chevalier, de Fieuzal, Haut-Bailly (red only), Haut Brion, Laville Haut Brion (white only), Malartic-Lagravière, La Mission Haut Brion (red only) and Pape-Clement.

Graves starts in the suburbs of Bordeaux with the most famous château, Haut Brion. Like the neighbouring La Mission Haut Brion, La Tour Haut Brion and Laville Haut Brion, it is surrounded by houses, and is next to the university – they don't have any problems recruiting students to pick the grapes at vintage time! After that, the region fans out west and south to include many great names.

## ∽ RED WINES ∽

The red wines of Graves are light and elegant, capable of producing wines of complexity and interest. But when they are dull, they are very dull! Having said that, many of Bordeaux's most interesting winemakers are, and have been, based in the Graves – Pierre Coste, Dubourdieu, Christian Médéville, Peter Vinding-Diers, Gérard Gribelin, André Lurton and Claude Ricard among them.

*Domaine de Chevalier, where Claude Ricard and Olivier Bernard are producing top class white as well as red wines.*

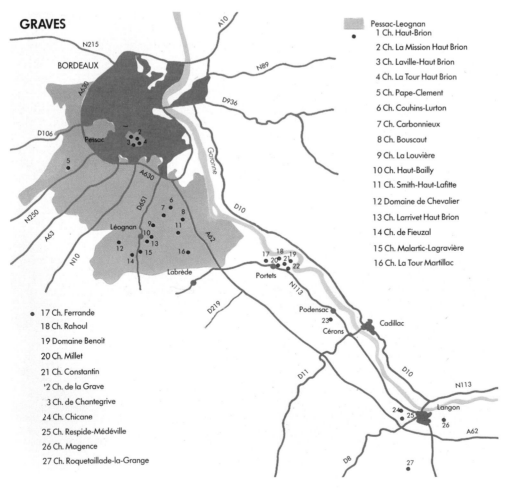

**GRAVES**

Pessac-Leognan
1 Ch. Haut-Brion
2 Ch. La Mission Haut Brion
3 Ch. Laville-Haut Brion
4 Ch. La Tour Haut Brion
5 Ch. Pape-Clement
6 Ch. Couhins-Lurton
7 Ch. Carbonnieux
8 Ch. Bouscaut
9 Ch. La Louvière
10 Ch. Haut-Bailly
11 Ch. Smith-Haut-Lafitte
12 Domaine de Chevalier
13 Ch. Larrivet Haut Brion
14 Ch. de Fieuzal
15 Ch. Malartic-Lagravière
16 Ch. La Tour Martillac

17 Ch. Ferrande
18 Ch. Rahoul
19 Domaine Benoit
20 Ch. Millet
21 Ch. Constantin
'2 Ch. de la Grave
3 Ch. de Chantegrive
24 Ch. Chicane
25 Ch. Respide-Médéville
26 Ch. Magence
27 Ch. Roquetaillade-la-Grange

## ❧ WHITE WINES ❧

When the white wines are well made they are sensational, a match for the very best white Burgundies and capable of lasting for decades. Indeed, Claude Ricard and Olivier Bernard of Domaine de Chevalier have recently decided to call their Second Wine Bâtard Chevalier, mimicking the great Grand Crus of Burgundy, Bâtard-Montrachet and Chevalier-Montrachet. And there has been a minor revolution in these wines over the last few years, all down to vinification techniques, inspired by a handful of great winemakers like Ricard.

All the best whites, without exception, are fermented in new oak casks rather than tanks. This has been semi-traditional in some of the great châteaux (like Domaine de Chevalier) for some time, but now a few of the 'lesser' properties are hauling themselves up the quality ladder by adopting similar techniques. The pioneer's greatest innovator is Peter Vinding-Diers (ex of Châteaux Rahoul, Constantin, Domaines Benoit and de la Grave), who is joined by Gérard Gribelin (de Fieuzal), Pierre Coste (several châteaux), André Lurton (Couhins-Lurton), and Christian Médéville (Respide-Médéville). Their disciples in recent vintages include Châteaux Bouscaut, Cabannieux, Carbonnieux, Ferrande, La Louvière, Roquetaillade-la-Grange, Smith-Haut-Lafitte and La Tour Martillac.

There are very few other great whites worth mentioning as most still cling to yesterday's boring and outmoded techniques. But there is plenty of young blood coming into the region. In recent years there has been an upsurge in quality wines coming from so called lesser châteaux, many of which put their classed growth neighbours to shame. If this trend continues, white Graves will once again become 'worth a detour'.

---

### VINTAGE CHART – GRAVES

| | |
|---|---|
| 1988 Excellent | 1975 Very good – better |
| 1987 Average, but some | than the Médoc |
| good early-maturing | 1974 Poor |
| wines made | 1973 Poor |
| 1986 Very good/outstanding | 1972 Poor |
| 1985 Outstanding | 1971 Excellent |
| 1984 Poor | 1970 Outstanding |
| 1983 Very good | 1969 Poor |
| 1982 Outstanding | 1968 Abysmal |
| 1981 Very good, great value | 1967 Average, drink up |
| 1980 Poor, with a few | 1966 Very good |
| exceptions | 1965 Abysmal |
| 1979 Good, but not great | 1964 Very good |
| 1978 Outstanding | 1963 Abysmal |
| 1977 Dreadful | 1962 Very good but drink up |
| 1976 Good | 1961 Outstanding |

Other exceptional older vintages that are still drinking well: 1949, 1947, 1945, 1929, 1928.

---

### RECOMMENDED WINES – GRAVES

Unless otherwise noted, all the following châteaux produce both red and white wine.

| | |
|---|---|
| Domaine Benoit | Château Larrivet Haut Brion |
| Château Bouscaut | Château La Tour Haut Brion |
| Château Carbonnieux | (red only) |
| Château de Chantegrive | Château La Tour Martillac |
| Domaine de Chevalier | Château Laville-Haut Brion |
| Château Chicane | (white only) |
| Château Constantin | Château Magence |
| Château Couhins-Lurton | Château Malartic-Lagravière |
| Château Ferrande | Château Millet |
| Château de Fieuzal | Château Pape-Clement |
| Château de la Grave | Château Rahoul |
| Château Haut-Bailly (red only) | Château Respide-Médéville |
| Château Haut-Brion | Château Roquetaillade-la- |
| Château La Louvière | Grange |
| Château La Mission Haut Brion (red only) | Château Smith-Haut-Lafitte |

---

### THE CLASSIFICATION OF GRAVES (1953)

Some of the châteaux only classified for one colour of wine in fact produce both red and white, and the red/white split of the classification has now largely been superseded. An example is Château de Fieuzal which now produces one of the top five white wines of Graves, better than many of the classified whites, although only its red was classified in 1953.

| *RED WINES* | *WHITE WINES* |
|---|---|
| Château Bouscaut | Château Bouscaut |
| Château Carbonnieux | Château Carbonnieux |
| Domaine de Chevalier | Domaine de Chevalier |
| Château de Fieuzal | Château Couhins |
| Château Haut-Bailly | Château Haut-Brion |
| Château Haut-Brion | Château La Tour Martillac |
| Château La Mission Haut Brion | Château Laville-Haut-Brion |
| Château La Tour Haut Brion | Château Malartic-Lagravière |
| Château La Tour Martillac | Château Olivier |
| Château Malartic-Lagravière | |
| Château Olivier | |
| Château Pape-Clement | |
| Château Smith-Haut-Lafitte | |

# St Emilion

$S$t Emilion produces some of the Bordeaux region's most exciting and also some of its most boring wines. ■ Surely not, I hear you cry: a wine with the words St Emilion on the label *must* be good! Unfortunately, St Emilion's far-reaching history and touristic attractions have meant that many of the region's small vineyards cash in on the area's name without paying much attention to the actual quality of the contents of the bottle. And even today, when more and more Bordeaux producers are improving their quality, rural St Emilion lags behind, although the top wines are stunning.

One of the main problems is the size of the vineyards. Because they are often only a tenth of the size of those in the Médoc they do not have the same financial muscle to make the necessary investment in new equipment and techniques. But when it's good, St Emilion is delicious – it produces soft, velvety wines of world-beating quality, based on the Merlot grape. They tend to be softer and more approachable when young than the wines of the Médoc, because of the violet, sometimes chocolatey, flavour found in the earlier-maturing Merlot. The wines of St Emilion and Pomerol often appeal to people who don't like the harsh bitterness of the Médoc wines. And Burgundy lovers will often prefer St Emilions because of their charm.

## ∾ THE MAIN GRAPE VARIETIES ∾ AND TYPES OF WINE

St Emilion is dominated by the Merlot and Cabernet Franc grapes, with the Cabernet Sauvignon playing only a background role. There is some Malbec but the Petit Verdot, found in many Médoc properties, is totally absent. Only red wine is produced, no white at all.

Merlot and Cabernet Franc both produce soft, relatively early-maturing wines, and because of this St Emilions can be drunk quite young. But don't be deceived by the relative accessibility of the wines – the best can last decades and in 1988 I tasted a superb 1928 Cheval Blanc that showed no signs of fading even after 60 years. Many supposedly more robust Médocs couldn't compete with that!

## ∾ THE GEOGRAPHY OF ST EMILION ∾

St Emilion is split into three main areas – the Graves (not to be confused with the appellation to the south of the Médoc of the same name), the Côte and the Plateau. The greatest wines tend to come from one of the first two areas, and are typified by the two First Growths (A), Châteaux Cheval Blanc and Ausone. The Graves wines, so-called because of the gravelly outcrop on which they are situated,

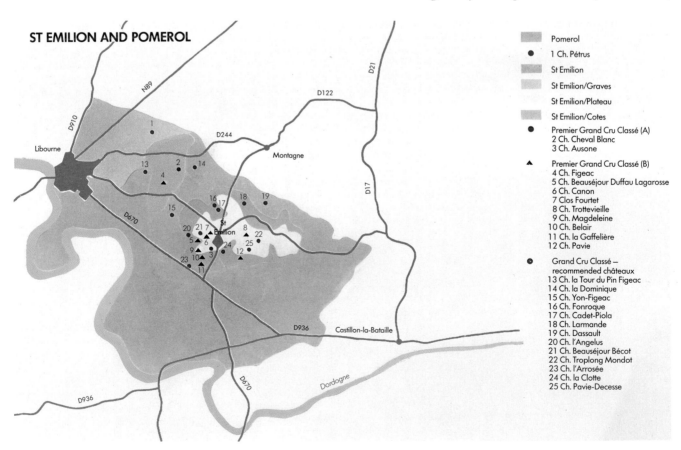

ST EMILION AND POMEROL

Pomerol
● 1 Ch. Pétrus
St Emilion
St Emilion/Graves
St Emilion/Plateau
St Emilion/Cotes
● Premier Grand Cru Classé (A)
    2 Ch. Cheval Blanc
    3 Ch. Ausone
▲ Premier Grand Cru Classé (B)
    4 Ch. Figeac
    5 Ch. Beauséjour Duffau Lagarosse
    6 Ch. Canon
    7 Clos Fourtet
    8 Ch. Trottevieille
    9 Ch. Magdeleine
  10 Ch. Belair
  11 Ch. la Gaffelière
  12 Ch. Pavie
● Grand Cru Classé –
    recommended châteaux
  13 Ch. la Tour du Pin Figeac
  14 Ch. la Dominique
  15 Ch. Yon-Figeac
  16 Ch. Fonroque
  17 Ch. Cadet-Piola
  18 Ch. Larmande
  19 Ch. Dassault
  20 Ch. l'Angelus
  21 Ch. Beauséjour Bécot
  22 Ch. Troplong Mondot
  23 Ch. l'Arrosée
  24 Ch. la Clotte
  25 Ch. Pavie-Decesse

are characterized by a more full, robust, style, whereas those of the Côte (the escarpment surrounding the town of St Emilion) are much lighter and more elegant in style. The wines of the Plateau are a mixture of the two styles.

## ∾ THE CLASSIFICATIONS OF ST EMILION ∾

The St Emilion classification is re-assessed every ten years (in theory) and, unlike the Médoc classification, changes *have* been known to have been made. The most radical in recent years happened in the 1985 reassessment, with the controversial declassification of Château Beauséjour-Bécot from First Growth (B) down to *Grand Cru Classé*.

The classification is different in structure to that of the Médoc in that it does not have simply classes one through to five, but instead the following divisions:

### Premier Grand Cru Classé (A)

There are only two châteaux here – Cheval Blanc and Ausone – both producing wines of outstanding quality, although in totally different styles.

### Premier Grand Cru Classé (B)

This class includes nine châteaux, some of which warrant their classification more than others. The best are Châteaux Figeac (which used to boast Cheval Blanc as part of its estate), Magdelaine (owned by the Moueix family of Pétrus fame), Belair (under the same ownership as Ausone) and Canon (owned by the Fournier family).

*Château Ausone in St Emilion, one of only two châteaux to have Premier Grand Cru Classé (A) status. The other château is Cheval Blanc and while both produce excellent quality wines they are totally different in style.*

---

**THE ST EMILION CLASSIFICATIONS OF 1958, 1969 AND 1985**

The classifications shown below are as they are at the time of writing, and do not include châteaux which have merged with other properties, or which have been demoted to *Grand Cru*.

**PREMIER GRAND CRU CLASSE (A)**

Château Cheval Blanc
Château Ausone

**PREMIER GRAND CRU CLASSE (B)**

Château Beauséjour Duffau Lagarosse
Château Belair
Château Canon
Clos Fourtet
Château Figeac
Château la Gaffelière
Château Magdelaine
Château Pavie
Château Trottevieille

**GRAND CRU CLASSE**

Château l'Angélus
Château l'Arrosée
Château Balestard la Tonnelle
Château Bellevue
Château Bergat
Château Berliquet
Château Beauséjour-Bécot
Château Cadet-Piola
Château Canon la Gaffelière
Château Cap de Mourlin

Château le Châelet
Château Chauvin
Château la Clotte
Château la Clusière
Château Corbin
Château Corbin Michotte
Château le Couvent
Château Couvent des Jacobins
Château Croque Michotte
Château Curé Bon la Madeleine
Château Dassault
Château la Dominique
Château Faurie de Souchard
Château Fonplégade
Château Fonroque
Château Franc-Mayne
Château Grand Barrail Lamarzelle
Château Grand Corbin Despagne
Château Grand Corbin
Château Grand Mayne
Château Grand Pontet
Château Guadet St Julien
Château Haut-Corbin
Château Haut-Sarpe
Clos des Jacobins
Château Laniote

Château Larcis Ducasse
Château Larmande
Château Laroze
Clos la Madeleine
Clos St-Martin
Château Lamarzelle
Château Mauvezin
Château Moulin du Cadet
Château Pavie Decesse
Château Pavie Macquin
Château Pavillon-Cadet
Château Petit-Faurie-de-Souchard
Château le Prieuré
Château Ripeau
Château St Georges
Château Sansonnet
Château la Serre
Château Soutard
Château Tertre Daugay
Château la Tour Figeac
Château la Tour du Pin Figeac (Giraud-Belivier)
Château la Tour du Pin Figeac (Moueix)
Château Trimoulet
Château Troplong Mondot
Château Villemaurine
Château Yon-Figeac
Clos de l'Oratoire

---

### Grand Cru Classé

There were 64 *Grands Crus Classés* in the original 1958 classification, varying in quality from the outstanding to the indifferent. The best included Châteaux Beauséjour-Bécot, l'Angélus, l'Arrosée, Cadet-Piola, la Clotte, Dassault, la Dominique, Fonroque, Larmande, Pavie-Decesse, Troplong Mondot and Yon-Figeac.

### Grand Cru

This name hides a multitude of sins, and don't be misled into thinking that a wine with '*Grand Cru*' on the label will necessarily be of high quality. Yes, there certainly are some excellent *Grand Cru* St Emilions (for example Château Fombrauge), but most do not merit special attention. There are too many of them to list here!

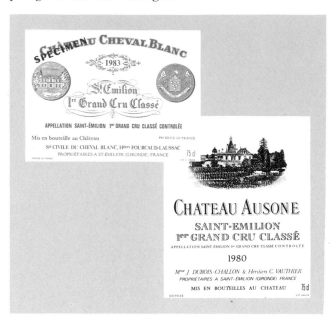

| VINTAGE CHART – ST EMILION | |
|---|---|
| 1988 Excellent | 1975 Very inconsistent – |
| 1987 Above average, some |     generally poor |
|     good early-maturing | 1974 Poor |
|     wines made | 1973 Average |
| 1986 Average | 1972 Poor |
| 1985 Outstanding | 1971 Outstanding |
| 1984 Poor | 1970 Good |
| 1983 Average | 1969 Poor |
| 1982 Exceptional | 1968 Abysmal |
| 1981 Very good, great value | 1967 Average: drink up |
| 1980 Poor, with a few | 1966 Good |
|     exceptions | 1965 Abysmal |
| 1979 Very good | 1964 Very good |
| 1978 Great potential | 1963 Abysmal |
| 1977 Dreadful | 1962 Very good but drink up |
| 1976 Some very good wines | 1961 Outstanding |

Other exceptional older vintages that are still drinking well: 1949, 1947, 1945, 1929, 1928.

# $\mathcal{P}$OMEROL

$\mathcal{P}$omerol is a small region to the north-east of Libourne, and most of its vineyards are tiny in comparison with those of the Médoc, and are more like those in neighbouring St Emilion.

Pomerol has no palatial or historically fascinating châteaux, like Château Margaux in the Médoc, Haut-Brion in the Graves or Ausone in St Emilion, and most of the châteaux are merely small farmhouses like Château Pétrus. Many are not occupied most of the time, and very few have cellars.

The region has only really come into its own since the Second World War, before which it was hardly known. Old vintages of Pomerol are extremely rare, and are hardly ever seen. Nonetheless this youngster boasts one of the world's most famous and expensive wines, Château Pétrus. And some of its other properties like Châteaux Lafleur, Trotanoy, L'Evangile, Certan de May, Vieux Château Certan and Le Pin come close to achieving superstar status, often selling for higher prices than top Médoc wines.

Surprisingly, no-one has ever come up with a classification of Pomerol, although Château Pétrus has worldwide First Growth status, and its price is often higher than the official First Growths.

Pomerol's wines have a very distinctive style. Although they share the same dominant grape variety (the Merlot) as those of St Emilion, they are very different. They exhibit the same soft velvetiness as St Emilion wines, but they tend to have a meatiness and structure that is seldom found in St Emilion.

Most of Pomerol's châteaux are owned by 'locals', and there is little outside influence, unlike the Médoc where it is not uncommon to have English-, American-, Japanese- or insurance company-owned châteaux. The only notable non-Pomerol owner is Bruno Prats (of Cos d'Estournel) who owns (and produces superlative wine at) Château Petit-Village.

One of the Pomerol's most important influences has been that of the Moueix family, headed by Jean-Pierre Moueix, and now actively involving Christian and Jean-Jacques. Since the war their company has been responsible for Château Pétrus's rise to fame, and in turn the reputation of the area as a whole. They are wholly responsible for, or heavily involved in, all of the following, with only a few exceptions the cream of Pomerol's wines: Bourgneuf-Vayron, Clos l'Eglise, la Fleur Pétrus, le Gay, la Grave Trigant de Boisset, Lafleur-Gazin, Lafleur, Lagrange (à Pomerol), Latour-à-Pomerol, Pétrus and Trotanoy. And they are one of the few Bordeaux winemaking families to become actively involved in New World wines, with Christian Moueix's Californian wine, Dominus.

*A helicopter helps dry the grapes in the vineyards of Château Pétrus during harvest time. This is the top wine in Pomerol and the most expensive wine produced in Bordeaux. No expense is spared in its making.*

## RECOMMENDED CHATEAUX – POMEROL

Château le Bon Pasteur
Château Bourgneuf-Vayron
Château Certan de May
Château Certan-Giraud
Château Clinet
Clos du Clocher
Château La Conseillante
Château La Croix
Château La Croix de Gay
Clos l'Eglise
Château l'Enclos
Château l'Evangile
Château l'Eglise-Clinet
Château Feytit-Clinet
Château la Fleur Pétrus
Château le Gay
Château Gazin

Château la Grave Trigant
  de  Boisset
Château Lafleur-Gazin
Château Lafleur
Château Lagrange
  (à Pomerol)
Château Latour-à-
  Pomerol
Château Mazeyres
Château Moulinet
Château Petit-Village
Château Pétrus
Château le Pin
Château Plince
Château Trotanoy
Vieux Château Certan
Château la Violette

## VINTAGE CHART – POMEROL

1988 Excellent
1987 Average, some good early-maturing wines made
1986 Not successful for Merlot
1985 Outstanding
1984 Poor
1983 Not special
1982 Exceptional
1981 Very good, great value
1980 Poor, with a few exceptions
1979 Very good
1978 Great potential
1977 Dreadful
1976 Better than the Médoc – good

1975 Very inconsistent – be careful
1974 Poor
1973 Average
1972 Poor
1971 Outstanding
1970 Outstanding
1969 Poor
1968 Abysmal
1967 Average: drink up
1966 Good
1965 Abysmal
1964 Very good
1963 Abysmal
1962 Very good but drink up
1961 Outstanding

Other exceptional older vintages that are still drinking well: 1949, 1947, 1945, 1929, 1928.

# *S*AUTERNES

### A load of Noble Rot?

So what exactly is this noble rot that everyone talks about? And, assuming it's a good thing (which it doesn't sound like!), how do the producers ensure their grapes become affected by it every vintage?

Noble rot, or *Botrytis cinerea* to give it its correct Latin name, is fundamental to the great wines of Sauternes. They are not just very sweet (anyone can add sugar to make a wine like that) but have a remarkable complexity and depth of flavour that is unequalled by any other sweet wine in the world. The only wines that come close in style are the great Beerenauslesen of Germany, but they are made from the Riesling grape, not from Sémillon, Sauvignon Blanc and Muscadelle like Sauternes. Naturally, the New World producers have tried hard to imitate the phenomenon, and some have made admirable efforts (de Bortoli in Australia and Quady in California for example), but none can match the magnificence of Château d'Yquem in a top vintage.

Botrytis only occurs when certain climatic conditions prevail. The ideal conditions are the damp, misty morn-ings (the river helps provide this) and sunny afternoons which happen in Sauternes in the late autumn and early winter. The already super-ripe grapes become infected by noble rot, puncturing the skins and covering them with a fine, wispy beard of mould. As they shrivel the acidity reduces and the sugar content increases because of the loss of water in the grapes. High sugar concentration means lots of potential alcohol, and many Sauterne grapes have very high levels of around 17 per cent to 25 per cent, giving a final alcohol content of 13 to 15 per cent.

Because noble rot spreads unevenly, the best producers will pick the grapes individually, rather than in bunches, and the very best producers (like Château d'Yquem) will go through the vines as many as ten times (known as 'tries') to make sure they obtain the maximum number of botrytis-infected grapes. It's a sticky business for the pickers! Once the grapes have been fermented, the best châteaux will age the wines in new oak barrels, giving them extra finesse and complexity.

Because noble rot only appears later on, in November, making Sauternes is a problem for this dedicated bunch of

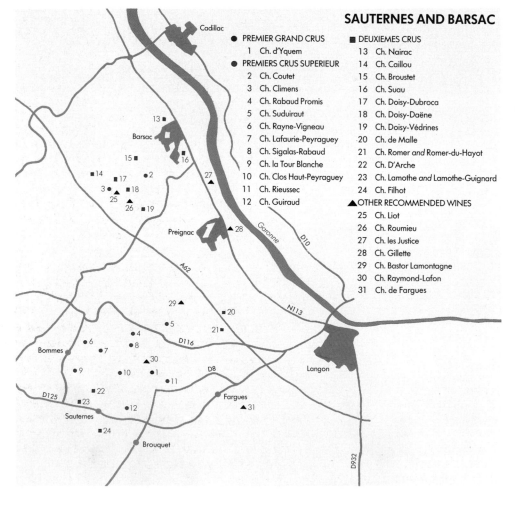

**SAUTERNES AND BARSAC**

● PREMIER GRAND CRUS
1 Ch. d'Yquem

● PREMIERS CRUS SUPERIEUR
2 Ch. Coutet
3 Ch. Climens
4 Ch. Rabaud Promis
5 Ch. Suduiraut
6 Ch. Rayne-Vigneau
7 Ch. Lafaurie-Peyraguey
8 Ch. Sigalas-Rabaud
9 Ch. la Tour Blanche
10 Ch. Clos Haut-Peyraguey
11 Ch. Rieussec
12 Ch. Guiraud

■ DEUXIEMES CRUS
13 Ch. Nairac
14 Ch. Caillou
15 Ch. Broustet
16 Ch. Suau
17 Ch. Doisy-Dubroca
18 Ch. Doisy-Daëne
19 Ch. Doisy-Védrines
20 Ch. de Malle
21 Ch. Romer *and* Romer-du-Hayot
22 Ch. D'Arche
23 Ch. Lamothe *and* Lamothe-Guignard
24 Ch. Filhot

▲ OTHER RECOMMENDED WINES
25 Ch. Liot
26 Ch. Roumieu
27 Ch. les Justice
28 Ch. Gillette
29 Ch. Bastor Lamontagne
30 Ch. Raymond-Lafon
31 Ch. de Fargues

*A*BOVE RIGHT: *Sugar intensified 'noble rot' (Botrytis cinerea) infected grapes, soon to be harvested to make the world's most famous sweet white wine, Sauternes.*

producers. First, they have to pray that the weather during September and October will be warm and sunny to build up the natural sugar level. Then, assuming the grapes are ripe enough, they have to wait for the Botrytis to set in, risking decimation of their entire crop by hail, storm or other bad weather. It's rather like playing Russian Roulette – if they harvest too early the wines do not have enough botrytis character, but each day they leave them they increase the risk of losing the entire crop. So even the greatest of the Sauternes producers cannot ensure that the particular freak weather conditions described above happen every year.

How does noble rot affect the taste of the resulting wine? Good Sauternes and Barsac have a honeyed, slightly coconutty, flavour with a pleasant underlying musty/earthy vegetal taste. Sauternes' legendary taste is even more difficult to describe than the wine is to make! Great vintages can last for decades, even centuries, and with age the wine develops a deep golden colour, becoming drier as it gets older. But in years when there is little botrytis, or even none at all, the wines are not as rich and sticky and, while being very enjoyable, do not have the depth of flavour of a great year.

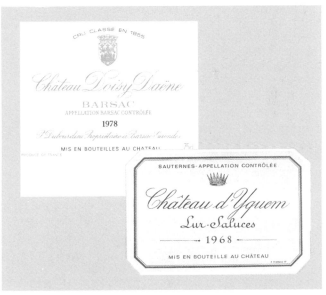

### THE GEOGRAPHY OF SAUTERNES

The appellation of Sauternes includes a number of smaller communes: Barsac, Preignac, Bommes and Fargues. As can be seen from the classification table many of the wines we know as Sauternes do not actually come from the Sauternes commune itself, but from one of the smaller ones. The appellation of Sauternes is situated to the south-east of

the town of Bordeaux, surrounded by the enormous spread of the Graves region. The nearest large town is Langon, on the eastern side of the Sauternes region, and the river Garonne forms the north-eastern boundary of the appellation.

As well as Sauternes itself, there are two other smaller, less classic, regions over the river which also produce sweet wine, Loupiac and Ste-Croix-du-Mont. Both of these can be excellent value as less expensive alternatives to Sauternes. There is also the very basic quality level of Premières Cotes de Bordeaux across the river, which also makes red wine.

*LEFT: Château d'Yquem, the world's finest Sauternes. Only 750 bottles of wine per hectare, are produced here. BELOW RIGHT: Wooden tubs full of harvested Botrytis infected grapes. Because the 'noble rot' spreads unevenly, these grapes are usually picked individually, rather than in bunches.*

## ∾ THE MAIN GRAPE VARIETIES ∾

The two main grapes used in the production of Sauternes and Barsac are Sémillon and Sauvignon, although of the two, the Sémillon is more susceptible to rot because of its thin skins. Most producers also grow a small proportion of sweet Muscadelle, which adds an exotic, floral nuance. The permitted yield in Sauternes is very low at only 25 hectolitres per hectare, less than half that allowed in the Médoc, although it's extremely rare that producers have problems with over production. Château d'Yquem, for instance, produces just 750 bottles a hectare!

## ∾ THE CLASSIFICATION OF SAUTERNES ∾

Sauternes and Barsac were classified at the same time as the Médoc and Graves in the 1855 classification. Yquem has a classification all to itself, First Great Growth, and is followed by 11 First Growths and 14 Second Growths. There is no class below Second Growth, and the difference between the Classified Growths and the Unclassifieds is much more marked than in the Médoc.

### Sauternes – a business proposition or not?
It is difficult to see how anyone in Sauternes makes any money. The production figures are tiny – the entire production of the Classified Growths is only about 115,000 cases a year. That's less than the total produced just by the big seven First Growths from the Médoc, Graves and St Emilion (Mouton, Latour, Lafite, Margaux, Haut-Brion, Cheval-Blanc and Ausone)! It is only in certain years that noble rot sets in at all, and half the time the entire crop can be wiped out by bad weather later on in the season. Sauternes has more than its fair share of real eccentrics – take

Château Gilette, for instance. They do not even bottle their wine until it is 20 years old! The cashflow implications of that kind of policy are mind-boggling, even if the results are stunning.

As Tom Heeter (the ex-proprietor of Château Nairac) has often been quoted as saying, you have to be half-crazy to make Sauternes. But somehow, when you've a glass of really good Sauternes in hand, its delicious richness and subtle balance of sweetness and acidity makes you realize why the proprietors persist.

### VINTAGE CHART

Without the spread of noble rot, vintages in Sauternes cannot be great, so as this is not a regular occurrence it's very important to remember about vintages especially if paying a high price.

| | |
|---|---|
| 1988 Outstanding | 1973 Much better than for red wines |
| 1987 Average | |
| 1986 Very good | 1972 Poor, but some attractive wines |
| 1985 Very good | |
| 1984 Poor | 1971 Outstanding |
| 1983 Outstanding | 1970 Very good |
| 1982 Average | 1969 Poor |
| 1981 Average | 1968 Disastrous |
| 1980 Very good | 1967 Very good (but Yquem outstanding) |
| 1979 Good | |
| 1978 Average | 1966 Good |
| 1977 Poor | 1965 Terrible |
| 1976 Very good | 1964 Good |
| 1975 Superb | 1963 Abysmal |
| 1974 Poor | 1962 Excellent |
| | 1961 Average |

Other notable vintages: 1921.

## THE 1855 CLASSIFICATION OF
## THE WHITE WINES OF THE GIRONDE

*PREMIER GRAND CRU* (First Great Growth)
Château d'Yquem

*PREMIERS CRUS SUPERIEURS* (Superior First Growths)
Château la Tour Blanche, Bommes
Château Lafaurie-Peyraguey, Bommes
Château Clos Haut-Peyraguey, Bommes
Château Rayne-Vigneau, Bommes
Château Suduiraut, Preignac
Château Coutet, Barsac
Château Climens, Barsac
Château Guiraud, Sauternes
Château Rieussec, Fargues
Château Rabaud-Promis, Bommes
Château Sigalas-Rabaud, Bommes

*DEUXIEMES CRUS* (Second Growths)
Château Myrat, Barsac
Château Doisy-Daëne, Barsac
Château Doisy-Dubroca, Barsac

Château Doisy-Vedrines, Barsac
Château D'Arche, Sauternes
Château Filhot, Sauternes
Château Broustet, Barsac
Château Nairac, Barsac
Château Caillou, Barsac
Château Suau, Barsac
Château de Malle, Preignac
Château Romer, Preignac
Château Romer-du-Hayot, Fargues
Château Lamothe, Sauternes
Château Lamothe-Guignard, Sauternes

*SAUTERNES & BARSAC*
 – Recommended wines

Château Bastor Lamontagne, Preignac
Château Broustet, Barsac
Château Coutet, Barsac
Château Climens, Barsac
Château Doisy-Daëne, Barsac
Château Doisy-Vedrines, Barsac
Château de Fargues, Fargues

Château Filhot, Sauternes
Château Gilette, Preignac
Château Guiraud, Sauternes
Château Clos Haut-Peyraguey, Bommes
Château les Justices, Preignac
Château Lafaurie-Peyraguey, Bommes
Château Lamothe, Sauternes
Château Lamothe-Guignard, Sauternes
Château Liot, Barsac
Château Nairac, Barsac
Château Rabaud-Promis, Bommes
Château Raymon-Lafon, Sauternes
Château Rayne-Vigneau, Bommes
Château Rieusscc, Fargues
Château Romer, Preignac
Château Romer-du-Hayot, Fargues
Château Roumieu, Barsac
Château Sigalas-Rabaud, Bommes
Château Suduiraut, Preignac
Château la Tour Blanche, Bommes
Château d' Yquem, Sauternes

# Bordeaux – Other, non-classic areas

Apart from the well-known classic areas of Bordeaux, there are other regions producing large amounts of wine, some very good, some uninteresting.

Wines with just Bordeaux or Bordeaux Supérieur on the label can come from just about anywhere in the region, and can be virtually any style! The only way to choose these is to find a handful that you enjoy, and then to stick to those, experimenting with others from time to time.

The best regions are described below, with a shortlist of the top châteaux within each. Each region produces red wine only, unless otherwise indicated.

### ～ Cotes De Bourg & Blaye ～

These two areas, Bourg being relatively small and Blaye substantially larger, produce mostly red wine which is sold at relatively inexpensive prices. The areas are next to each other on the east bank of the Gironde estuary, facing the Médoc. Many of their wines can be excellent value, and tend to resemble the wines of the Libournais, rather than the Médoc, in style.

| | |
|---|---|
| Château de Barbe, Bourg | Château Haut-Sociando, Blaye |
| Château Bourdieu, Blaye | Château les Heaumes, Bourg |
| Château de Bousquet, Bourg | Château Mercier, Bourg |
| Château Brûle Sécaille, Bourg | Château Peychaud, Bourg |
| Château Caruel, Bourg | Château Peyredoulle, Blaye |
| Château Charron, Blaye | Château Rousselle, Bourg |
| Château Croute Courpon, Bourg | Château Rousset, Bourg |
| Château Grand Barrail, Blaye | Château Segonzac, Blaye |
| | Château Tayac, Bourg |
| | Château de Thau, Bourg |
| | Château la Tonnelle, Blaye |

### ～ Cotes De Castillon ～

A large area to the east of St Emilion, and only slightly smaller in size. The wines produced are of a fairly basic quality, and are in the style of lesser St Emilions. But some of the better producers, like those listed here, produce great-value, soft wines for early drinking.

| | |
|---|---|
| Château de Clotte | Château Robin |
| Château Lesacques | Château la Terrasse |
| Château de Pitray | |

### ～ Cotes De Francs ～

Not yet well-known, with only about six châteaux, but an area with great potential. Dominated by the Merlot grape and situated to the north-east of Côtes de Castillon. Two of the best châteaux (see above) are both owned by the

Thienpont family (of Vieux Château Certan in Pomerol), and produce wines of a better quality than many St Emilions, as does Château la Prade, owned by Patrick Valette of Château Pavie.

| | |
|---|---|
| Château Laclaverie | Château la Prade |
| Château Puygueraud | |

*Château de la Rivière in Fronsac, one of the châteaux showing how good the red wines from this appellation can be. Well worth laying down, the best wines from Fronsac and Canon-Fronsac are excellent value for money.*

## ∾ ENTRE DEUX MERS ∾

An enormous region producing huge quantities of wine, between the Garonne and Dordogne rivers. Both red and white are produced, although the majority is white. With modern cold-fermentation methods white Entre-Deux-Mers can be good value – crisp and dry – and the reds are mostly soft, Merlot-based wines. Entre-Deux-Mers wines are never expensive, and good producers offer great value.

| | |
|---|---|
| Château Bonnet | Château Latour |
| Château Canet | Château Launay |
| Château le Gardera | Château Moulin de Launay |
| Château Goumin | Château Peyrebon |
| Château Grand Montheil | Château Thieuley |

## ∾ FRONSAC & CANON-FRONSAC ∾

These appellations are two of the most exciting in the Libournais district. They are both due for a renaissance, and in five or ten years' time could well be achieving the fame (and prices) of St Emilion and Pomerol. Well worth buying now and laying down.

Château Bodet, Canon-Fronsac
Château Canon de Brem, Canon-Fronsac
Château Canon-Moueix, Canon-Fronsac
Château Dalem, Fronsac
Château de la Dauphine, Fronsac
Château de la Huste, Canon-Fronsac
Château Junayme, Canon-Fronsac

Château Mazeris-Bellevue, Canon-Fronsac
Château de la Rivière, Fronsac
Château Rouet, Canon-Fronsac
Clos du Roy, Fronsac
Château Toumalin, Canon-Fronsac
Château Vrai-Canon-Boyer, Canon-Fronsac
Château Villars, Fronsac

## ∾ LALANDE-DE-POMEROL ∾

Neighbouring Pomerol to the north-east, Lalande-de-Pomerol produces some very exciting, meaty, Merlot-based wines which are great value when compared to Pomerol's prices.

| | |
|---|---|
| Château des Annereaux | Château Haut-Chatain |
| Château de Bel-Air | Château Haut-Surget |
| Château Belles-Graves | Château la Fleur St Georges |
| Château Garraud | Château Moncets |
| Château Grand-Ormeau | Clos des Templiers |
| Château Haut-Ballet | Château Tournefeuille |

## ∾ ST EMILION SATELLITES ∾

Of the various St Emilion satellites (Montagne-, St Georges-, Lussac-, Puisseguin- and Parsac-St Emilion), only St Georges-St Emilion deserves a special mention, and that only for two châteaux, Château St Georges and Château Tour du Pas St Georges. Both properties produce stunning wines of better quality than many Grand Cru Classé St Emilion wines, and they can last for decades.

# Burgundy

Burgundy's Côte d'Or is a far more attractive area to visit than Bordeaux, with the possible exception of historic St Emilion. Tiny little villages and walled vineyards (known as *clos*) abound and driving through the villages is rather like reading through a fine wine list. On a first visit to Burgundy the speed at which famous vineyards flash by is incredible. It is, admittedly, sometimes difficult to discover which vineyard you are passing, as very few of them have name signs!

## ⤬ THE GEOGRAPHY OF BURGUNDY ⤬

The vineyards of Burgundy are split up geographically into six distinct regions. They are, travelling from north to south, Chablis, the Côte de Nuits, the Côte de Beaune, the Côte Chalonnaise, the Côte Mâconnais and Beaujolais. Each has its own very individual style.

The region is not big – for example, the entire Côte d'Or (that's to say the Côtes de Nuits and Beaune) is the same size as St Emilion, and boasts well over a hundred appellations producing both red and white wines. Because of this the production of many of the appellations is tiny, making it difficult for you, the consumer, to find your way around. There are few impressive châteaux in the region, and some of the smaller growers make their wines in what are really no more than converted garages!

The ownership structure of the vineyards is very complicated because of France's archaic inheritance laws, and because there are very few châteaux, one often finds that there can be up to 90 owners in just one appellation. A classic example of this is Clos de Vougeot, with over 80 different owners. Because of this, many different styles of wine are produced with the same name on the label. Unlike Bordeaux, where the château name takes precedence on the label, Burgundy wine labels highlight the appellation. This involved system means that it is essential to choose your Burgundy primarily by the producer, not the appellation.

## ⤬ THE PRODUCERS ⤬

There are two distinct types of producer in Burgundy – the growers and the *négociants* – and opinion is split as to which produces the better wine.

In the bad old days it was the *négociants* who sold virtually all Burgundy, buying grapes and wine from the growers under contract, and often adulterating the wines they made by adding wines from the Rhône and elsewhere. But this practice was stopped in the early 1970s by the enforcement of the laws of *Appellation Contrôlée*, which obliged producers to make wines only from the allowed grapes.

Throughout the 1970s a lot of really dreadful wine was produced, especially red wine, one of the main reasons being that the producers were no longer allowed to adulterate it. They had to discover new winemaking methods that worked with the authentic grapes!

During this period many of the growers did not renew their contracts with the *négociants*, and started marketing their wines themselves. We now have the situation where there are many fabulous wines made in the region, although there are still too many poor quality ones. Whether the good wines are made by *négociants* or by smaller growers depends on the region. The Côte d'Or's best wines tend to come from growers, whereas those from the Côte Chalonnaise and the Mâconnais, Beaujolais and Chablis can come from either growers or *négociants*.

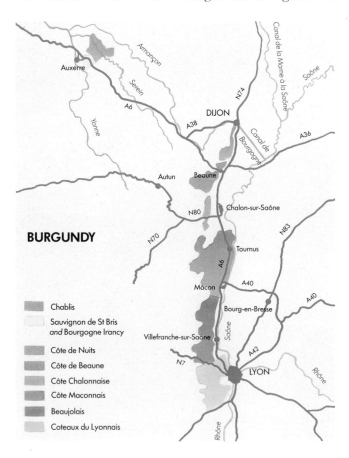

**BURGUNDY**

- Chablis
- Sauvignon de St Bris and Bourgogne Irancy
- Côte de Nuits
- Côte de Beaune
- Côte Chalonnaise
- Côte Maconnais
- Beaujolais
- Coteaux du Lyonnais

## ⁓ THE TYPES OF WINE ⁓

Burgundy produces red and white wines, the former made from the Pinot Noir or Gamay (Beaujolais only), and the latter from the Chardonnay or Aligoté. There is also some sparkling wine produced, red, rosé and white. The two most important grapes are Pinot Noir and Chardonnay, although the Gamay is responsible for all of the delicious red wines of Beaujolais. Red and white wines are split geographically, with one colour generally dominating an area. Chablis: mostly white; Côte de Nuits: mostly red; Côte de Beaune: red and white; Côte Chalonnaise: red and white; Mâconnais: mostly white; Beaujolais: mostly red.

Chardonnay is fairly easy to grow, and producers worldwide have attempted, with varying degrees of success, to imitate the great white wines of the Côte d'Or like Le Montrachet or Meursault. The grape produces wines with a pronounced buttery, white-currant flavour, and the top wines (mostly from the Côte d'Or) are often aged in new oak barrels, giving them seductive spicy, vanilla overtones and added complexity.

Pinot Noir, on the other hand, is much more difficult to grow, and there are few other wine-producing countries with more than a handful of successful Pinot Noir wines. The red wine produced from the Pinot Noir (when good) is delicate with a deliciously ripe, concentrated raspberry/strawberry flavour, and can have 'farmyardy' overtones. The best producers in the Côte d'Or age it in new oak barrels before bottling, giving even more depth of flavour. The colour is normally pale, the opposite to the wines of Bordeaux, and often takes on more depth with age.

But it's difficult to be precise about Pinot Noir's flavour and style because more than 1,000 different clones of the Pinot Noir grape are grown in Burgundy, making the already complicated task of choosing your red Burgundy even worse! All these clones produce widely varying styles of wine, from the heavy, jammy and obvious, to the concentrated and fine, to the light and insipid, to the light, delicate and complex. It's *very* important to buy from the right producer, and not to rely just on the appellation.

As well as the famous, well-known names, Burgundy produces a large amount of ordinary 'generic' wine, which comes from the appellations listed in the table on this page. If from a good producer (normally a *négociant*) these can be very good indeed, especially white and red A C Bourgogne. But beware the misleading name of Bourgogne Grand Ordinaire – the 'Grand' doesn't mean what you might think it does: it refers to 'Ordinaire'; in other words, *very* ordinary!

## ⁓ THE CLASSIFICATION SYSTEM OF BURGUNDY ⁓

Burgundy's classification system works by vineyard, not by owner or château, and has two categories – *Grand Cru* (equivalent to Bordeaux's *Premier Cru*) and *Premier Cru* (equivalent to Bordeaux's *Deuxièmes* to *Cinquièmes Crus*). But it can be confusing – for instance, in Bordeaux one finds Château Latour which is classified a First Growth, and happens to be in the Pauillac appellation. In Burgundy

*The famous tiled roof of the Hospice de Beaune found in Beaune, the centre of Burgundy production.*

the vineyard area of Le Montrachet is classified as a Grand Cru, and also has its own appellation (Le Montrachet). The problem is that there are a number of different owners of Le Montrachet, all of whom produce different styles of wine! So, as with the appellations mentioned above, it is most important to look out for the producer's name on the label.

### GENERIC BURGUNDY APPELLATIONS

All produce both red and white unless otherwise indicated.

| | |
|---|---|
| Bourgogne | + rosé |
| Bourgogne-Aligoté | white only |
| Bourgogne Grand Ordinaire | |
| Bourgogne Mousseux | sparkling red only |
| Bourgogne Ordinaire | |
| Bourgogne Passetoutgrains | red and rosé only |
| Crémant de Bourgogne | sparkling white and rosé only |

### VINTAGE CHART – BURGUNDY

| | | | |
|---|---|---|---|
| 1988 | Excellent | 1978 | Outstanding |
| 1987 | Average to good | 1977 | Dreadful |
| 1986 | Good to very good, especially whites | 1976 | Not as good as was thought originally – average |
| 1985 | Outstanding | | |
| 1984 | Average, but much better than Bordeaux | 1975 | Poor |
| | | 1974 | Poor |
| 1983 | Excellent, but some rot and overripeness | 1973 | Average |
| | | 1972 | Good, with some stunning wines |
| 1982 | Good, but some dilution | | |
| 1981 | Average | 1971 | Outstanding, although now mature |
| 1980 | Average to good, with some superb wines | | |
| | | 1970 | Average |
| 1979 | Good | 1969 | Outstanding |

Other earlier particularly good years: 1964, 1962, 1959, 1957, 1953, 1952, 1949, 1947, 1945.

# The Chablis Region

Chablis, named after the town of the same name, is probably not only Burgundy's most famous white wine but one of France's too. It's one of the most northerly vineyard areas in France and purists will argue that it's not actually part of Burgundy because it is so far away and is, in fact, closer to Champagne.

The Chardonnay reigns supreme in the vineyards producing Chablis, which are situated in the Yonne department, to the east of the town of Auxerre. It is said to be the distinctive soil (calcareous Kimmeridgian and Portlandian clay) of this area which gives the wines their characteristic dry, steely flavour.

Chablis has become a worldwide favourite and high demand has undoubtedly led to a reduction in quality. Its popularity has also meant higher prices for what are sometimes indifferent wines although more recently prices have returned to a more sensible level. In both California and Australia producers took the term Chablis to mean a crisp dry white wine, normally made from Chardonnay, and the name was frequently bastardized on their labels.

There are in Chablis two different styles of winemaking. One favours the use of oak barrels for ageing to make a more complex, richer, later-maturing wine and the other uses stainless steel vats, bottling the wine for early drinking.

## ❧ THE APPELLATIONS OF CHABLIS ❧

### Chablis
This is the standard appellation, which must have a minimum alcohol level of 10 degrees. As in any appellation, both good and bad wines are made. Most standard Chablis is made to be drunk young, up to five years old. Light green in colour, Chablis is dry with high acidity, reflecting the northerly position of these vineyards.

### Chablis Grand Cru
Grand Cru Chablis is the highest classification and is above Premier Cru. The wines while dry, are rich and should have considerably more depth of character than straight Chablis. Yields are lower than for the other Chablis appellations and the minimum alcohol level is higher at 11 degrees. There are seven Grand Crus in total, all situated to the north of Chablis on the hillside overlooking the town. The name of the Grand Cru will appear on the label, but wines from the same cru can differ depending on how they are made and who makes them. The seven Grand Crus, all of which have different characteristics, are Blanchot, Bougros, Les Clos, Grenouilles, Les Preuses, Valmur and Vaudésir.

### Chablis Premier Cru
These vineyards can be found on both sides of the river Serein, around the town of Chablis. The wines should be better quality than standard Chablis, although again this depends on the vineyard site and the winemaker. There are 30 Premier Crus, although they tend to be sold under 12 of the most best-known names: Beauroy, Côte de Léchet, Fourchaume, Les Fourneaux, Mélinots, Montée de Tonnerre, Montmains, Mont de Milieu, Vaillons, Vaucoupin, Vau de Vey and Vosgros.

### Petit Chablis
Petit Chablis wines are generally regarded as coming from the less good Chablis vineyards, although many originally within this appellation have now been upgraded to the

*ABOVE RIGHT: The Chablis region, where the Chardonnay grape reigns supreme. The distinctive soil of this region, Kimmeridgian clay, is said to give the wines their distinctive dry, steely flavour.*

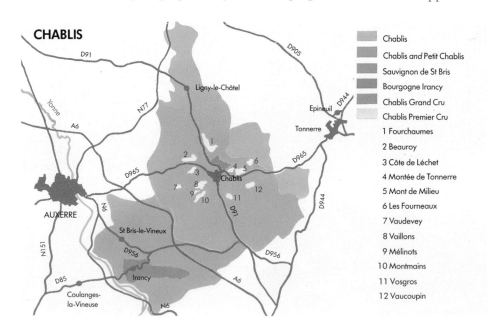

**CHABLIS**

- Chablis
- Chablis and Petit Chablis
- Sauvignon de St Bris
- Bourgogne Irancy
- Chablis Grand Cru
- Chablis Premier Cru

1 Fourchaumes
2 Beauroy
3 Côte de Léchet
4 Montée de Tonnerre
5 Mont de Milieu
6 Les Fourneaux
7 Vaudevey
8 Vaillons
9 Mélinots
10 Montmains
11 Vosgros
12 Vaucoupin

Chablis appellation. The wines produced are generally light in style, and often do not justify their high price.

### Sauvignon de St Bris

This is one of the oddities produced in the Chablis region, as it is made from the Sauvignon and not the Chardonnay grape. Although VDQS status rather than AC, the wines made in this village are of excellent quality and have the characteristic smokey gooseberry-like flavour of the Sauvignon grape with added nuances of chocolate.

### Bourgogne Irancy

This is the red wine of the region, made from Pinot Noir and an old grape variety known as César. The wines are light and fruity, in the main suitable for everyday drinking.

---

### CHABLIS AND DISTRICT APPELLATIONS

| | |
|---|---|
| Bourgogne Coulanges-la Vineuse | red, white & rosé |
| Bourgogne Epineuil | red, white & rosé |
| Bourgogne Irancy | red only |
| Chablis | white only |
| Chablis Grand Cru | white only |
| Chablis Premier Cru | white only |
| Petit Chablis | white only |
| Sauvignon de St Bris VDQS | white only |

---

### RECOMMENDED PRODUCERS

| | |
|---|---|
| Bersan et Fils | Domaine de la Maladière |
| Domaine Brocard | Louis Michel |
| La Chablisienne | Domaine de la Moutonne |
| Dauvissat | Albert Pic |
| Etienne Defaix | J-M Raveneau |
| Jean-Paul Droin | A. Regnard |
| Joseph Drouhin | Marcel Servin |
| Jean Durup | Simmonet-Febvre |
| William Fèvre | Luc Sorin |
| Domaine de la Jouchère | Philippe Testut |
| Labouré-Roi | Thomas-Bassot |
| Domaine Laroche | Robert Vocoret |
| Domaine Long-Depaquit | |

---

# THE CÔTE D'OR

*T*he Côte d'Or, made up of the Côte de Nuits and the Côte de Beaune, is one of the smallest of Burgundy's wine-growing zones in area, and is responsible for only about 10 per cent of the region's entire production. But its wines are among the best-known in the world, boasting names like Meursault, Nuits St Georges, Beaune, Volnay and Montrachet. And they can also be among the most expensive in the world!

There is much confusion surrounding Burgundy (see page 70 and following) but the great wines are worth saving up for, and the Côte d'Or is the home to most of these.

## ∾ THE GEOGRAPHY OF THE CÔTE D'OR ∾

The Côte d'Or is a narrow strip of gently sloping, mostly east-facing, hilly land that starts just south of Dijon (yes, that's where the mustard comes from) at the north end of the Côte de Nuits, becoming the Côte de Beaune further south, which itself ends to the north of the town of Chalon-sur-Saône and the Côte Chalonnaise.

There are few impressive buildings in the Côte d'Or, although the historic walled town of Beaune is well worth a visit. And while there are a few decent-sized châteaux among the vineyards, there is nothing like the number of impressive buildings that one sees throughout the Bordeaux region.

The Côte d'Or is very confusing for the traveller, because the vineyards run into each other in a haywire fashion, and it's difficult to know which vineyard belongs to which appellation or *cru*. There is the odd exception like the walled vineyard of Clos Vougeot or Le Montrachet, but in most cases it's as clear as mud!

## ∾ THE TYPES OF WINE ∾

The Côte d'Or produces red and dry white wine, from fairly basic wines to some of the most fabulous wines in the world. The reds are all made from the Pinot Noir, and the best whites from the Chardonnay. There is also a small amount of Aligoté grown, and an even smaller amount of Pinot Gris.

The best reds have a smooth, silky texture, with a pronounced flavour of raspberries and strawberries. They are relatively light in body and colour, but the best can last for decades. The whites exhibit typical Chardonnay character, with a rich, buttery flavour and overtones of white-currants. Both red and white are often aged in new oak barrels, giving them added complexity and interest.

One of the real joys of good Côte d'Or wines is that they can last for decades, yet are often very drinkable when young. Unlike the top Bordeaux wines, you don't have to wait for ten years before you can even begin to think of drinking them.

## ∾ THE CLASSIFICATION OF THE CÔTE D'OR ∾

The classification of the Côte d'Or is two-tier: *Grand Cru* (the best) and *Premier Cru*. Beneath this level are the so-called *village* wines. But because of the complexity created by different producers owning parts of the same vineyard (or *Grand* or *Premier Cru*), there is an anomaly in that a village wine from a good producer can often be better than a *Premier* or *Grand Cru* from an indifferent one!

### *The future*
In the Côte d'Or the growers have really come into their own in recent years. There is now a whole hoard of young *vignerons*, trained at university and eager to achieve high quality, who have stepped into their parents' shoes and are now producing some of the best wine that has come out of the Côte d'Or in living memory.

Côte de Nuits
1 Marsannay-la-Côte
2 Fixin
3 Gevrey-Chambertin
4 Morey-St-Denis
5 Chambolle-Musigny
6 Vougeot
7 Vosne-Romanée
8 Flagey-Echézeaux
Hautes Côtes de Nuits
Côte de Beaune
9 Pernand-Vergelesses
10 Savigny-les-Beaune
11 Aloxe-Corton
12 Ladoix
13 Chorey-lès-Beaune
14 Pommard
15 St Romain
16 Auxey-Duresses
17 Monthélie
18 Volnay
19 Meursault
20 St Aubin
21 Blagny
22 Puligny-Montrachet
23 Chassagne-Montrachet
24 Santenay
25 Cheilly-lès-Maranges
Hautes Côtes de Beaune

CÔTE D'OR

DIJON
Canal de Bourgogne
Nuits-St-Georges
Beaune
Nolay
Chagny

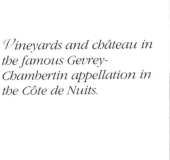

*Vineyards and château in the famous Gevrey-Chambertin appellation in the Côte de Nuits.*

It's certainly time to rediscover the Côte d'Or and in the following pages you will see that I have singled out and listed various producers for special mention.

While this will never be an exhaustive list (new growers are appearing virtually every week) you will not go far wrong if you take the time to seek out those mentioned.

### ❧ THE COTE DE NUITS ❧ & THE HAUTES-COTES DE NUITS

The Côte de Nuits, the most northerly of the two *côtes* that go to make up the Côte d'Or, produces mostly red wines. And what red wines!

The most famous red Burgundy estate, a producer of some of the world's best known wines, is based in this small strip of land – Domaine de la Romanée-Conti. The wines all fetch megabuck prices, and most are out of reach of the average pocket. But if you can possibly justify it, it's worth saving up for a bottle or two of some of the top wines like La Tâhe or Echézeaux from Domaine de la Romanée-Conti or Morey St Denis from Domaine Dujac.

The Côte de Nuits itself runs north–south along a narrow strip of hillsides, with the town of Nuits St Georges as its southern base.

Just to the south-west of Nuits St Georges itself is a region producing increasingly interesting and very good value wines – Hautes-Côtes de Nuits. Moreover, while the wines will never have the firmness, complexity or power of the Côte de Nuits wines themselves, they are a very useful alternative, with the added advantage that they won't break the bank.

### *The Appellations of the Côte de Nuits & Hautes-Côtes de Nuits*

There is not room here for a full description of each appellation, so an outline of their general styles and quality levels must suffice (see overleaf). '+ 1er Cru' indicates that the appellation includes *Premier Cru* wines as well.

**Bourgogne Hautes-Côtes de Nuits** Fairly full red (fuller than the Hautes-Côtes de Beaune), and a very small amount of white. Good value.

**Chambolle-Musigny and its Grands Crus (Bonnes Mares and Musigny)** Full, solid wines, although the *Premier* and *Grand Crus* have great style. + 1er Cru.

**Vougeot & Clos de Vougeot (Grand Cru)** The best can have incredible elegance and delicacy.

**Côte de Nuits-Villages** Firm, fully-flavoured generic wines whch can be good value.

**Echézeaux & Grands Echézeaux (Grands Crus)** Fabulous wines which can be very tannic and muscular when young, but which mature very well.

**Fixin** Normally rather obvious reds and whites, but the best are great value.

**Gevrey-Chambertin and its Grands Crus (Chambertin, Clos de Bèze, Chapelle-, Charmes-, Griottes-, Latricières-, Mazis-, Mazoyères- and Ruchottes -Chambertin)** Fabulous, silky red wines with great ageing potential. + 1er Cru.

**Marsannay** This appellation used to be known only for its rosé, but it is now producing good-value reds and, recently, some white.

**Morey-St-Denis and its Grands Crus (Clos St-Denis, Clos des Lambrays, Clos de la Roche and Clos de Tart)** Some of my favourites among the great Burgundies. Incredible complexity and delicacy combined. A very small amount of superb white is also made. + 1er Cru.

**Nuits-St-Georges** Much of the wine commonly found here is dull, relying on its name to sell. But the best are firm, muscular wines which will keep well. + 1er Cru.

## RECOMMENDED GROWERS – COTE DE NUITS

| | |
|---|---|
| Bernard Bachelet | Henri Leclerc |
| Domaine Bertagna | Domaine Leflaive |
| Guy Berthaut | Georges Lignier |
| Bryczek | Henri Magnien |
| Alain Burguet | Alain Michelot |
| Bruno Clair | Mongeard-Mugneret |
| Clair-Daü | Mortet et Fils |
| Raoul Dau | Réné Mugneret |
| Drouhin-Laroze | Gérard Mugnier |
| Guy Dufouleur | Charles Noellat |
| Domaine Dujac | Domaine Parizot |
| Engel | Domaine Ponsot |
| Faiveley | Remoriquet |
| Henri Gouges | Daniel Rion |
| Machard de Gramont | Domaine de la Romanée-Conti |
| Jean Grivot | Joseph Roty |
| Jean Gros | Georges Roumier |
| Henri Hudelot | Armand Rousseau |
| Alain Hudelot-Noellat | Domaine Serveau |
| Henri Jayer | Domaine Tortochot |
| Jacqueline Jayer | Louis Trapet |
| Robert Jayer-Gilles | J Truchot-Martin |
| Henri Lamarche | Domaine des Varoilles |
| Domaine des Lambrays | Comte Georges de Vogüé |

## RECOMMENDED NEGOCIANTS – COTE DE NUITS

| | |
|---|---|
| Joseph Drouhin | Moillard |
| Jaffelin | Mommessin |
| Labouré-Roi | Charles Viénot |

*LEFT: Harvesting Pinot
Noir grapes in the Côte de
Beaune.
BELOW LEFT: Every year
after the famous wine
auction there is a dinner
held in Clos Vougeot. All
the proceeds from the
auction are donated to
the Hospices de Beaune.*

**Vosne-Romanée and its Grand Crus (La Romanée, La
Romanée-Conti, Romanée-St-Vivant, Richebourg and La
Tâche)** Some of Burgundy's most famous reds – silky
rich with great depth of flavour. + 1er Cru.

### THE COTE DE BEAUNE
### & THE HAUTES-COTES DE BEAUNE

The Côte de Beaune is most southerly of the two *côtes* that
go to make up the Côte d'Or, and produces mostly white
wines; indeed all its *Grand Crus* except Corton (red or
white) are white. Names like Le Montrachet, Meursault,
Puligny, Chassagne and Corton-Charlemagne conjure up
visions of vinous feasts, although unfortunately, like the
reds from the Côte de Nuits, the prices are usually sky-
high. In the Côte de Beaune, however, one can find more
good value, less well-known wines than in the Côte de
Nuits, and certain appellations like St-Aubin, Santenay, St-
Romain, Auxey-Duresses, Pernand-Vergelesses, Monthelie
and Savigny-lès-Beaune can be a relative bargain both for
red and white.

The Côte de Beaune is a slightly wider area than the
Côte de Nuits, and runs south from just below Nuits-St-
Georges with Beaune as its only sizable town. But like the
Côte de Nuits, it also has to its west a region known as the
Hautes-Côtes (de Beaune) which produces lighter, but
arguably better value, wines than the Côte itself. In com-
mon with all Burgundy's regions it is essential to pay atten-
tion to the grower's name and not just to the appellation.

### The Appellations of the Côte de Beaune & Hautes-Côtes de Beaune

There is not room here for a full description of each appellation, so an outline of their general styles and quality levels must suffice. '+ 1er Cru' indicates that the appellation includes *Premier Cru* wines as well.

**Aloxe-Corton, Chorey-lès-Beaune and Corton (Grand Cru)** These appellations are the most northerly of the Côte de Beaune, producing firm, full reds which can be outstanding, and a tiny amount of white (see Corton-Charlemagne). Chorey-lès-Beaune can be excellent value. + 1er Cru.

**Auxey-Duresses** One of Burgundy's best-kept secrets. Fabulous reds and whites from next door to Meursault, and in the same style. + 1er Cru.

**Beaune** Mostly red, but a small amount of superb white (especially Drouhin's Clos des Mouches). The reds are relatively light, and many sell on their name, not their quality. + 1er Cru.

**Blagny** Good value but seldom seen reds from a commune next to Meursault.

**Bourgogne Hautes-Côtes de Beaune** Good value, relatively light reds and white from outside the main Côte de Beaune.

**Chassagne-Montrachet** Often superb whites, ordinary reds. + 1er Cru.

**Cheilly-lès-Maranges** Light reds, virtually no white. + 1er Cru.

**Corton-Charlemagne & Charlemagne (Grands**

---

### COTE DE NUITS APPELLATIONS

Some of the more obscure and infrequently used appellations have been excluded from this list. All those listed produce both red and white unless otherwise indicated. GC by an appellation's name means that it is a *Grand Cru*.

| | | | | | |
|---|---|---|---|---|---|
| Bonnes Mares GC | red only | Clos Vougeot GC | red only | Musigny GC | |
| Bourgogne Hautes-Côtes de Nuits | | Côte de Nuits-Villages | | Nuits | |
| | | Echézeaux GC | red only | Nuits Premier Cru | |
| Chambertin GC | red only | Fixin | | Nuits-St-Georges | |
| Chambertin-Clos de Bèze GC | red only | Fixin Premier Cru | | Nuits-St-Georges Premier Cru | |
| | | Gevrey-Chambertin | red only | | |
| Chambolle-Musigny | red only | Gevrey-Chambertin Premier Cru | red only | Richebourg GC | red only |
| Chambolle-Musigny Premier Cru | red only | | | La Romanée GC | red only |
| | | Grands Echézeaux GC | red only | Romanée-Conti GC | red only |
| Chapelle-Chambertin GC | red only | Griottes-Chambertin GC | red only | Romanée-St-Vivant GC | red only |
| Charmes-Chambertin GC | red only | Latricières-Chambertin GC | red only | Ruchottes-Chambertin GC | red only |
| Clos de Bèze GC | red only | Marsannay | | La Tâche GC | red only |
| Clos des Lambrays GC | red only | Marsannay la Côte | | Vosne-Romanée GC | red only |
| Clos de la Roche GC | red only | Mazis-Chambertin GC | red only | Vosne-Romanée Premier Cru | red only |
| Clos St-Denis GC | red only | Mazoyères-Chambertin GC | red only | | |
| Clos de Tart GC | red only | Morey-St-Denis | | Vougeot | |
| Clos de Vougeot GC | red only | Morey-St-Denis Premier Cru | | Vougeot Premier Cru | |

**Crus)** Sensational, tiny production of white wine. Heavier than the Montrachet *Grand Crus*.

**Côte de Beaune & Côte de Beaune-Villages** Large production of lightish red and white (-Villages red only), of average quality.

**Ladoix** Some good, full-bodied reds and a little white. Can be good value. + 1er Cru.

**Meursault, Meursault-Blagny** Most famous for its superb whites, but also makes red wines of note. + 1er Cru.

**Monthelie** Good value reds and some white produced. + 1er Cru.

**Le Montrachet and other neighbouring Grands Crus (Bienvenues-Bâtard-Montrachet, Bâtard-Montrachet, Chevalier-Montrachet, Criots-Bâtard-Montrachet)** Probably the world's most famous and most sought-after white wines. A tiny production of rich, toasted, nutty liquid gold! Each *Grand Cru* produces a slightly different style of wine.

**Pernand-Vergelesses** Great value full-bodied reds and whites from next door to Corton. + 1er Cru.

**Pommard and Volnay** Superb, rich, velvety reds from these neighbouring communes. Volnay is slightly lighter. + 1er Cru.

**Puligny-Montrachet** Fabulous whites and some dull red. + 1er Cru.

**St-Aubin** Delicious, relatively light reds and whites not dissimilar to those of Puligny. Good value for money. + 1er Cru.

**St-Romain** Good value reds, great value whites.

**Santenay** Undervalued reds and whites which can be delicious. + 1er Cru.

**Savigny and Savigny-lès-Beaune** Superb wines and great value, especially the reds. + 1er Cru.

---

### RECOMMENDED GROWERS – COTE DE BEAUNE

| | |
|---|---|
| Robert Ampeau | Latour-Giraud |
| Marquis d'Angerville | Vincent Leflaive |
| Bernard Bachelet | Domaine Leroy |
| Simon Bize | Chantal Lescure |
| Blain-Gagnard | Bonneau de Martray |
| Henri Boillot | Domaine Matrot |
| Chandon de Briailles | Château de Mercey |
| Domaine Chartron | Prince de Mérode |
| Chavy-Chouet | Hubert de Montille |
| Henry Clerc | André Morey |
| Raoul Clerget | Bernard Morey |
| Coche-Dury | Pierre Morey |
| Michel Colin-Déleger | Morot |
| Domaine Diconne | Domaine Mussy |
| Dubreuil-Fontaine | Michel Niellon |
| Gagnard-Delagrange | Domaine Parent |
| Gaunoux | Domaine de la Pousse d'Or |
| Jean Girardin | Jacques Prieur |
| Girard-Vollot | Henri Prudhon |
| Alain Gras | Roland Rapet |
| Jessiaume Père et Fils | Domaine de la Romanée-Conti |
| Michel Lafarge | Guy Roulot |
| Comte Lafon | Etienne Sauzet |
| Marquis de Laguiche | Tollot-Beaut |
| Laleure-Piot | Michel Voarick |

### RECOMMENDED NEGOCIANTS – COTE DE BEAUNE

| | |
|---|---|
| Chartron et Trébuchet | Olivier Leflaive |
| Joseph Drouhin | Leroy |
| Louis Jadot | Moillard |
| Jaffelin | Patriarche Père et Fils |
| Louis Latour | Remoissenet |

---

### COTE DE BEAUNE APPELLATIONS

Some of the more obscure and infrequently used appellations have been excluded from this list. All those listed produce both red and white unless otherwise indicated. GC by an appellation's name means that it is a *Grand Cru*.

| | | | | | |
|---|---|---|---|---|---|
| Aloxe-Corton | | Chevalier-Montrachet GC | white only | Pommard | red only |
| Aloxe-Corton Premier Cru | | Chorey-lès-Beaune | | Pommard Premier Cru | red only |
| Auxey-Duresses | | Chorey-lès-Beaune-Côte | red only | Puligny-Montrachet | |
| Auxey-Duresses-Côte de | Red only | de Beaune | | Puligny-Montrachet-Côte | red only |
| Beaune | | Corton GC | | de Beaune | |
| Auxey-Duresses Premier Cru | | Corton-Charlemagne GC | white only | Puligny-Montrachet | |
| Bâtard-Montrachet GC | white only | Côte de Beaune | | Premier Cru | |
| Beaune | | Côte de Beaune-Villages | red only | St-Aubin | |
| Beaune Premier Cru | | Criots-Bâtard-Montrachet GC | white only | St-Aubin-Côte de Beaune | red only |
| Bienvenues-Bâtard- | white only | Ladoix | | St-Aubin Premier Cru | |
| Montrachet GC | | Ladoix-Côte de Beaune | red only | St-Romain | |
| Blagny | red only | Ladoix Premier Cru | | St-Romain-Côte de Beaune | red only |
| Blagny-Côte de Beaune | red only | Meursault | | Santenay | |
| Blagny Premier Cru | red only | Meursault-Blagny | | Santenay-Côte de Beaune | red only |
| Bourgogne Hautes-Côtes | | Meursault-Côte de Beaune | red only | Santenay Premier Cru | |
| de Beaune | | Meursault Premier Cru | | Savigny | |
| Charlemagne GC | white only | Meursault-Santenots | | Savigny-Côte de Beaune | red only |
| Chassagne-Montrachet | | Monthlie | | Savigny-lès-Beaune | |
| Chassagne-Montrachet-Côte | red only | Monthlie-Côte de Beaune | red only | Savigny-lès-Beaune-Côte | red only |
| de Beaune | | Monthlie Premier Cru | | de Beaune | |
| Chassagne-Montrachet | | Montrachet GC | white only | Savigny Premier Cru | |
| Premier Cru | | Le Montrachet GC | white only | Savigny-lés-Beaune Premier | |
| Cheilly-lès-Maranges | | Pernand-Vergelesses | | Cru | |
| Cheilly-lès-Maranges-Côte | red only | Pernand-Vergelesses-Côte | red only | Volnay | red only |
| de Beaune | | de Beaune | | Volnay Premier Cru | red only |
| Cheilly-lès-Maranges | | Pernand-Vergelesses | | Volnay-Santenots | red only |
| Premier Cru | | Premier Cru | | | |

# CÔTE CHALONNAISE

## OR REGION DE MERCUREY

The Côte Chalonnaise is often said to produce wines like mini-Côte d'Or wines. But this is only partly true, because while some can be of very high quality (and great value) I have only ever tasted one wine from this region that approaches the complexity of a good Côte d'Or wine – a Rully *Premier Cru* from Michel Juillot.

Côte Chalonnaise wines are better drunk for what they are – honest red and white wines made from Pinot Noir and Chardonnay, which have a robust style all of their own. Three of the five appellations produce both red and white wines, whereas Montagny and Bourgogne Aligoté Bouzeron just produce whites, the latter from the Aligoté rather than Chardonnay.

Much of the best basic AC Bourgogne comes from this area, with producers like Antonin Rodet making particularly good examples.

---

## CÔTE CHALONNAISE APPELLATIONS

All produce both red and white unless otherwise indicated.

| | |
|---|---|
| Bourgogne Aligoté Bouzeron *white only* | Montagny *white only* |
| Givry | Montagny Premier Cru *white only* |
| Mercurey | Rully |
| Mercurey Premier Cru | Rully Premier Cru |

---

## RECOMMENDED PRODUCERS

| | |
|---|---|
| Bouchard Père et Fils | Louis Latour |
| Cave de Buxy | Noel-Bouton |
| Emile Chandesais | Jean Maréchal |
| Chanzy Frères | Bernard Michel |
| Pierre Cogny | J-P Muelin |
| Alain Constant | Antonin Rodet |
| André Delorme | Château de Rully |
| Derain | Domaine Saier |
| Faiveley | Baron Thénard |
| Louis Jadot | Aubert de Villaine |
| Michel Juillot | |

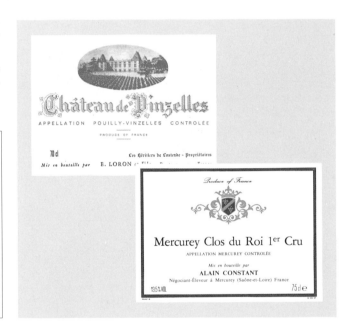

---

# THE MÂCONNAIS

### ∽ TYPES OF WINES ∽

If you like white Burgundy but don't like its price, then the white wines of Mâcon are a good bet. This region produces predominantly white wine, the most important quantity of any Burgundy region by a long way. Mâcon wines are excellent for everyday drinking, particularly if you know which names to look out for. Don't expect them to have the same richness and opulence of the top Côte d'Or wines but, at their price level, Mâcons compare favourably with Chardonnay-based wines from elsewhere in the world. Mâcon whites are generally not oak-aged, with the exception of Pouilly-Fuissé, and some St-Véran and Pouilly-Vinzelles. There are also some reds made in the region, although these have more in common with

Beaujolais than red Burgundies as they are made mainly from the Gamay grape.

### ∽ THE GEOGRAPHY OF THE MÂCONNAIS ∽

Situated roughly equidistant between Lyon and Beaune, the Mâconnais stretches along the west of the river Saône from the north of Tournus down to Romanèche-Thorins. Most of the vineyards in the Mâconnais lie to the west of the river.

#### *The Appellations of Mâcon*

**Mâcon** The wines in this appellation can be either red or white (and even some rosé), and are designed for easy everyday drinking.

**CÔTE CHALONNAISE AND MÂCONNAIS**

Côte Chalonnaise
- Bourgogne Aligoté Bouzeron
- Rully
- Mercurey
- Givry
- Montagny
- Mâconnais
- Mâcon
- Mâcon-Villages
- St Véran
- Pouilly-Fuissé
- Pouilly-Loché
- Pouilly-Vinzelles

*ABOVE: Harvesting Pinot Noir in Rully, one of the appellations of the Côte Châlonnaise.*

**Mâcon-Villages**   Only dry white wines are made within this appellation, which covers 42 villages. Wines made entirely from single village vineyards may use the village name, instead of 'Villages' as a suffix. Among the best are Mâcon-Chardonnay, -Clessé, -Fuissé, -Igé, -Lugny, -Péronne, -Prissé, -Solutré, -Uchizy, -Vinzelles, and -Viré.

**Mâcon-Supérieur**   These wines are not necessarily better than straight Mâcon, as all that is required by law is an extra degree of alcohol! Both red and white are made.

**Pouilly-Fuissé**   People often mistake Pouilly-Fuissé with the Loire wine of a similar name, Pouilly-Fumé. But while the Loire version is made from the gooseberry-flavoured Sauvignon grape, Pouilly-Fuissé is made from Chardonnay and is a much richer, fuller-bodied wine. One producer, Vincent at Château Fuissé, makes an exceptional wine from *vieilles vignes* ('old vines') which produce a robust, fuller bodied wine. Until recently Pouilly-Fuissé was vastly overpriced, and better value could be obtained (and often still can be) from neighbouring Pouilly-Vinzelles, St-Véran, Mâcon-Fuissé and Pouilly-Loché.

**Pouilly-Vinzelles, St-Véran and Pouilly-Loché**   Three satellites of the more famous Pouilly-Fuissé, producing similar, but cheaper wines. Good value.

---

### MACONNAIS APPELLATIONS

All produce both red and white unless otherwise indicated.

| | |
|---|---|
| Mâcon | Pinot Chardonnay-Mâcon |
| Mâcon-Villages *white only* | *white only* |
| Mâcon + Village Name | Pouilly-Fuissé *white only* |
| + *rosé* | Pouilly-Loché *white only* |
| Mâcon-Supérieur | Pouilly-Vinzelles |
| Mâcon-Supérieur + Village | *white only* |
| Name | St-Véran *white only* |

---

### RECOMMENDED PRODUCERS

| | |
|---|---|
| André Bonhomme | Roger Lucquet |
| Georges Burrier | Producteurs de Lugny |
| Cave Cooperative de | René Michel |
| Chardonnay | Daniel Rousset |
| Collin et Bourisset | Producteurs de Prissé |
| Domaine Corsin | Signoret |
| Jacques Dépagneux | Jean Thévenet |
| Georges Duboeuf | J-J Vincent |
| Roger Lasserat | Château de Vinzelles |
| Louis Latour | Cave Cooperative de Viré |
| Château de Loché | Château de Viré |
| Loron et Fils | |

---

### CHALONNAIS AND MACONNAIS VINTAGE CHART

NB: The older vintages (pre-1985) are only worth buying for top wines like Pouilly-Fuissé or St-Véran.

| | |
|---|---|
| 1988 Outstanding | 1982 Average, a bit dilute |
| 1987 Good, but light | 1981 Good |
| 1986 Very good | 1980 Good |
| 1985 Excellent, but some rot | 1979 Average |
| 1984 Average | 1978 Excellent |
| 1983 Very good | |

# ℬEAUJOLAIS

*B*eaujolais is a fun wine, one to be glugged with friends, enjoyed rather than pondered over! The reason Beaujolais is one of France's best known wines is that everyone has heard of Beaujolais Nouveau (or Primeur), the brilliant marketing idea thought up by producers in the early 1960s to improve their cashflow. It's given the region enormous prominence, especially since every bottle produced carries the name Beaujolais, unlike Bordeaux, for example, with its many different appellations. Now more than 50 per cent of all Beaujolais is sold as Nouveau in November of the year of the vintage. And ignore that old adage about drinking it before Christmas – good Nouveau will happily keep (and improve) for a year or two.

### ∾ THE GEOGRAPHY OF BEAUJOLAIS ∾

Situated below Mâcon, Beaujolais is the most southerly region of Burgundy, sprawling over the granite hills above Lyon. The region is roughly thirty miles long by nine miles across and the latest figures show that well over half of the entire production of the Burgundy region is provided by Beaujolais.

### ∾ THE TYPES OF WINE ∾

Beaujolais is primarily a red-wine-producing region, and the red wine is made from the Gamay grape. It's the only region in France (and the world) where Gamay produces impressive results.

But current thinking suggests that the style of wine is not so much due to the grape and the soil alone, but to the special method of vinification which is widely used, known as *macération carbonique*.

### Macération Carbonique

*Macération carbonique* works as follows. The grapes are picked in whole bunches and then placed in vats complete with their stalks. Those at the bottom of the vat are crushed by the weight of the others and fermentation starts, giving off carbon dioxide. The heat of the fermentation starts all the other grapes fermenting inside the skins. The result of this type of vinification is a deep coloured, purple, fruity wine, with low tannins (because these skins have not been pressed) and high acidity and a type of bubblegum aroma. Apart from some of the top *crus*, these wines are designed to be drunk young.

### *The Appellations of Beaujolais*

**Beaujolais & Beaujolais Supérieur**   This is the basic wine of the region that can go into Nouveau or simply labelled with the vintage. Fresh and fruity, this kind of Beaujolais is refreshing and is often drunk chilled in the region. Beaujolais Supérieur wines simply have 1 degree more alcohol and are not generally of higher quality.

**Beaujolais-Villages**   There are 38 villages whose wines can carry the appellation Beaujolais-Villages, mainly in the north of the region. Slightly more expensive than straight Beaujolais, Villages wines have rather more depth of fruit.

**Coteaux du Lyonnais**   Although not strictly speaking in the Beaujolais region, the Coteaux du Lyonnais is immediately to the south and produces a large quantity of perfectly acceptable light red wine made from the Gamay variety of grape.

*Georges Duboeuf, of the company of the same name. This company was largely responsible for the early success of Beaujolais nouveau, but like most of the Beaujolais producers it also produce excellent 'cru' wines.*

## THE CLASSIFICATION OF BEAUJOLAIS

The Beaujolais classification is very straightforward, thank goodness! There are just ten names, all of which are known simply as *crus*. The *cru* wines are generally more full bodied than straight Beaujolais and some are still made by traditional vinification techniques. They are by far the most impressive wines of the region and those from a good producer in a good vintage can last well. Yields are restricted and the wines are rarely released for sale until the beginning of the year following the harvest. The ten *crus* are as follows:

**Brouilly**   This is the largest and most southerly *cru*, producing sound earthy wines.

**Chénas**   Named after the oak trees that used to fill the slopes above the village of Moulin-à-Vent, this is the smallest *cru*. Reasonably full bodied wines with charm.

**Chiroubles**   Lighter bodied than most, with a light delicate aroma and flavour.

**Côte de Brouilly**   More full bodied and longer lasting than Brouilly, and made from vines grown on the slopes around the village of Brouilly.

**Fleurie**   One of the most popular of the Beaujolais *crus*, perhaps because its name is easy to pronounce, and known as 'The Queen of Beaujolais'. It has fragrant fruit and can age for a good few years.

**Juliénas**   Powerful, well-structured wines that develop richer flavours with age, often tannic when young.

**Morgon**   Relatively full-bodied wines that can have a seductive, plummy, cherry-like flavour and aroma when young. Can age well.

**Moulin-à-Vent**   Known as 'The King of Beaujolais', this is the most long-lived of the *crus*, with a hard, relatively tannic structure and immense fruit. After ten years or so of ageing these wines can take on a spicy, almost sweet aroma and flavour, more reminiscent of the Côte d'Or Pinot Noir wines than Gamay.

**Régnié**   This is the tenth and most recent member of the élite Beaujolais *cru* club, Régnié makes mid-weight wines that don't as yet seem to have as much individuality as the other *crus*.

**St-Amour**   The most northerly *cru*, loved by many because of its evocative name. One of the lighter wines, it is aromatic, elegant and complex.

### BEAUJOLAIS AND REGION APPELLATIONS

All produce both red and white unless otherwise indicated.

| | |
|---|---|
| Beaujolais | Côte de Brouilly *red only* |
| Beaujolais + village name | Coteaux du Lyonnais |
| Beaujolais Nouveau *red only* | *red only* |
| Beaujolais Primeur *red only* | Fleurie *red only* |
| Beaujolais Supérieur | Juliénas *red only* |
| Beaujolais-Villages | Morgon *red only* |
| Brouilly *red only* | Moulin-à-Vent *red only* |
| Chénas *red only* | Régnié *red only* |
| Chiroubles *red only* | St-Amour *red only* |

### RECOMMENDED PRODUCERS

| | |
|---|---|
| Brac de la Perrière | Pierre Ferraud |
| Chanut Frères | Sylvain Fessy |
| Thomas la Chevalière | Jacky Janodet |
| André Cologne | Loron et Fils |
| Jacques Dépagneux | Château du Moulin-à-Vent |
| Dessalle | Robert Sarrau |
| Georges Duboeuf | Louis Tête |
| Eventail de Producteurs | Trenel |

### VINTAGE CHART

| | |
|---|---|
| 1988 Very good | 1986 Very good |
| 1987 Pleasant, light wines for drinking now | 1985 Outstanding |
| | 1984 Poor |

**BEAUJOLAIS** (map)

Beaujolais *and* Beaujolais-Villages
Beaujolais *crus*
1 St Amour
2 Juliénas
3 Chénas
4 Moulin-à-vent
5 Fleurie
6 Chiroubles
7 Régnié
8 Morgon
9 Brouilly
10 Côte de Brouilly
Coteaux du Lyonnais

MÂCON
Villefranche-sur-Saône
LYON
Rhône

# CHAMPAGNE

*T*he pop of a Champagne cork instantly conjures up an atmosphere of celebration, the wine's dancing bubbles adding glamour even to the most ordinary occasions. I have to admit I've long had a love affair with Champagne, a product that is very dear to my heart. It firmly earned its place as my desert island wine during the year I spent working in Reims in the Champagne region when I was 18.

It's the only true celebration drink. I always think it's a great shame when it's smashed over bows of ships or sprayed around by jubilant racing drivers – I prefer to drink it!

Champagne is not just any old sparkling wine – it has to be produced in the region of the same name, the most northerly appellation in France. While other regions in France and around the world make sparkling wines by the same method as the Champenoise, under EEC law they are not permitted to use the word Champagne on the label. Champagne producers, who have fought many a battle to protect their name over the years, have now persuaded the EEC to go one stage further. Other sparkling wines will soon not be allowed to carry the words *méthode champenoise* on the label, despite the fact that the term describes the production process itself!

## ∾ THE HISTORY OF CHAMPAGNE ∾

Thank goodness for the Romans. For it is they who are credited with planting the vines in the Champagne region, situated 90 miles north east of Paris. In those days Champagne was not the dancing bubbly product we now know, but a still wine. Even today, nobody in the Champagne region is entirely sure exactly when the sparkle was invented. After the Romans, the other most important human factor in the history of Champagne was the Church. In the local community the monks often made the wine, and not just in France – the Domesday Book reports many monastery wineries in England too.

Enter the wine world's most sparkling legend, Dom Pérignon, a 17th century monk from Hautvillers Abbey, close to Epernay, who is credited with the creation of Champagne, the world's most stylish drink. If he were alive today his version of the story would undoubtedly be different and it is unlikely that he would lay claim to 'inventing' Champagne. But he noticed that the wine of the region had a natural tendency to sparkle in the bottle in springtime when the weather warmed up. Visit Moët & Chandon's museum at Hautvillers and you'll see that Dom

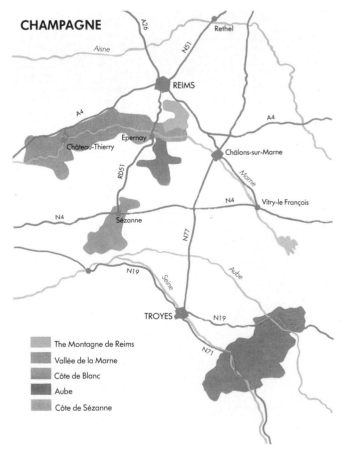

**CHAMPAGNE**

The Montagne de Reims
Vallée de la Marne
Côte de Blanc
Aube
Côte de Sézanne

Pérignon was an extremely perceptive man. He realized that a sparkling wine needed a much stronger bottle to withstand the pressure, and that a cork (rather than a cloth and a peg) was more effective in keeping the magical bubbles in the bottle. Even more fundamental to Champagne was his innovation of blending wines from different grapes and vineyards. One hopes that Dom Pérignon would be both flattered by his recognition and impressed that his work is being continued even today by the Champagne industry as a whole, whose members are continually working on research into vine clones, soils and new technology.

### ☙ THE GEOGRAPHY OF CHAMPAGNE ❧

What, you may ask, apart from its closely guarded name, makes Champagne so different from any other sparkling wine? Its secret lies in the soil and the underlying rock which is chalk, part of the same chalk outcrop as the white cliffs of Dover. To make really good sparkling wine requires a fairly acidic, tart wine to start with. It is the combination of the northerly situation of the vines and lack of sunshine, as well as the natural presence of lime in the soil, that produces grapes with high acidity – ideal for Champagne.

In the region there were traditionally four main areas of production, although a fifth at the southern limit of the appellation now exists.

**The Montagne de Reims**   This is where the Pinot Noir, which flourishes mainly on north and north-eastern facing slopes, is gently warmed by rising hot air from the valley.

*ABOVE: One of the wine world's most sparkling monks, Dom Pérignon. He takes some of the credit for discovering how to keep the all important bubbles in the bottle of Champagne as we know it today.*
*LEFT: Vineyards showing the chalky soil that produces an acidic, tart wine, the ideal base wine for Champagne.*

These grapes add structure, body and depth of flavour to the blend. In this region one of the best villages, Verzenay, boasts the only one remaining windmill in the region while another village, Bouzy, is a name difficult to forget!

**Vallée de la Marne** While all three Champagne grapes are grown in this area, mainly to the west of Epernay, it is the Pinot Meunier that reigns supreme. It produces relatively soft, easy drinking wines. It is, however, an essential part of the blend in Champagne and is suited to the climate of the valley as it is fairly frost-resistant.

**The Côte des Blancs** As its name would suggest, these vineyards produce the essential Chardonnay, the one white grape used in Champagne. These are the most coveted grapes in the region and add elegance, depth, richness and longevity, natural characteristics that make it one of the world's most fashionable grape varieties.

**The Aube** Situated along the southern limit of the appellation, this part of the region enjoys more sunshine than the rest. While many houses have in the past dismissed the wines of this region as inferior and rather obvious, even harsh, all the wine is sold, some of it to the very companies who criticize it. But the criticism is only relative and, when blended well, wines from the Aube add good aroma and ripeness of fruit.

**Côte de Sézanne** This area situated to the south-west of Epernay has only relatively recently become an important source of Chardonnay.

## THE CLASSIFICATION OF CHAMPAGNE

Within the Champagne region there is a vineyard classification system that ranges from 100 per cent down to 80 per cent. There are only 17 of the best 100 per cent vineyards (known as *Grands Crus*) and 140 *Premiers Crus* that are rated 90 per cent. The 80 per cent vineyards are found mainly in the Aube region. The price a grower receives for his grapes depends on these ratings and decreases proportionally. Every year the C.I.V.C. (*Comité Interprofessionnel des Vins de Champagne*) sets the price for grapes – those from 100 per cent rated vineyards sell for this price, 90 per cent rated at 90 per cent of the price, and so on.

## MAKING CHAMPAGNE

Many people are surprised to learn that Champagne is made from a blend of three grapes, two of which are black, the Pinot Noir and Pinot Meunier, and the world's most fashionable white grape, the Chardonnay.

### Pressing the grapes
After picking, pressing is carried out as soon as possible so that the grapes do not have time to oxidize. The first pressing, known as the *cuvée*, yields the best juice which in theory goes into the best Champagnes. Then second and third pressings are made, known as the *première* and *deuxième taille*.

### The first fermentation
The wine then ferments naturally in large stainless steel tanks, a process that originally took place in wooden barrels, now only used by a few companies like Krug. After the first alcoholic fermentation the resulting wine is still, and has a harsh acidic flavour. By the following March or April the *assemblage*, or blending of wines from different grape varieties and different vineyards, is complete. The most difficult skill of all is blending a consistent non-vintage wine, using the current vintage wines plus several older reserve wines.

### The second fermentation
But where, you may well ask, are the all important bubbles? That comes next. The still wine is bottled together with the addition of yeast and sugar and sealed with a crown cap (like the ones on beer bottles). The bottles are then transported down to the miles and miles of cellars hewn out of the chalk, many of which have been there since Roman times. Then the yeast sets to work and the wine begins to re-ferment. The yeast eats up the sugar in the wine and then in effect burps, transforming it into tiny bubbles of carbon dioxide that are imprisoned inside the bottle. This dead yeast gives the Champagne a richer, sometimes biscuity flavour.

### Remuage – collecting the yeast
Once this fermentation is complete (the length of time can vary from ten days to three months) it's time for the really tricky bit – how to take out all the tiny particles of dead yeast that are trapped inside the bottle without losing the bubbles. It is assumed that during Dom Pérignon's day everyone drank their Champagne complete with bits. It was much later that La Veuve Clicquot, the widow that Champagne drinkers all over the world ought to thank, invented *remuage* as a way of removing the bits. Bottles are placed horizontally neck first in hinged wooden racks that look like inverted V shapes. Then over a period of around two months the bottles are twisted by hand, one by one, to loosen the sediment until they are virtually vertically upside down, and all the sediment is resting inside the crown cork.

Automatic *remuage* in large steel cages has now replaced the traditional hand-turning in many houses, and experiments are currently being carried out to avoid this stage of the process completely by putting the yeast into tiny capsules of alginate that will simply fall back into the neck of the bottle when tipped up, ready for *dégorgement*.

### Dégorgement – removing the dead yeast
The bottles are then placed neck first into a freezing solution which freezes an inch or so of Champagne and imprisons the dead yeast. Quickly turned the right way up before the ice melts, the crown corks are flipped off and the ice plug pops out complete with the sediment.

The wine is now clear, but the bottles need to be topped up to ensure we all get a full bottle of Champagne. It is at this stage that the sweetness of the wine can be altered. Traditionally even the driest Champagne, known as Brut, has a little bit of sugar added at this stage, together with some reserve wine, whereas Demi-Sec wines, the sweetest style, have much more added. Today there are some totally dry Champagnes made (with names like Brut Zero or Ultra-Brut) but they are nothing like as palatable as standard Brut.

*Many people are surprised to learn that two-thirds of the grapes that make Champagne are black grapes. By removing the skins from the juice soon after pressing the colour pigment in the skins does not stain the juice.*

### Popping in the cork

Finally the bottles are sealed with the famous Champagne cork which has to be leashed down with wire to prevent it flying out. To open a bottle of Champagne the trick is to keep your thumb on the top of the cork and turn the bottle, not the cork. That way you are in control and the cork will come out with a gentle pop, the signal that a celebration is about to start!

### ∾ THE DIFFERENT STYLES OF CHAMPAGNE ∾

### Non-vintage Champagne

Non-vintage Champagnes account for almost 90 per cent of production. These are a blend of several different vintages and should taste the same year after year. Each Champagne house has a different style ranging from light, delicate aperitif Champagnes to richer, heavier, more creamy Champagnes which go well with food.

### Vintage Champagne

Unlike other areas of France the Champagne region does not declare a vintage every year, only doing so in the very best years. Vintage Champagne made from the grapes of a single year shows more of the style of the vintage than the producer.

### Rosé Champagne

Traditionally rosé Champagne was made by leaving the skins of the black grapes in contact with the juice to enable the natural pigments to colour it. Using this method, however, it is very tricky to control the exact colour. Although a few of the more traditional Champagne houses still use this method, it's much more common to see producers mixing red wine produced in the region with white Champagne and adjusting the amounts depending on the required colour. Rosés can vary from pale onion skin through to salmon pink to deep reddy pink. Many rosés have a higher proportion of black grapes in them and some are made without any white grapes at all. Tasting rosé Champagne with your eyes closed it can be very difficult to detect the difference between rosé and white Champagne – rosé Champagne's biggest asset is its fun colour.

### Blanc de Blancs

This simply means white of white – a Champagne made entirely from the Chardonnay grape.

### Blanc de Noirs

This sounds like a contradiction in terms, meaning white of black, but it simply means the Champagne has been made entirely from black grapes although the resulting colour is white.

### Prestige Cuvées or Deluxe Cuvées

These are the Champagne houses' top-of-the-range wines and therefore their price reflects this. As they are generally vintage wines made from grapes from the best vineyards you have to be fairly wealthy to develop a taste for them.

### Crémant Champagnes

For those of you who like a less fizzy Champagne, Crémants are the answer as they are about half as bubbly, with around 3.5 atmospheres of pressure compared with the normal 5.5 to 6. The word Cramant is not a variation on the same theme, but the name of a village in the Côte des Blancs. Confusingly it is possible to find Crémant de Cramant, which can be excellent.

## THE COMMERCIAL STRUCTURE OF CHAMPAGNE

There are four main types of producer involved in the making of Champagne and you can tell which one has produced the bottle of Champagne in front of you by looking at the small letters on the bottom of the label.

**The Champagne Houses (NM)**    Also known by the sinister-sounding title *négociants-manipulants*, all the big, well-known names belong to this group. Traditionally the large houses did not own vineyards, preferring to have regular buying contracts with growers. Now, however, many do have their own vineyards which account for varying percentages of their production.

**Récoltants-Manipulants (RM)**    These are the growers that also make their own wine, part of which they sell under their own name and the rest they sell to the big houses or the co-operatives. In the past ten years more growers have decided to sell wine under their own label rather than letting the larger houses reap the financial benefit.

**Coopératives-Manipulants (CM)**    These are the smaller growers' co-operatives and can sell grapes, juice and wine under a variety of different labels.

**Marque Auxiliaire (MA)**    A huge category of wines come into this section which covers all the BOBs (buyer's own brands) sold by retailers like supermarkets who want their own label. These wines are generally bought by wholesale merchants who then sell the Champagne under a variety of different labels. Champagnes falling into this category have increased dramatically over the last few years because of the huge increase in supermarket own-label sales.

### VINTAGE GUIDE – CHAMPAGNE

Because of supply and demand, many vintage Champagnes are released for sale at their minimum permitted age of only three years old. But many need a lot longer to mature and really good vintage Champagne can last for years.

Not every year is declared a vintage and it is up to each particular house whether they declare one or not. Vintage Champagne will last longer than non-vintage wines, and are well worth laying down. They mature and are still recognizable as Champagne up to ten years old. After that they become a deeper yellow colour, lose their fizz and develop a remarkable nutty richness. Old Champagne is an acquired taste, and I love it – the oldest Champagne I have drunk was a stunningly youthful 60-year-old!

Non-vintage Champagne will also benefit from extra bottle age, so if you've a favourite brand lay down a few cases in your cellar taking care to write the date you bought them on the boxes.

1983  Excellent, almost as good as 1982, good ageing potential
1982  Superb, especially Chardonnay
1981  Good, Pinot Noir particularly successful
1979  Superb
1978  Not many houses declared a vintage – not a great success
1976  Superb. Big crop, high alcohol, very full and rich
1975  Excellent, declared by most producers but not long lasting
1973  Excellent, better than the vintage in most other wine regions
1971  Very good, although not outstanding
1970  Very good, rich and full

## RECOMMENDED PRODUCERS

| Main name | Prestige Cuvées | Rosé? | Other specials |
|---|---|---|---|
| Henri Abelé | Grand Marque Impériale | Yes | – |
| Ayala & Co | – | Yes | Blanc de Blancs |
| Besserat de Bellefon | – | Yes | Crémant |
| Billecart-Salmon | Cuvée N F Billecart | Yes | Blanc de Blancs |
| Bollinger | 'R.D.', Année Rare | Yes | Vieilles Vignes, Blanc de Noirs |
| Bricout & Koch | – | Yes | – |
| Canard Duchêne | Charles VII Brut | No | Blanc de Blancs |
| Cheurlin | Special Reserve | No | – |
| De Castellane | Cuvée Commodore | Yes | Blanc de Blancs |
| Deutz and Gelderman | Cuveé William Deutz | Yes | Blanc de Blancs |
| Duval-Leroy | – | Yes | Crémant + Blanc de Blancs |
| Georges Gardet | – | Yes | – |
| Gosset | Cuvée 4ème Centenaire | Yes | Blanc de Blancs |
| Georges Goulet | Cuvée du Centenaire | Yes | Crémant + Blanc de Blancs |
| Alfred Gratien | – | Yes | Crémant |
| Charles Heidsieck | Champagne Charlie | Yes | Blanc de Blancs |
| Heidsieck Monopole | Diamant Bleu | Yes | – |
| Henriot | Réserve Baron de Rothschild, Cuvée Baccarat | Yes | Blanc de Blancs |
| Jacquart | La Renommé | Yes | – |
| Jacquesson & Fils | Brut Zéro Blanc de Blancs, Signature | Yes | Blanc de Blancs |
| Krug | Clos du Mesnil Blanc de Blancs | Yes | Krug Collection |
| Lanson Père & Fils | Spécial Cuvée | Yes | |
| Laurent-Perrier | Grande Siècle, Millésime Rare | Yes | Crémant + Ultra Brut |
| Abel Lepitre | Prince A de Bourbon Parme | Yes | Crémant Blanc de Blancs |
| Mercier | Réserve de l'Empereur | Yes | Crémant |
| Moët & Chandon | Dom Pérignon | Yes | Crémant |
| G H Mumm & Co | René Lalou | Yes | Crémant de Cramant |
| Bruno Paillard | – | Yes | Crémant Blanc de Blancs |
| Joseph Perrier | Cuvée Cinquantenaire, Cuveé Royale | Yes | Blanc de Blancs |
| Perrier-Jouët | Belle Epoque | Yes | Extra Brut |
| Philipponnat | Clos de Goisses | Yes | Blanc de Blancs |
| Piper-Heidsieck | Florens-Louis, Rare | Yes | Brut Sauvage |
| Pol Roger | Cuvée Winston Churchill, Spéciale Réserve | Yes | – |
| Pommery & Greno | Louise Pommery | Yes | |
| Louis Roederer | Cristal | Yes | Blanc de Blancs |
| Ruinart Père & Fils | Dom Ruinart Blanc de Blancs | Yes | – |
| Salon | 'S' | No | – |
| Taittinger | Comtes de Champagne Blanc de Blancs | Yes | Collection |
| Veuve Clicquot-Ponsardin | Grande Dame | Yes | – |

*ABOVE LEFT: Vineyards on the banks of the river Marne, where the Pinot Meunier reigns supreme. RIGHT: Bottles are placed neck first in hinged wooden racks known as 'pupitres', gently twisted and tilted until all the dead yeasts lie in the neck of the bottle.*

# The Loire Valley

The valley of the Loire, France's longest river, is one of the most attractive wine-producing regions of France, famous for the fairytale châteaux which adorn its banks. It's not really surprising to learn that is was once the playground of the kings and queens of France who not only built fabulous châteaux there but wined and dined in true majestic style on the delicious river fish and a wide variety of the region's wines.

The Loire is also one of the most versatile wine-producing regions of France, making a much wider gamut of wines than many people give it credit for. Whether you want white, red, rosé, dry, semi-dry or sweet sparkling or still wine, you can find it in the Loire valley.

If you follow the river Loire from its source in the Cévennes mountains, along 1000km (625 miles) until it reaches the Atlantic Ocean, you will pass through 12 different *départements* and lose count of the many wine regions. If you attempt to try all the wines of the Loire, you'll have a very long but enjoyable trip!

Often looked down on by the more traditional wine drinker, the Loire Valley produces many excellent value for money wines, many from little known *appellations*. All areas in the Loire have to contend with the cold northern climate and the wine's taste reflects this. White grapes had to predominate in the Loire Valley. One of the Loire's top white grape varieties, the Chenin Blanc, is immensely versatile producing crisp, dry, through to lusciously sweet whites. The sheer range of different styles of white Loire wines is very impressive.

There are some reds (indeed, with *phylloxera* in the 19th century all Sancerre was red) but they are light, with none of the staying power of the more southerly reds like those from Bordeaux or the Rhône Valley.

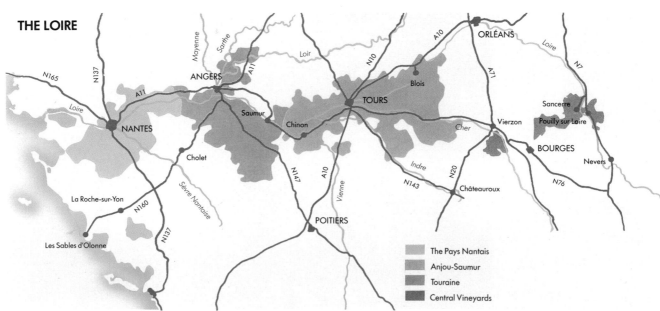

**THE LOIRE**

- The Pays Nantais
- Anjou-Saumur
- Touraine
- Central Vineyards

*The villages of Chavignol and Sancerre in the Loire Valley, one of France's most versatile wine-producing regions. Vineyards adorn its banks as it travels through many appellations.*

## ✤ THE GRAPE VARIETIES ✤

In different areas of the Loire even the same grapes can produce very different wines due to changes in microclimate and soil. The four most important grape varieties grown in the Loire are:

**Chenin Blanc** This is probably the most versatile. High in acidity, it can produce dry whites, still and sparkling, semi-dry and rich, and sweet luscious pudding wines.

**Sauvignon Blanc** Produces flinty, dry, grassy whites with a distinct aroma of gooseberries and asparagus.

**Cabernet Franc** *The* red variety of the Loire. Wines have marked red-fruit flavours of raspberries and strawberries with a touch of earthy violets.

**Gamay** The Beaujolais grape that fares well in the Loire and produces light, fruity wines which are ideal for everyday drinking. Some Pinot Noir is grown, but mainly around Sancerre.

### The Winemakers
Like Burgundy, the Loire can be confusing because it's not enough just to buy its wines according to the appellation. There are small growers and huge *négociants*, all producing different styles of wine. Again, like Burgundy, sometimes it's the *négociant* who makes the best wine, sometimes the grower. You just have to keep an eye on the name on the label!

*ABOVE: Vineyards in Sancerre, an area originally predominantly planted with black grapes that were replaced with white grapes after the onslaught on the vine-eating louse phylloxera.*
*LEFT: Vineyards in the Coteaux du Loir, where luscious sweet wines are made from the Chenin Blanc grape.*
*RIGHT: Vineyards in the Pays Nantais, the home of Muscadet. Many of the smaller producers still use horses in preference to tractors.*

# THE PAYS NANTAIS

*P*art of the Loire-Atlantique (where the river Loire flows into the Atlantic Ocean), the Pays Nantais lies to the south-east of Nantes and is the home of Muscadet, the crisp dry white wine made from the grape of the same name and grown almost exclusively in this region.

Muscadet's origins are unclear, although locals suggest that the grape's other name, 'Melon de Bourgogne', relates to a legend which tells of shipwrecked sailors en route from Burgundy who just happened to have some vine cuttings with them. As luck would have it, it seems that they had just the perfect vine clone to hand, as few other vines could survive the climatic conditions of the Pays Nantais, one of France's most northerly wine-producing regions.

Muscadet really came into its own in France around the 1950s when many more people started drinking wine, and the restaurants of Paris could not keep up the supply of expensive white Burgundy. Instead, they looked to the Pays Nantais for a ready supply of large quantities of Muscadet, washed down by the bucket-load in 'Gai Paris', accompanied by dozens of oysters.

Muscadet is a dry, crisp wine with high acidity. The best examples combine this acidity with good fruit although poorly made Muscadet can be dry and tart with little flavour. The best area for Muscadet production is the Sèvre-et-Maine district, which accounts for over 80 per cent of the production. It is more hilly than others parts of the Pays Nantais, so the grapes have slightly more exposure to ripening sunshine. You'll also find Muscadets from the Coteaux de la Loire, a district further north centred around the town of Ancenis, but they are rarely as good as those from Sèvre-et-Maine.

### Sur lie

To give their wines more fruit and body, the best producers leave them in contact with their lees (the natural dead yeast particles that result from fermentation), until 15 February following the harvest, when the wine is bottled. The resulting wines have *sur lie* printed on their label and have a greater depth of yeasty flavour than normal Muscadet. Often they have a slight spritz when young, the result of the natural carbon dioxide produced during fermentation, some of which is captured in the juice while left on its lees. It's well worth paying the extra for a Sur Lie Muscadet as the added depth of flavour means it will complement many more dishes.

Another wine made and drunk widely in the region but rarely seen elsewhere is Gros Plant, which is rather like a dilute and more acidic version of Muscadet.

---

### THE APPELLATIONS OF THE PAYS NANTAIS

There are also some VDQS wines in the Pays Nantais, also producing light, very dry whites, namely Coteaux d'Ancenis, Fiefs Vendéens and Gros Plant.

Muscadet
Muscadet des Coteaux de la Loire
Muscadet de Sèvre-et-Maine

---

### VINTAGES

Pays Nantais wines should always be drunk young and fresh, so vintages are of little importance. Avoid any wines more than three or four years old.

---

### RECOMMENDED PRODUCERS

| | |
|---|---|
| Aubert Frères | Marquis de Goulaine |
| Donatien Bahaud | Jacques Guindon |
| Barré Fils | Domaine des Herbanges |
| Château la Berrière | Louis Métaireau |
| Chereau Carré | Château la Noë |
| Château de Chantrié | Château de l'Oiselinière |
| Michel Chiron | Château de la Ragotière |
| Jean Dabin | Sauvion et Fils |
| Guilbaud Frères | Domaine de Tourmaline |

# Anjou-Saumur

Anjou. No, don't groan – there is more to this region than boring old Anjou Rosé, a sweetish blended rosé gulped down by the container-load in Britain but not drunk much by the locals over there! Made well, it can be a pleasant enough drink, but made badly for the cheapest possible price it can be very unpleasant.

Cabernet d'Anjou is generally of a better quality than Anjou Rosé. And ironically, in the past Anjou was better known for the quality of its white wines than rosés. But the district contains several other appellations and their wines are far more interesting.

The most important are as follows:

**Anjou Blanc** Made predominantly from the Chenin Blanc grape, this is a pleasant, undemanding wine, generally dry, with a honeysuckle, slightly earthy flavour.

**Anjou Rouge** This can be made from several grape varieties, often with a high percentage of the Cabernet Franc grape producing light to medium bodied wines with a flavour of earthy red fruits.

**Anjou Gamay** As its name would suggest this is made from the classic Beaujolais grape, the Gamay. It is a light, easy quaffing red.

**Coteaux du Layon** This appellation produces mainly great value medium-sweet and sweet white as well as some rosé. Made from the Chenin Blanc grape, the best sweet whites can be rich, luscious and nutty and last for years. The grapes in this region are left on the vines long after the harvest in the hope that they will develop noble rot. Also look out for similar wines from two other appellations within this region, Bonnezeaux and Quarts de Chaume.

*ABOVE: Château de la Roche-aux-Moines, one of two Grand Crus of the Savennières appellation, with Chenin Blanc vines in the foreground. The vines here are planted on steep slopes so they benefit from maximum exposure to the sun.*
*LEFT: The impressive castle in Saumur which looks out on to the Loire.*
*ABOVE RIGHT: Chenin vines in the Coteaux du Layon appellation. The grapes in this region are left on the vines in the hope that they develop noble rot. The town of Rochefort-sur-Loire can be seen in the background.*

**Savennières**  Situated on the north bank of the Loire, the vines of Savennières are planted on steep slopes so they benefit from maximum exposure to the sun. Made from the Chenin Blanc grape, these wines can appear dry when young and become honeyed and sweeter when mature. The two *Grand Crus* of the appellation are Coulée de Serrant and la Roche aux Moines.

**Saumur Rouge**  Made predominantly from the earthy, red fruit-tasting grape, Cabernet Franc, these are pleasant, drinkable reds. The best villages in the area produce Saumur Champigny, the best red wine produced in the Anjou and Saumur region. The beauty of it is that it is extremely fruity and refreshing when young, with all the best characteristics of the Cabernet Franc grape, but will mature into a softer more full bodied wine over a period of five to ten years.

**Sparkling Saumur**  Apart from the ubiquitous Anjou Rosé, the sparkling wines of Saumur are probably the best known wines from this region. And in this case, rightly so. Producers in Saumur claim they were making naturally sparkling wines before the Champenois and even used to sell them their grapes. Both regions certainly have the ideal base product from which to make the best sparkling wine: a raw, tart, acidic liquid readily available in this district from the Chenin Blanc grape. Both districts also share similar calcareous soil and underlying rock, which not only gives the grapes the required high acidity, but also provide natural caves for use as cellars after the local tufa (limestone) was quarried for building.

Although made mainly from the Chenin Blanc grape, Saumur d'Origin (the term you'll see on the label) producers are allowed up to 20 per cent of other grape varieties such as Sauvignon and Chardonnay (which is being planted increasingly in this area). Sparkling Saumur is one of the best *méthode champenoise* wines produced in France, especially if drunk when young. It has a much more pronounced flavour than Champagne with more of an earthy tang. Also look out for the rosé Saumur, made like rosé Champagne with the addition of red wine made from the Cabernet Franc grape.

---

### THE APPELLATIONS OF ANJOU-SAUMUR

All produce both red and dry white unless otherwise indicated.

| | |
|---|---|
| Anjou | + rosé and sweet white |
| Anjou Coteaux de la Loire | white only |
| Anjou Gamay | red only |
| Anjou Mousseux | sparkling white and rosé only |
| Anjou Pétillant | sparkling white and rosé only |
| Bonnezeaux | sweet white only |
| Cabernet d'Anjou | rosé only |
| Cabernet de Saumur | rosé only |
| Coteaux de l'Aubance | sweet white only |
| Coteaux du Layon | sweet white only |
| Coteaux du Layon-Chaume | sweet white only |
| Coteaux du Layon Villages | sweet white only |
| Coteaux de Saumur | sweet white only |
| Quarts-de-Chaume | sweet white only |
| Saumur | + sweet white |
| Saumur-Champigny | red only |
| Saumur Pétillant | sparkling white only |
| Saumur Mousseux | sparkling white and rosé only |
| Savennières | dry to sweet white only |

---

### RECOMMENDED GROWERS

*Anjou-Saumur (general)*
Château des Fesles
Logis de la Giraudière
Moulin Touchais

*Saumur-Champigny*
Claude Daheuiller
Domaine Filliatreau
Domaine des Roches Neuves
Domaine des Varinelles

*Bonnezeaux, Coteaux du Layon and Quarts de Chaume*
Domaine des Baumards
Château de Beaulieu
Château de Belle Rive

Clos de Sainte Catherine
Château des Fesles
Domaine des Rochelles
Clos des Rochettes
Moulin Touchais

*Savennières*
Château de la Bizolière
Clos du Papillon
La Roche-aux-Moines
Coulée de Serrant

*Sparkling Saumur*
Jean Douet
de Neuville
Langlois Château

# TOURAINE

*T*ouraine produces high quality red, dry white and sweet white wines. The best reds are on a par with Saumur-Champigny and are among the best of the Loire's red wines. The whites range from dry, fresh, zingy Sauvignons and Chevernys to lusciously sweet Vouvrays and Montlouis.

**Chinon** This is the first appellation (going upstream) in the Touraine region and the home of the red wines referred to above. Along with the kings and queens of France, the writer Rabelais was a devotee of the wines of Chinon. 'Chinon, Chinon, little town, great renown' is a much quoted line of his.

The town of Chinon is fascinating to visit with many ancient timber-framed houses, narrow streets and an impressive château which gives a good view of the surrounding vineyards.

Cabernet Franc is in its element in this region and produces ripe earthy reds, often with a flavour of ripe strawberries, raspberries and a touch of violets that can be enjoyed while young but the best of which will last a good decade and more. Many of the wines that last the longest have been aged in oak barrels that make the wines even more bitter when young. Try buying a few bottles from a good producer and laying them down for a few years. You may well be surprised how much the earthy flavour softens in bottle into a mature wine which, when tasted blind, can almost resemble an old claret.

**Bourgueil** Just opposite the appellation of Chinon, on the other side of the river, is the home of Loire's other excellent red, Bourgueil. The village of the same name still boasts its ancient Benedictine chapel originally built in AD 990. Local vignerons do not only grow grapes but supplement their income with large crops of fruit and vegetables, which thrive in this pocket of the Loire Valley that enjoys relatively warm temperatures for the region. There are eight communes which produce wine with this name, and just one (the best one) St-Nicholas de Bourgueil, has its own appellation.

The wines of Bourgueil can be almost too harsh and earthy when young but come into their own with age. Because of their natural Cabernet Franc-flavoured fruit and acidity they are a good foil for strong fish dishes such as sardines, mackerel or pike and meaty casseroles.

**Touraine**

Many different styles of wine carry the Touraine appellation. While Chenin Blanc is still grown in this region, the crisp grassy Sauvignon Blanc takes precedence. Good examples of Touraine Sauvignon can rival less good Sancerres with an unmistakable aroma and flavour of gooseberries.

In Touraine the Gamay takes over from the Cabernet Franc in terms of importance and produces some deliciously gulpable light reds, which are best drunk chilled as they are in the region. In general they are much lighter than Beaujolais which is also made from Gamay.

Look out for the white dry and sweet wines produced in Azay-le-Rideau, made mainly from the Chenin Blanc grape which can be sumptuous, especially when old.

**Vouvray** Driving out of the city of Tours towards Vouvray it's hard to miss the numerous caves, cut into the side of the tufa hills, some of which are still inhabited by locals. Many houses have also been built into the sides of hills and have natural cellar extensions stretching back underground.

In Vouvray the Chenin Blanc grape is grown, a grape capable of producing every style of white: dry, medium-dry and sweet. Grapes are picked late in this area in an attempt to encourage the development of noble rot (see *Sauternes*, pages 64-67), which gives the wines a distinctive flavour.

*BELOW LEFT: The spectacular Château de Chenonceaux on the river Cher.*
*RIGHT: The picturesque town of Chinon with the river Vienne in the foreground.*

Many producers, aware that the consumer has become confused as to whether Vouvray is a dry or sweet wine, now label their wines *sec, demi-sec* or *doux* (dry, semi-dry or sweet). But because of the high acidity content which can mask the fruit it can be difficult to ascertain whether a young wine is dry or sweet. And this is sometimes further complicated by the fact that wines that are dry when young can become more honeyed and sweeter with age. In middle age Chenin Blanc develops a strange sort of 'rusty' or musty aroma, while young Chenin can be crisp, earthy and delightful. The hotter the vintage the sweeter the wine generally is, and wines from hot vintages such as 1947 and 1976 can last for years, helped by their natural high acidity.

The same acidity, as in Saumur, lends itself to the production of sparkling wines, again made here by the *méthode champenoise*. Sparkling Vouvray (*pétillant* or *mousseux*) has a more marked aroma and flavour of Chenin than Saumur sparkling wines, with a slightly peachy, melon, honeysuckle flavour.

**Montlouis** In good vintages this appellation, just to the south of Vouvray, produces wines equal in quality to the best Vouvrays.

## THE APPELLATIONS OF TOURAINE

All produce both red and white unless otherwise indicated.

| | |
|---|---|
| Bourgueil | red and rosé only |
| Cheverny | + rosé and sparkling red, white and rosé |
| Chinon | + rosé |
| Coteaux du Loir | |
| Jasnières | white only |
| Montlouis | white only |
| Montlouis Mousseux | sparkling white only |
| Montlouis Pétillant | sparkling white only |
| St-Nicholas-de-Bourgueil | red and rosé only |
| Touraine | + rosé |
| Touraine Amboise | + rosé |
| Touraine Azay-le-Rideau | white and rosé only |
| Touraine-Mesland | + rosé |
| Touraine Mousseux | sparkling white and rosé |
| Touraine Pétillant | sparkling white and rosé |
| Vouvray | white only |
| Vouvray Mousseux | sparkling white only |
| Vouvray Pétillant | sparkling white only |

## RECOMMENDED GROWERS

*Chinon*
Audebert & Fils
P-J Druet
Couly-Dutheil
Clos de l'Echo
Guy Lemaire
Pierre Manzagol
Jean-François Olek
Plouzeau et Fils
Mme Jean Spelty
Serge Sourdais

*Bourgueil, St-Nicholas-de-Bourgueil and Touraine-Mesland*
Clos de l'Abbaye
Audebert & Fils
Aimé Boucher
Raphael Galteau
Pierre Grégoire
Jean-Jacques Jamet
Marc Mureau

*Vouvray and Montlouis*
Domaine des Barguins
Marc Brédif
Gaston Huet
Château Montcontour
Château de Montlouis
Prince Poniatowski (Clos Baudoin)

# THE CENTRAL VINEYARDS

*I*n the upper stretch of the river Loire the Chenin Blanc grape gives way to the Sauvignon Blanc, which produces better wines here than anywhere else in the Loire. This is the home of the Loire's most famous whites after Muscadet: Sancerre and Pouilly-Fumé.

The Central Vineyards (so-called because they are in the middle of France, *not* the centre of the Loire Valley) are predominantly white-wine regions, although a little red and rosé is produced. In fact, Sancerre used to produce mostly red. But then, in the mid- to late-19th century, the phylloxera louse hit Europe, decimating Sancerre's vineyards. The growers were faced with a dilemma: whether to replant with red grape vines, or to replant with Sauvignon Blanc vines which produced fruit much more quickly. They chose the latter option which is why today most Sancerre is white! As well as the well-known Sancerre and Pouilly-Fumé there are three other appellations further away from the river Loire itself, producing alternatives from the same grapes, and rivalling Sancerre in terms of value for money.

**Reuilly**   Like Sancerre, Reuilly is also situated on a hill surrounded by vineyards. Not to be confused with the white Burgundy of a similar name (Rully), Reuilly is rather lighter in style than Sancerre and often more austere.

**Quincy**   Just as in the rest of the Loire where the soil type can change every few miles, six miles east of Reuilly the soil changes and as a result so do the wines. With slightly less lime in the soil the Sauvignon wines of Quincy (pronounced can-see) are somewhat rounder, smoother, less harsh and austere than those of Reuilly

**Menetou-Salon**   This region also produces whites from the Sauvignon Blanc grape, which here takes on a floral aroma and a curious, almost chocolatey, flavour which gives the wines more immediate charm than some Sancerres. It is still relatively good value as, despite its proximity to Sancerre it is nothing like as well known. Look out also for the red wines of Menetou-Salon made from the Pinot Noir grape, which tend to be light quaffable reds, best drunk chilled.

**Sancerre**   Good white Sancerre is crisp and dry with masses of gooseberry flavour. However, this wine has suffered a drop in quality as a result of its own popularity and is not the good value it once was, with only a few exceptions. Rosé Sancerre is normally insipid but red Sancerre (made from the Pinot Noir grape) can be delicious from a good producer.

**Pouilly-Fumé**   On the right bank of the Loire, just across the river from Sancerre, lies the village of Pouilly-sur-Loire. Once a busy village with the main N7 running through it, a bypass was built and now it is quiet. Some of the best white wines from the entire Loire valley come from this region which, up until the early 1970s, was relatively unknown. I prefer Pouilly-Fumé to Sancerre as it has more finesse and, after a few years in bottle, develops a more complex flavour of flinty grassiness, with a touch of smokey fennel on the aftertaste. Don't confuse this with Pouilly-Fuissé from Burgundy, which is a totally different white wine. Pouilly-Fumé can also be known as Blanc-Fumé de Pouilly, Blanc-Fumé de Pouilly-sur-Loire and Pouilly Blanc Fumé.

*ABOVE: The fairytale Château de Nozet where de Ladoucette Pouilly-Fumé is produced.*
*LEFT: Harvesting Sauvignon Blanc grapes at Sancerre.*
*RIGHT: Vineyards above the river Loire at Pouilly where the dry white wine Pouilly-Fumé is produced.*

# $A$LSACE

$S$top anyone in the street and ask them what country Alsace is in and you'll get one of two answers: France or Germany. But considering the number of times the region has changed hands over the years perhaps this is hardly surprising. As far as the style of the wines goes (rather than of the architecture) it seems only right and fitting that today Alsace is very much part of France. Unfortunately the wines still suffer from an identity crisis because of the Germanic-looking tall, fluted bottles and the Gothic print that still exists on many labels.

In an oft-quoted line, Johnny Hugel, one of the top wine-makers in the region says 'we are specialists in white wines and wars'. During the First World War Alsace was part of France, but just over 22 years later the Germans took control again until the end of the Second World War. As a result, both French and German are spoken in the region, as well as a local dialect impossible to understand! While now under French ownership, the region does sometimes look Germanic with its small cobbled streets and rows of half-timbered houses.

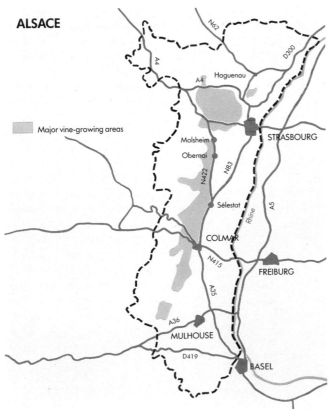

## ∽ THE GEOGRAPHY OF ALSACE ∽

Alsace is a narrow strip of land that lies between the Vosges mountains to the west and the river Rhine to the east, with most of the vineyards situated in the foothills of the Vosges. Roughly eighteen miles wide by eight miles long, the region ends in the south near the Swiss border. Records in the area show that winemaking dates back to Roman times.

Although Alsace is quite far north, the vineyards are protected by the Vosges mountains that modify the influences of the Atlantic Ocean and reduce the rainfull so that the region enjoys relatively warm, sunny summers. The Alsaciens were the first winegrowers in France to promote and differentiate between their wines by using the names of the grape varieties. In this respect they were ahead of the Californians and Australians who are often credited as being responsible for increasing our varietal awareness.

## ∽ THE WINEMAKERS ∽

There are over 9,000 growers in Alsace, the majority of whom grow other crops as well as wine, as the average size of a holding is little more than 2 acres. The best grapes are produced in the Haut-Rhin, in the south of the region, where most vineyards are planted on south and south-east facing vineyards and gain maximum sun exposure. Over

95 per cent of the production is white wine and, as mentioned earlier, since the First World War, the majority are made from single grape varieties. Many of the smaller growers sell their grapes to the *négociants* who make the wine and bottle it under their own label. Around 30 per cent of the production is handled by the various co-operatives in the region, although there is an increasing trend for smaller growers to market their wines under their own label.

## ∽ THE TYPES OF WINES ∽

Most Alsace wine is made to be drunk young – they tend to be dry, spicy whites. But there are a few wines that deserve a special mention.

### Grand Cru
A relatively recent phenomenon (since 1983) has been the emergence of *Grand Cru* status for certain vineyards, and ever-increasing numbers are being authorized. Like the Burgundy classification, *Grand Cru* status appertains to the vineyard, not the winemaker, so there is no guarantee that a *Grand Cru* will be better than an ordinary AC wine. In practice, however, most *Grands Crus* do deserve their status.

### Vendange Tardive
This means literally 'late-picked', and the wines allowed to put these words on the label must be made from the Riesling, Pinot Gris or Gewürztraminer grapes. *Vendange Tardive* wines are only made in exceptional years, as the grapes need to have high natural sugar levels to achieve the required potential alcohol levels of 12.9 degrees for

Riesling, and 14.3 degrees for Pinot Gris and Gewürztraminer. In order to achieve this, grapes are left on the vines long after the harvest has finished. *Vendange Tardive* wines can be either rich and sweet, or dry but with rich fruit, and they are always aromatic and powerful.

### Sélection de Grains Nobles
This is the best of them all, and the wines are equivalent to a top Sauternes or Beerenauslese. The wines are always lusciously sweet, and the grapes must have enough natural sugar for potential alcohol levels of 15.1 degrees for Riesling and 16.4 degrees for Pinot Gris and Gewürztraminer. These wines are very rare indeed, only being made in exceptional vintages like 1976 or 1983.

## ∽ THE GRAPE VARIETIES ∽

**Pinot Blanc (also known as Klevner and Clevner)** An underrated grape variety, dismissed by many as being boring, the Pinot Blanc can produce some deliciously soft and complex wines, especially with wood ageing. Without wood ageing its aroma is light, the sugar content fairly low and acidity high, all characteristics that make it ideal for sparkling wine production. Much of it vanishes into *Edelzwicker* (literally 'noble mixture'), the only blended wine of the region. Picked early and on the right sites it can have the refreshing characteristic spiciness of Alsace wines.
**Pinot Auxerrois** Confusion surrounds this grape, the fourth most widely planted variety of the region. According to Jancis Robinson in her book *Vines, Grapes and Wines* many growers believe that it is related to the Chardonnay or Sylvaner grapes. Pinot Auxerrois is grown mainly in the north of the region and it is principally used

*Setting up wires; the training system used for vines in Riquewihr, Alsace.*

*LEFT: Grapes arriving at Trimbach's cellars in Ribeauvillé in Alsace. RIGHT: Fertilizing vines near Kaysersberg. The vines here are protected by the Vosges mountains.*

blending in Edelzwicker or for the sparkling Crémant d'Alsace.

**Gewürztraminer** Gewürztraminer is the grape that encapsulates the essence of Alsace – spiciness and ripeness from the long warm summers. Gewürztraminer is not a grape that can be mimicked (the Muscat is its closest) and it is so distinctive that people either love it or hate it. Smelling Gewürztraminer is like sticking your nose into a bowl of tropical fruit salad with a magical aroma of lychees, mangoes and peaches. It is the richest and most full-bodied of the Alsace grape varieties and has a high natural sugar content, enabling it to make both dry and sweet wines, normally high in alcohol. Because of the natural sugar found in the grape, the dry varieties still appear to be off-dry. The spiciness of the grape makes it the ideal partner to ethnic spicy food, especially Thai and Chinese. Because of the sunshine, Alsace Gewürztraminers tend to be more full-bodied and luscious than the German examples.

**Riesling** Tasting a young Alsace Riesling in no way prepares one's palate for its later glories. Young Riesling can be acidic, unapproachable and gives no hint that it can be transformed into a luscious, rich, oily and complex wine in later years, helped along the road to maturity by its high acidity. A variety of styles of Riesling are produced in Alsace, many reflecting the varying soil structure of the region. Clay produces the richest, most oily wines, and limestone the more elegant and stylish.

**Sylvaner** This grape, together with the two preceding grape varieties, accounts for over 65 per cent of the production of the area. It is thought to have originated in Austria, although there is little evidence of it there today. If you are thirsty and don't want to drink the excellent Alsace beer, Sylvaner is the wine to drink as it is fresh, clean and zippy, often with a slight spritz.

Certain producers like Marc Kreydenweiss are now making oak-aged Sylvaner that is excellent, adding a lot more body and definition to the grape's flavour. While the Pinot Blanc is low in acidity, Sylvaner has high acidity and is popular with growers whose vineyards are situated on the flat fertile plains of the Bas-Rhin where it is a regular and higher cropper. Because its natural high acidity loses its edge in very hot vintages, Alsace Sylvaner can be a good bet in lesser years when it retains its acidic edge.

**Muscat** In Alsace the main variety of Muscat grown is the Muscat Ottonel, a different strain of Muscat than that used in the fashionable dessert wines of Beaumes de Venise. This other variety, Muscat Blanc à Petits Grains, is, however, also grown in Alsace and tends to produce the more

tion of the vineyards planted. With medium acid levels this is one of the few grapes that makes the fabulously rich, spicy *Vendange Tardive* wines so characteristic of Alsace. The Common Market was of the opinion that the vine's local name 'Tokay d'Alsace' should be abandoned in favour of Pinot Gris, despite the fact that the vine has been so called for a good 400 years. They have now rescinded their decision and will allow producers to use the term on the label only if it is accompanied by the name Pinot Gris.

**Chasselas** This grape variety is of decreasing importance in the Alsace region and today is rarely seen on the label. The majority of it finds its way into Edelzwicker, the blended white wine of the region. Generally it produces rather thin, bland wines without any distinctive aroma, and in other areas Chasselas grapes are mainly grown for eating.

**Crémant d'Alsace** This is the popular sparkling wine of the region, having had its own appellation since 1976, and is made by the *méthode champenoise* described in the section on Champagne (pages 84-9). It can be made from a variety of grapes (Chardonnay, Pinot Auxerrois, Pinot Blanc, Pinot Gris, Pinot Noir and Riesling), although the most common blend is Pinot Auxerrois and Pinot Blanc. The majority of Crémants d'Alsace are pleasant, if somewhat bland, often lacking the spiciness that has become the region's hallmark. The rosés made with Pinot Noir can be far more aromatic and interesting, sometimes difficult to distinguish from Champagne.

aromatic of the Muscat wines. Muscat Ottonel is slightly less perfumed and more earthy, although it still has the characteristic grapey, peachy smell of Muscat. Alsace dry Muscats are delicious and until relatively recently were the only examples of their kind, although now both the Australians and the Portuguese (namely Peter Bright at João Pires) are emulating them, using early picking and cold fermentation.

Alsace Muscats can also be sweet and luscious, especially if late picked (*Vendange Tardive*).

**Pinot Noir** Alsace's main red variety, Pinot Noir, takes on different characteristics to those it flaunts in Burgundy. Used to make both red and rosé wines (often a producer's red wine looks like browny, rust-coloured rosé) the wines are relatively light. However, examples from the top producers have shown that these wines can become darker with age and transform themselves into very seductive wines. Alsace rosé is deliciously fresh, with all the red fruit aromas of Pinot Noir but without the creaminess found in oak-aged Burgundies. The more recent style of deeper coloured reds are now aged in oak and are beginning to show more depth and structure.

**Pinot Gris (Tokay d'Alsace)** After Riesling and Gewürztraminer, Pinot Gris is rated to be the next finest variety grown in Alsace although it represents only a tiny propor-

---

**RECOMMENDED PRODUCERS**

| | |
|---|---|
| Adam | Marc Kreydenweiss |
| Lucien Albrecht | Kuehn |
| Becker | Lorentz |
| Leon Beyer | Jos Meyer |
| Blanck | Mittnacht |
| Bott Frères | Muré |
| Joseph Cattin | Preiss-Henn |
| Theo Cattin | Preiss-Zimmer |
| Deiss | Rentz |
| Dopff & Irion | Reinhart |
| Dopff au Moulin | Schaller |
| Engel | Schleret |
| Faller | Schlumberger |
| Gaschy | Schmidt |
| Rolly Gassman | Sick Dreyer |
| Louis Gisselbrecht | Siffert |
| Willy Gisselbrecht | Louis Sipp |
| Hartmann | Pierre Sparr |
| Louis Hauller | Stempfel |
| Heim | Trimbach |
| Hugel | Weinbach |
| Kientzler | Zind-Humbrecht |

---

**VINTAGE CHART**

Most of Alsace's wines are made to be drunk young, and so vintages aren't that important. Make sure you don't buy wines that are more than five or six years old, unless they are from a top producer and a top vintage. The two best Alsace vintages in recent years are 1983 and 1976, and *Vendange Tardive* or *Sélection de Grains Nobles* wines from either are well worth buying.

# THE RHONE VALLEY

*I*n the past Rhône's wines, particularly those from the Northern Rhône, have been overlooked. But today those in the know realize that wines like Hermitage and Côte Rôtie from top producers like Chave, Guigal and Paul Jaboulet Aîné are every bit as good quality as First Growth Clarets and top Burgundies.

Few areas can boast the diversity of wines produced in the Rhône Valley that stretches 140 miles from Vienne in the north down to Avignon in the south. Here, one black grape variety in particular, rarely found elsewhere in France, comes into its own: the Syrah. The other most frequently found grape is the Grenache, ubiquitous in the southern areas of France.

## ∽ THE GRAPES OF THE RHONE ∾
### (North and South)

**Syrah**    The Syrah grape is one of the most powerful grape varieties around, with its own distinctive style. Thought to have Middle Eastern origins, it is not widely grown in France and accounts for less than 2 per cent of all vines planted. It produces very tannic, full-bodied wines with earthy, tarry overtones. Top vintages often take years to mature and an aficionado of the best Rhône wines has to be very patient.

**Viognier**    This is the top white grape of the Rhône and produces the rare wines of Condrieu and Château Grillet. It is not found outside the Rhône Valley and produces full-bodied whites, musky and aromatic, which can be both sweet or dry.

**Grenache**    The mainstay grape of the southern Rhône, the Grenache is rarely seen on its own but is used in blending. Capable of producing a wide variety of wines from open fruity reds to full-flavoured rosés, the Grenache is a popular grape variety in southern France because it has the quality of being able to produce acceptable wine in hot temperatures.

## ∽ THE PRINCIPAL APPELLATIONS ∾
### OF THE NORTHERN RHONE

**Château Grillet and Condrieu**    Château Grillet is one of the smallest single estate appellations in France and, like Condrieu, makes a rather special white wine from the Viognier grape. Both are planted on very steep vineyards and the production is tiny, hence the high price. Both can start life as dry, but then develop a rich, honeysuckle and peach aroma.

**Clairette de Die** Both still and sparkling wines are made in this appellation. The still wines are made from 100 per cent Clairette and are dull – high in alcohol and low in acidity without any noticeable flavour. The sparkling wine known as Clairette de Die Tradition is a variation on *méthode champenoise* made from 50 per cent Muscat à Petits Grains, blended with the Clairette grape.

**Cornas** The steep vineyards of Cornas are believed to be among the oldest in France. The wines are made from 100 per cent Syrah and are intensely deep in colour and concentrated. The wines are very tough, tannic and tarry in their youth and often need around ten years to soften to maturity.

**Côte Rôtie** The 'roasted slopes' of Côte Rôtie are among the most impressive vineyards in the world. Visible from the town of Ampuis, it seems incredible that anyone could have dreamt of planting vines there as the slopes are so steep. They are cultivated by hand – a tractor would tip over immediately. Côte Rôtie is complex with its mixture of rich, ripe *cassis*, plummy earthy aromas and flavours, and can last for decades. It is made from Syrah and, although producers are allowed to add up to 20 per cent of

*The steep slopes of Côte Rôtie, one of the top appellations of the Northern Rhône.*

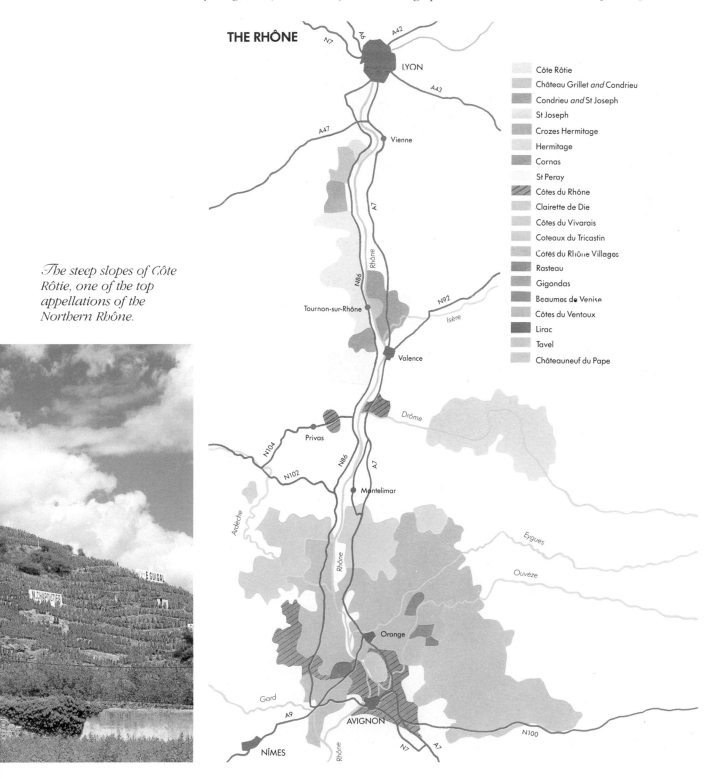

**THE RHÔNE**

- Côte Rôtie
- Château Grillet *and* Condrieu
- Condrieu *and* St Joseph
- St Joseph
- Crozes Hermitage
- Hermitage
- Cornas
- St Peray
- Côtes du Rhône
- Clairette de Die
- Côtes du Vivarais
- Coteaux du Tricastin
- Côtes du Rhône Villages
- Rasteau
- Gigondas
- Beaumes de Venise
- Côtes du Ventoux
- Lirac
- Tavel
- Châteauneuf du Pape

the white grape Viognier, few use more than five to ten per cent.

There are two slopes, the Côte Blonde and the Côte Brune, said to be named after two sisters. The wines of the Côte Brune are generally the heavier, with more obvious aroma and tannin than the Côte Blonde, whose wines are more delicate and elegant (within the context of Côte Rôtie). On the hillside are named *lieux dits*, the most famous of which are Guigal's La Mouline in the Côte Blonde and La Landonne in the Côte Brune.

**Crozes-Hermitage** The appellation of Crozes-Hermitage is on the east side of the river Rhône, surrounding the more famous appellation of Hermitage (see below), and can be superb value. The climate and grapes are the same for both appellations: Syrah for the reds and Marsanne and Roussanne for the whites. Generally Crozes- is less full-bodied than Hermitage although a top Crozes- (like Jaboulet's Domaine de Thalabert) can beat lesser Hermitages in blind tastings. The whites should be drunk when first in bottle and do not benefit from long ageing.

**Hermitage** The best known of the Northern Rhône appellations, and the wine with the highest profile. The south-facing granite hill of Hermitage is a sight that has to be seen to be believed – incredibly steep terraced vineyards, definitely not suitable for pickers with vertigo!

Hermitage is made from the Syrah grape, to which a small percentage of Marsanne and Roussanne grapes can be added. Few growers take up this option, however, preferring to use their white grapes for their white Hermitage.

The best-known Hermitage comes from the steepest part of the slopes and is known as La Chapelle, after the chapel that can be found on the top of the hill.

Because of the weight and tannin produced by the Syrah grape few growers use new oak barrels, preferring the gentler, softer effect of older oak to make this full, smokey, tarry, meaty red which normally needs to be kept for many years before it is drinkable.

**St Joseph** The wines from the appellation of St Joseph represent some of the best value-for-money wines in the Rhône Valley and have the added attraction that they can

be drunk relatively early.

The appellation covers a large area on the west bank of the river with the best vineyards near Mauves and Tournon. St Joseph wines are generous with lashings of blackberry and plummy fruit, with body but without excessive tannin.

**St-Péray** This region, the most southerly appellation of the Northern Rhône, makes both still and sparkling white wines from the Marsanne and Roussanne grapes, neither of which are very highly rated.

| THE APPELLATIONS OF THE NORTHERN RHONE | |
|---|---|
| Château Grillet | Côtes-du-Rhône |
| Châtillon-en-Diois | Côte Rôtie |
| Clairette de Die | Crozes-Hermitage |
| Clairette de Die Mousseux | Hermitage |
| Clairette de Die Tradition | St-Joseph |
| Condrieu | St-Péray |
| Cornas | St-Péray Mousseux |

| RECOMMENDED PRODUCERS | |
|---|---|
| Gilles Barge | Guigal |
| Guy de Barjac | Paul Jaboulet Aîné |
| Roger Burgaud | Robert Jasmin |
| Chapoutier | R Michel |
| Bernard Chave | M Multier |
| Jean-Louis Chave | R Ogier |
| Clape | J Pinchon |
| P Dazamat | H Sorrel |
| J Fayolle | Georges Vernay |
| Château Grillet | A Voge |

| VINTAGE CHART – NORTHERN RHONE | |
|---|---|
| 1988 Potentially exceptional | 1983 Outstanding |
| 1987 Soft, early maturing wines | 1982 Very good |
| | 1981 Average |
| 1986 Good, but not great | 1980 Some very good wines |
| 1985 Outstanding | 1979 Very good |
| 1985 Average | 1978 Outstanding |

*The ruined château of Châteauneuf-du-Pape. Vines flourish among the large stones, which reflect the intense sunlight and radiate heat during the night.*

## ∾ THE PRINCIPAL APPELLATIONS OF ∾ THE SOUTHERN RHONE

The Southern Rhône's terrain is flat, with only the occasional hilltop village, in total contrast to the Northern Rhône. The region is much hotter, more akin to the fashionable sunny south of France. The Mediterranean influence can be seen in the hot scorched vegetation and the abundance of wild herbs.

While the Northern Rhône is famous for its breathtakingly steep, vineyard-covered slopes, the Southern Rhône is famous for the large stones that make up many of the vineyards, particularly in Châteauneuf-du-Pape. Although it looks as if nothing could flourish among the mini-boulders, some as large as melons, the vines love it and the stones reflect the intense heat of the sunlight as well as providing excellent drainage for the vines.

The Southern Rhône is the blender's dream, where many different grape varieties are grown and no one variety dominates. Varieties include Syrah (nothing like as important or impressive as it is in the north), Grenache, Cinsault, Mourvèdre, and the less commonly seen Counoise, Muscardin, Terret and Vaccarèse for red wines. White grapes include Marsanne, Roussanne, Viognier, Grenache Blanc, Clairette, Picardin, Picpoul and Bourboulenc

**Châteauneuf-du-Pape** This is the best known of the Southern Rhône wines and can vary greatly in style because of the 13 different grape varieties permitted within the blend. Situated close to the city of Avignon, the appellation takes its name from the 'new château' that Pope John XXII built in the 14th century, planting a vineyard around it.

The styles of wines produced varies dramatically from rich, slightly sweet, full-bodied reds to light, thin, innocuous, concocted blends. The best are rich, redolent of liquorice, delicious with full-flavoured casseroles and gamey or spicy food. The white wines produced tend to be rather heavy and can lack acidity, although experiments with ageing the wines in new oak barrels seems to be producing interesting results.

**Côtes-du-Rhône** Côtes-du-Rhône wines account for as much as 80 per cent of the Rhône Valley's production and, although the wines can come from all over the Rhône, the vast majority come from the Southern Rhône. Many grapes are permitted and the best wines are made from a blend of Grenache, Syrah, Cinsault and Mourvèdre. The reds in the appellation can range from thin oxidized reds to full-bodied, jammy, easy-drinking pleasant reds. The whites and the rosés that are made from the same permitted grape varieties are less tired and oxidized than they used to be and seem to be getting better each vintage. On the whole Côtes-du-Rhône wines are designed for early drinking.

**Coteaux du Tricastin** The reds produced in this appellation are again blended wines made from the Grenache, Cinsault, Mourvèdre, Syrah, Picpoul and the Carignan. The reds are round and soft, peppery, crisp and refreshing without the weightiness of a top Châteauneuf-du-Pape. They can be drunk chilled, as they are in the region on hot sunny days. The small amount of white that is made is nothing like as good as the red.

**Côtes du Luberon** Some exciting wines are made in this area that has just been upgraded to *Appellation Controlée* status. There are good reds and rosés and some of the more progressive producers are starting to add Chardonnay to the whites. One of the best producers is Val-Joanis.

**Côtes-du-Rhône-Villages** There are 17 specific communes whose wines can add their own name to Côtes-du-Rhône-Villages. The wines have much more concentration than straight Côtes-du-Rhône, and have to achieve higher alcohol levels and lower yields. White wines are also made.

**Côtes du Ventoux** Mainly red wines, not dissimilar to Côtes-du-Rhône. Good value easy-drinking wines with lots of southern fruit.

**Côtes du Vivarais** Good basic fruity reds and sound rosés.

**Gigondas** The red wines from this appellation have a concentrated, spicy, plummy flavour and more depth of flavour than many others in the Southern Rhône.

**Lirac** One of the best rosés produced in the Rhône, dry and relatively full-bodied. A very good red wine is also made.

**Muscat de Beaumes-de-Venise** This appellation makes a sweet, luscious fortified wine from the Muscat grape – (see section on fortified wine, pages 178-187) as well as red Côtes-du-Rhône.

**Rasteau** Like Beaumes-de-Venise, this is a sweet fortified wine. The red wine is fairly basic and alcoholic.

**Tavel** Like Lirac, makes a very good dry rosé.

---

### THE APPELLATIONS OF THE SOUTHERN RHONE

| | |
|---|---|
| Châteauneuf-du-Pape | Gigondas |
| Coteaux du Tricastin | Lirac |
| Côtes du Lubéron | Muscat de Beaumes-de- |
| Côtes-du-Rhône | Venise |
| Côtes-du-Rhône-Villages | Rasteau |
| Côtes du Ventoux | Tavel |

---

### CHATEAUNEUF-DU-PAPE – RECOMMENDED PRODUCERS

| | |
|---|---|
| Beaucastel | Guigal |
| Berard | Paul Jaboulet Aîné |
| Chante Cigale | Château Rayas |
| Clos de l'Oratoire | Mont Redon |
| Clos des Papes | Roger Sabon |
| Fines Roches | La Solitude |
| Château Fortia | Vieux Télégraphe |
| Font de Michelle | |

---

### VINTAGE CHART – SOUTHERN RHONE

| | | | |
|---|---|---|---|
| 1988 | Potentially exceptional | 1983 | Outstanding |
| 1987 | Soft, early maturing wines | 1982 | Very good |
| | | 1981 | Poor |
| 1986 | Good, but not great | 1980 | Some very good wines |
| 1985 | Outstanding | 1979 | Very good |
| 1984 | Average | 1978 | Outstanding |

# PROVENCE

*I* find it impossible to write about Provence without instantly wanting to pack up the word processor and ■ catch the plane to Nice.

For me, Provence is sun and sand, fabulous hilltop villages like Les Baux and Aix-en-Provence, that intoxicating smell of wild herbs, thyme, fresh basil and rosemary, and of course the locally caught seafood washed down with delicious wines.

In the past, the food and scenery of Provence were far more appealing than its wines, which tended to suffer from an excess of sunshine, resulting in a stewed flavour and low acidity. But now, in common with many other areas in France, winemaking techniques have improved dramatically.

Many of the best producers now pick their grapes early to ensure good acidity levels, and cold fermentation has largely seen off the flabby oxidized whites and rosés of the past. Some of the co-operatives like Les Maîtres Vignerons de Saint Tropez make excellent dry rosés with lots of earthy Grenache-flavoured fruit.

The biggest problem with Provence's wines nowadays is that so much is sold locally to tourists that producers have no need to export their wines and price them very high for export. As a result, Provence wines are rarely good value when bought outside the region itself.

## ❧ STYLES OF WINE ❧

The best wines from Provence and its surrounding regions are red, although there are many pleasant rosés. There are many exciting red wines coming out of the south of France whose names might be unfamiliar but are well worth searching out.

The large appellation of Coteaux d'Aix-en-Provence produces full-bodied spicy reds, the ideal complement to full-flavoured spicy food. Wines from the village of Les Baux can add the village name to the appellation. Les Baux produces both dry whites and rosés as well as some excellent red wines. These are made predominantly from a variety of full-bodied black grape varieties like Grenache, Carignan, Cinsault, Mourvèdre and Cabernet Sauvignon. Look out especially for the organically made wines from Terres Blanches and the full-bodied, enormous reds from Domaine de Trévallon, made from Cabernet and Syrah, and grown in steep, rocky vineyards.

There are several good producers in Coteaux d'Aix-en-Provence. The wines from George Brunet's Château Vignelaure are among the best, although this is hardly surprising as he used to own the great Médoc property, Château La Lagune. Many tasters believe his wine, which contains a high proportion of Cabernet Sauvignon, has more of a

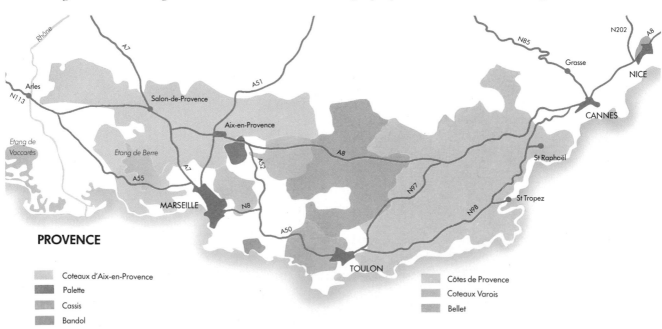

**PROVENCE**

- Coteaux d'Aix-en-Provence
- Palette
- Cassis
- Bandol
- Côtes de Provence
- Coteaux Varois
- Bellet

claret than a Provence flavour.

There is a host of wines which bear the Côtes de Provence appellation, reds, whites and rosés. Like the VDQS wines from Coteaux Varois they vary greatly in quality. Some of the best rosés for everyday drinking come from the co-operative Les Maîtres Vignerons de la Presqu'île de St Tropez. If you prefer a rosé with more depth and subtlety try Domaine Ott's rosé, Château de Selle. The reds, however, rarely disappoint whichever style you're looking for. If you fancy a soft, smooth plummy red for quaffing with your meal there are plenty to choose from – and if you're visiting the region be prepared to experiment with wines from different producers. More full-bodied red wines like Commanderie de Peyrassol are not made for immediate drinking and need laying down for a few years.

If you are after some of the more unusual wines from the south try the reds, whites or rosés from the tiny appellation of Bellet, to the north of Nice. Or go further south and try the full-bodied rich curranty reds from Cassis, whose breathtaking vineyards slope down to the sea, close to Marseille. Closer to Toulon are the wines of Bandol, where the red wines can last for years and are a good and moderately priced investment for future drinking.

Alternatively, make a note to look out for the wines of Palette, an appellation found about three miles from Aix. There, over 75 per cent of the vineyard's appellation is owned by a single property, Château Simon. Both the rich heavy reds that need keeping a few years and the crisp dry whites are excellent with plenty of character. There is much investment in the south of France as growers realize the importance of grape varieties. While the purists argue that this will lead to the region's wine losing their identity, it is focusing the grower's mind's on the importance of specific grape varieties (both local and otherwise). This can only lead to even better wines in the future.

---

### THE APPELLATIONS OF PROVENCE

All the following appellations make red, white and rosé unless otherwise indicated. Provence also produces some excellent *vin de pays* – see *French Country Wines*, page 110.

| | |
|---|---|
| Bandol | Coteaux d'Aix-en-Provence |
| Bellet | Coteaux Varois (VDQS) |
| Cassis | (no white) |
| Coteaux d'Aix-en-Provence-les-Baux | Côtes de Provence |
| | Palette |

---

### VINTAGES – PROVENCE

Vintages are relatively unimportant in hot wine-growing areas, and as a rule buy the youngest available white or rosé, and a red that is two to five years old.

The hilltop town of Les Baux in the heart of Provence.

# OTHER FRENCH WINES

*U*nder this admittedly rather general heading, which covers hundreds of different wines, I have included *vins de pays* (Country Wines), VDQS (*Vins Délimités de Qualité Supérieur*) and *Appellation Controlée*. The common factor is that they are all wines for everyday drinking that do not fall into the classic categories. Many are very good value, many are ordinary, but a good wine retailer will choose the best from this vast mixture of styles. For the sake of clarity I have broken down this chapter into just three areas: the Loire, Jura and Savoie, and the massive south of France. But first, what are 'French Country Wines'?

### ❧ FRENCH COUNTRY WINES ❧

*Vins de pays* covers a huge volume of wine. The estimated annual production is 640 million bottles and, in line with French drinking habits, around 70 per cent is red, 20 per cent white and 10 per cent rosé. *Vins de pays* wines are subjected to much stricter quality controls than *vins de table*, covering grape varieties, region of origin and yield. In addition they have to pass a test to qualify. More than 10 per cent fail this test, a factor that encourages growers to keep standards high. The concept of *vins de pays* was officially introduced in 1973, and expanded on in 1979. By 1976 there were 55 in total, a figure that has risen to 132 today.

Co-operatives account for over 60 per cent of the entire production, who by and large produce sound wines. It is, however, the smaller growers and estates (some making only a few hundred cases a year) who are producing the very best wines.

While these wines can come from over 38 different *départements*, over 75 per cent come from just four in the south of France: Aude, Gard, Hérault and Pyrénées-Orientales. While traditionally local grape varieties were used in the south, increasingly the classic noble varieties like Cabernet Sauvignon, Merlot, Sauvignon and Chardonnay are creeping into areas and on to labels.

### ❧ THE LOIRE – VIN DE PAYS ❧

The Loire Valley produces huge amounts of *vin de pays*, sold under the name of Vin de Pays du Jardin de la France. The best wines are the Sauvignon- and Chardonnay-based whites, both popular grape varieties, and they can be excellent value for money.

*Vineyards in Roussillon in the south of France where the best red wines offer exceptional value for money.*

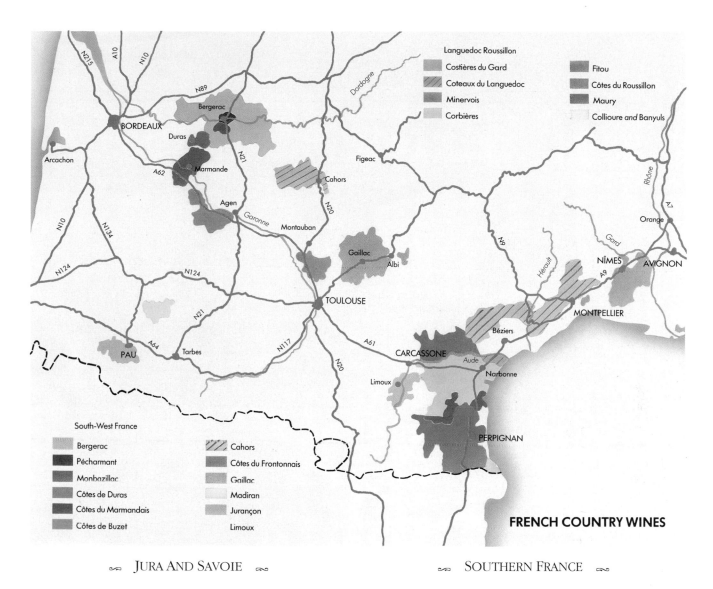

Languedoc Roussillon
- Costières du Gard
- Coteaux du Languedoc
- Minervois
- Corbières
- Fitou
- Côtes du Roussillon
- Maury
- Collioure *and* Banyuls

South-West France
- Bergerac
- Pécharmant
- Monbazillac
- Côtes de Duras
- Côtes du Marmandais
- Côtes de Buzet
- Cahors
- Côtes du Frontonnais
- Gaillac
- Madiran
- Jurançon
- Limoux

**FRENCH COUNTRY WINES**

## ❧ JURA AND SAVOIE ❧

Jura's best known wine, although produced in tiny quantities only, is a strange sherry-like wine called *vin jaune*, from AC Château-Chalon and others, but most of the dry white wines produced in this region are heavy and uninteresting. Savoie produces a good basic sparkling wine made in Seyssel and some of the red made in this area, from the full-bodied Mondeuse grape, can be quite fortifying after a good day's ski-ing – although it rarely tastes as good back home.

## ❧ SOUTHERN FRANCE ❧

This includes hundreds of *vins de pays*, covering the *départements* of Vaucluse, Var, Drôme, Bouches-du-Rhône, Hérault, Aude, Pyrénées-Orientales, Ardèche, Gard, Tarn, Pyrénées-Atlantiques, Haute-Garonne and Tarn-et-Garonne. Many of them can be great value, and generally speaking the full-bodied, flavourful reds are much better than the whites.

There are also some very good *Appellation Contrôlée* wines from South-West France and Languedoc-Roussillon.

### THE BEST APPELLATIONS OF SOUTH-WEST FRANCE

| | |
|---|---|
| Bergerac | Red, rosé and white (sec) |
| Blanquette de Limoux | Sparkling white |
| Buzet | Very good red, + white and rosé |
| Cahors | Full reds |
| Côtes de Duras | Very good red, white and rosé |
| Côtes du Frontonnais | Red and rosé |
| Côtes du Marmandais (VDQS) | Good red and white |
| Gaillac | Red, white, and rosé |
| Jurançon | Dry to sweet, good value |
| Madiran | Dense, meaty red |
| Monbazillac | Great value sweet white |
| Pécharmant | Good red |

### THE APPELLATIONS OF LANGUEDOC-ROUSSILLON

| | |
|---|---|
| Banyuls | France's equivalent to Port! |
| Collioure | Similar to Banyuls |
| Corbières | Good red, + white |
| Costières du Gard (VDQS) | Good red, white and rosé |
| Coteaux du Languedoc | Varying red, white and rosé |
| Côtes du Roussillon | Good red, + white and rosé |
| Faugères | Good red, + rosé |
| Fitou | Very good red |
| Maury | Red, white and rosé |
| Minervois | Good red, + white and rosé |
| Muscat de Frontignan | Very sweet white |
| Muscat de Rivesaltes | Very sweet white |
| St-Chinian | Good red, + rosé |

# GERMANY

ENTION GERMAN WINE and most people think of Liebfraumilch, the bulk-selling medium sweet white which has such popular appeal. It is one of the few German names that English speakers can pronounce, and is medium sweet, a taste that offends few new drinkers. Both these factors have made Liebfraumilch Germany's top-selling export wine. Current figures suggest that it accounts for nearly 50 per cent of German wine exports, although many Germans have never even heard of it. Quality German wine growers despair, and it is ironic that the wine that helped make fortunes for many of their competitors (albeit mainly *négociant*-type companies) made it an uphill battle to persuade wine-lovers to take German wine seriously and discover the delights that lie beyond Liebfraumilch.

Germany manages to grow vines in one of Europe's most northerly sites where, in particularly cold years, it is difficult for the grapes to ripen and achieve the important natural sugar content which balances the grapes' natural high acidity. Whereas the mass-market wines are produced and blended in bulk, the better wines are made in much smaller quantities from single grape varieties, with growers restricting yields to ensure a much higher quality.

The key to making successful German wine is to grow the right variety of grape on the right soil, one which is able to ripen and produce the required balance of fruit, extract, sugar and acidity.

Germany's vineyards, the most northerly in Europe, are to be found either side of the great river Rhine and its tributaries, stretching from the capital, Bonn, in the north down to Basel on the Swiss border in the south. One of the benefits of siting the vineyards near the rivers is that the sun's reflection off the water means the vineyards remain warm right through to the evening. In such a northerly climate any added heat is a great advantage.

*Most of the best vineyard sites in Germany are situated on the banks of the river Rhine, which reflects the sunlight and keeps the vineyards warm during the colder evenings.*

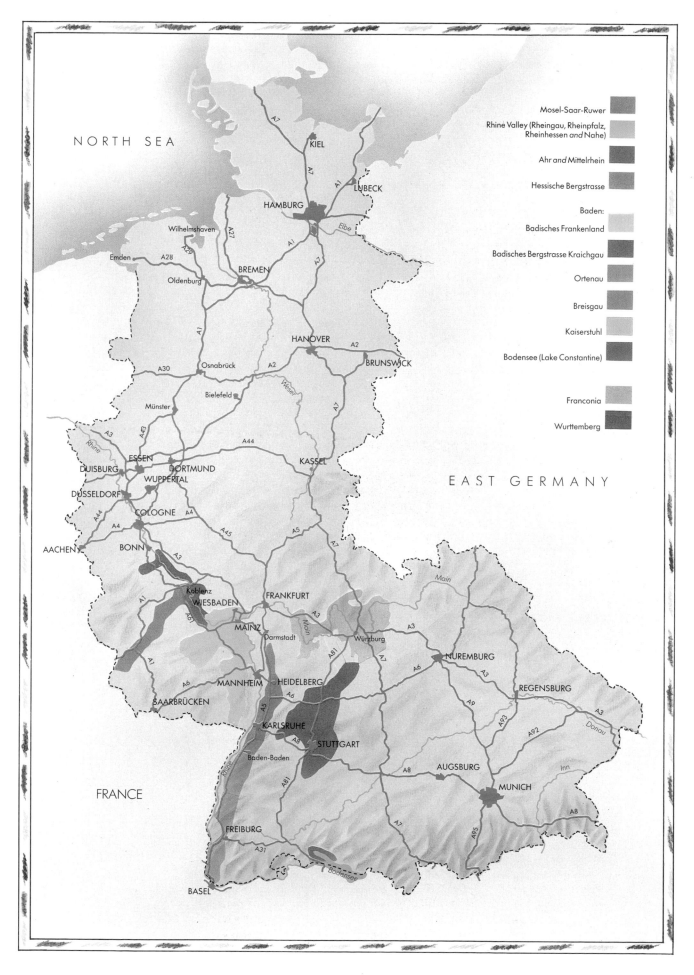

NORTH SEA

KIEL

LÜBECK

HAMBURG

Wilhelmshaven

Elbe

Emden

A28

A29

A27

BREMEN

A1

Oldenburg

A1

HANOVER

A2

Osnabrück

A30

A2

BRUNSWICK

Weser

Bielefeld

Münster

A7

A3

A43

A44

KASSEL

Rhine

ESSEN

DORTMUND

DUISBURG

WUPPERTAL

DÜSSELDORF

COLOGNE

A4

A4

A44

A45

A5

AACHEN

BONN

A3

A7

Koblenz

WIESBADEN

FRANKFURT

Main

Main

MAINZ

A3

A1

A61

Darmstadt

Würzburg

A3

EAST GERMANY

Main

A7

NUREMBURG

A6

A81

A1

MANNHEIM

HEIDELBERG

A6

A6

REGENSBURG

SAARBRÜCKEN

A5

KARLSRUHE

A9

A93

A3

Donau

A8

STUTTGART

A92

Baden-Baden

A81

AUGSBURG

Inn

A8

MUNICH

FRANCE

A7

A95

A8

FREIBURG

A31

Rhine

Bodensee

BASEL

Mosel-Saar-Ruwer

Rhine Valley (Rheingau, Rheinpfalz,
Rheinhessen and Nahe)

Ahr and Mittelrhein

Hessische Bergstrasse

Baden:

Badisches Frankenland

Badisches Bergstrasse Kraichgau

Ortenau

Breisgau

Kaiserstuhl

Bodensee (Lake Constantine)

Franconia

Wurttemberg

## ∾ QUALITY STRUCTURE ∾

Unlike France, whose vineyards are classified by region, German wines are classified according to the amount of sugar present when the grapes are picked. In ascending quality order they are:

**Deutscher Tafelwein**  German table wines from the biggest wine regions in Germany. Do not mix this up with EEC Tafelwein, a blended wine that can come from anywhere in the EEC.

**Landwein**  is a relatively new quality level, similar to French *vin de pays*. These wines can only be dry or medium, not sweet.

**Qualitätswein bestimmter Anbaugebiete (QbA)**  are wines from one of the 11 specified wine regions, and each region has a limited number of permitted grape varieties. All wines carry an AP number, which shows that they have undergone analytical and tasting tests.

**Qualitätswein mit Prädikat (QmP)**  This is above QbA level and producers are not allowed to add sugar (as opposed to Süssreserve) to the grape must to increase the alcohol level. On all quality levels below this producers are allowed to add sugar to the must. In order for a wine to be classified as QmP, the grapes must have a higher natural sugar level than those which make QbA wines. All QmP wines, with the exception of Beerenauslese, Trockenbeerenauslese and Eiswein, can be dry through to sweet, depending on the style the wine maker wants to achieve.

QmP wines are split into six categories, as follows:

*Kabinett*  These are the lightest QmP wines.

*Spätlese*  Literally translated, this means 'late picked'. The grapes are picked at least one week after the normal harvest starts and because they are riper the resulting wines are higher in sugar and therefore potential alcohol.

*Auslese*  Literally translated, this means 'selected' and refers to grapes that are riper than Spätlese and are sometimes affected by noble rot.

*Beerenauslese*  Wines made totally from botrytized or noble rot (*Botrytis cinerea*) infected grapes – as in Sauternes. Always very sweet.

*Trockenbeerenauslese* (known as 'TBA')  Wines made from botrytized grapes that have totally shrivelled up and look rather like raisins. Always ultra-sweet.

*Eiswein*  This is extremely rare and is made from frozen grapes, left on the vines sometimes until February, which must be harvested and pressed below −7°C (19°F). The water naturally present in the grapes is frozen and the ice crystals remain in the presses, resulting in an extremely high concentration of natural sugar.

But just to make life more complicated, there are two descriptive categories, Trocken and Halbtrocken (meaning dry and semi-dry), which can be added to the name of any wine up to and including the Spätlese quality level. This can be rather confusing, but now a large amount of Germany's wine is dry – about 45 per cent of all Franken wines and 24 per cent of those from Baden-Württemberg for example.

As mentioned above, the quality classification of a German wine has no relation to the area in which it was produced. However, Germany is split up into 11 wine producing areas (Anbaugebieten), whose borders are strictly determined according to the differing micro-climates and historic development. These areas are then further broken down into the smaller areas known as Bereich, Grosslage and Einzellage, all of which define areas of differing size.

*Anbaugebiet*  A main wine producing region, of which there are 11. They are, going from north to south: Ahr, Mittelrhein, Rheingau, Mosel-Saar-Ruwer, Nahe, Franken,

*LEFT: Many of Germany's vineyards are so steep that, during the harvest, pickers sometimes need the aid of climbing ropes.*
*RIGHT: Kaiserstuhl vineyards in Baden, an area now producing some exciting varietal wines.*

Rheinhessen, Hessische Bergstrasse, Rheinpfalz, Württemburg and Baden.

*Bereich* A large area of vineyards within an Anbaugebiet with similar growing conditions. Can be thousands of hectares big. For example the Anbaugebiet of Rheinpfalz, which covers 22,000 hectares (54,362 acres) of vines, contains only two Bereichs.

*Grosslage* A group of Einzellagen (or vineyard sites) situated around one or more wine growing villages, generally less than 10 hectares in size. The name of a Grosslage must always be preceded by the name of the village when it appears on the label. For example, the Bereich of Bernkastel contains the Grosslage of Badstube, which itself contains six Einzellagen. A wine from the general Grosslage would be called Bernkasteler Badstube (the -er suffix meaning from Bernkastel).

*Einzellage* A single vineyard site, all of which are officially listed.

### ∾ THE TWO MAIN GRAPE VARIETIES ∾

#### *Riesling*

In Germany the Riesling grape reigns supreme, and it can make anything from stylish crisp, steely dry wines to luscious sweet wines. Sadly, many people who drink German wine most of the time are not drinking Riesling – it's more likely they'll be drinking other boring grape varieties like Müller-Thurgau. Riesling, perhaps more so than any other white variety, takes on different characteristics depending on the type of soil in which it is grown.

Riesling is a late ripener, and therefore eminently suitable for Germany – the slow ripening aided by the cool climate brings out the best characteristics of the Riesling grape, whose personality relies heavily on a good balance of sugar and acidity. Riesling is also well suited to the region because it has the ability to withstand very cold winter temperatures down to −20°C (−44°F). It can produce wines with a very high *Oechsle* level (high natural sugar levels) and, at the same time, good acidity levels. Such wines are capable of ageing for years, and so they tend to be a good invesment.

#### *Müller-Thurgau*

Müller-Thurgau is a crossing, created in 1882, an attempt to produce a grape with the Silvaner's early ripening ability, combined with the flavour of the Riesling. It is Germany's most widely planted grape variety and is highly popular with producers because of its high yields. Many areas that were originally arable farm land are now planted with Müller-Thurgau, often on sites where other varieties like Riesling would not survive. This is particularly true in the Mosel. Müller-Thurgau is the workhorse of the German grape varieties and is suitable for blended wines because it is bland and inoffensive. However, grown on the right sites and well made, it can occasionally produce flowery wines with character. Unfortunately its potential quality has been sacrificed by many producers in favour of quantity.

**SUSSRESERVE** This is unfermented grape juice that is permitted to be added to wines of all qualities. Its purpose is to round off the unharmonious acidity of a wine – it's a tool for the winemaker to improve the quality. It is often misunderstood – people tend to assume that it is used to increase the actual alcohol level of a wine, but in fact it dilutes it, although it does add sweetness. Its use largely stems back to after the Second World War when people had no sugar and wanted something sweet.

### ∾ STYLES OF WINES PRODUCED ∾

Over 85 per cent of German wine production is white, although red wine production is gradually increasing (as is the quality of the wines produced). The styles of wine vary greatly from north to south, from the fresh light, fruity Riesling wines to the more full bodied French-style wines from Baden, and from raspingly dry to lusciously sweet.

The biggest change in Germany's wine style in recent years has been the introduction of oak-barrel-ageing by a small number of producers. Some of these wines, often produced from grape varieties not officially permitted, are fabulous and it will be worth waiting to see what the future will bring.

| VINTAGE CHART | |
|---|---|
| Because most German wine does not age well (with the exception of some Beerenauslesen and TBAs) this vintage chart only goes back to 1982. | |
| 1988 Excellent | 1984 Poor |
| 1987 Poor | 1983 Exceptional |
| 1986 Very good | 1982 Average |
| 1985 Outstanding | |

Other older particularly successful vintages worth seeking out provided the wines are at the top of the quality ladder, are 1971, 1975 and 1976.

# MOSEL-SAAR-RUWER

The Mosel river runs from Luxembourg down to Koblenz. This was the region that made German wine world-famous, and the tall, slim, flute-shaped green bottle became synonymous with quality German wine. The region boasts many pretty little villages dominated by slopes so steep that it is impossible to imagine how harvesters manage to pick the grapes, and harvesting machines are totally out of the question. In many vineyards pickers are issued with climbing ropes and no one who suffered from vertigo would last five minutes in this region. Their job is made even more difficult by the slippery slate soil. But it is exactly this soil which gives the Mosel's wines their typical steely acidity; it also retains heat, an important factor in such a northerly climate.

Along the meandering course of the Mosel it is the south-facing steep slopes that produce the best wine because the grapes ripen better. These vineyards also benefit from additional heat reflected from the river.

Over the last few years the area has suffered from a low-quality image. This is mainly due to the number of vineyards that were planted with Müller-Thurgau on the flat land in the valley floors. Mass production of grapes that have not been properly ripened has given the Mosel a bad name, and this includes once famous names like Piesporter-Michelsberg.

The Mosel is mainly a Riesling area, but the old variety of Elbling is now experiencing a renaissance in the upper regions near Luxembourg. And because of its lively acidity, Elbling is also used to make base wines for the German sparkling wine Sekt, produced widely throughout the region. The wines made from pure Riesling are light and elegant with a zippy level of acidity and the best will age well. Unhappily, large quantities of Müller-Thurgau are now planted in the poor-quality flat areas and account for the bulk of the mass produced wines in the Mosel.

Quite apart from the poor image created by high-production Müller-Thurgau, the Mosel has suffered from the recent wine scandals which have affected all German

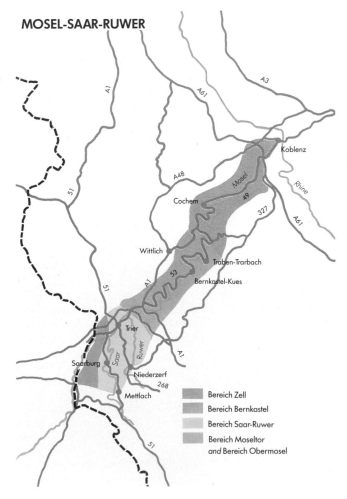

**MOSEL-SAAR-RUWER**

Bereich Zell
Bereich Bernkastel
Bereich Saar-Ruwer
Bereich Moseltor
and Bereich Obermosel

*ℬELOW LEFT: Grapes grown on the slopes of the Mosel have to be picked by hand because of the steepness of the slope. RIGHT: The Bernkastel Bereich is the biggest Bereich in the Mosel, which produces both everyday wines and some top wines like Bernakasteler Doctor.*

wine. The high production costs (caused by the steep slopes and small parcels of vineyards) make it difficult for the smaller, quality-conscious producers to survive. They are forced to sell their wines at low prices, making them great value. Many small vineyard owners sell their wine and/or grapes both to co-operatives and large companies, who blend them to make indifferent mass-produced wines like Piesporter-Michelsberg, once a light, elegant and individual wine but now so popular that it comes from a much larger region and has lost its original character.

But all is not lost for the Mosel – it also boasts some of Germany's finest vineyards like Bernkasteler Doctor.

## ∾ THE BEREICH ∾

**Bereich Moseltor** and **Bereich Obermosel** are the two most southerly Bereiche, neither of which produce anything of note. Very little Riesling is planted. Elbling dominates the vineyards and most of it is made into Sekt.

**Bereich Saar-Ruwer** produces many of the region's best quality wines on the steep, slatey slopes.

**Bereich Bernkastel** is the biggest of the region's Bereich. It produces both unexciting mass-produced wines (like Piesporter Michelsberg), and also some of Germany's top wines like Bernkasteler Doctor.

**Bereich Zell** produces very few exciting wines.

### RECOMMENDED PRODUCERS

| | |
|---|---|
| Bischöfliches Priesterseminar Trier | Leiwen |
| Bischöfliches Konvikt Trier | Leuz-Jahn |
| Eduard Bremm | Dr Loosen |
| Deinhard | Egon Müller zu Scharzhof |
| J. C. Erben | Peter Nicolay |
| Dr Weins-Prum Erben | J. J. Prüm |
| Friedrich-Wilhelm-Gymnasium | S. A. Prüm Erben |
| | Eddie Reverchon |
| Hohe Domkirche | Max F. Richter |
| Maxim Grünhaus | Von Schubert |
| Fritz Haag | St Nikolaus Hospital |
| Jungwinzer | Staatliche Weinbaudomäne |
| Reichsgraf von Kesselstatt | Dr H. Thanisch |
| J. Lauerburg | Zentralkellerei Bernkastel |

# THE RHINE VALLEY'S FAMOUS FOUR

## ∽ RHEINGAU, RHEINPFALZ, RHEINHESSEN ∽ AND NAHE

The wine-producing part of the Rhine Valley starts at Basel, and runs right down to just south of Bonn, in all covering a distance of well over 400 kilometres (250 miles). The first part of its journey takes it through the Baden region (see page 120) and then, to the south-east of Mannheim, the Rheinpfalz starts, followed by Reinhessen, Rheingau and Nahe. After that comes the Mittelrhein (see page 120).

It is these four areas that make up the wine region so well-known to tourists, with a fairytale castle appearing at virtually every turn of the river.

The style of wine produced in this large area varies from the light, fruity, high-acidity, high-quality wines of the Rheingau (similar in style to those of the Mosel but without the slatiness) through to the richer, heavier wines of the Rheinpfalz.

## ∽ GRAPE VARIETIES ∽

Both Müller-Thurgau and Riesling are widely planted here and together make up around 50 per cent of the grapes planted. Other grape varieties include Silvaner, and the red grapes Portugieser and Spätburgunder (Pinot Noir). As with every German wine-producing region, it is the Riesling that produces the best white wines, but some of the red wines now being produced here are very exciting.

## ∽ THE RHEINGAU ∽

Although the most famous of all Germany's regions, with a wine-producing history going back to the 12th century, the Rheingau is a relatively small region measuring roughly 50 km by 2 km, with just 3,300 hectares (8,150 acres) of vines (compared to the Rheinpfalz with 22,000 hectares [54,400 acres]). It runs east to west, with Hochheim at one end and Lorch at the other. Because, for once, the Rhine is flowing east-west, the Rheingau's vineyards face south, thus gaining better exposure to the sun. The Rheingau is the home of Hock (after the village of Hochheim), which was traditionally sold in brown bottles as opposed to the Mosel's green bottles. The wines are similar in style to the Mosel as they are high in acidity. The region of Rüdesheim is a tourist trap, with the old-wine producing town of Rüdesheim being especially popular.

Riesling and Spätburgunder produce the best wines of the region, and Riesling is by far the most widely planted

grape, reflecting the quality status of the region. The red wine area is Assmanshausen, producing some of Germany's finest light red wines.

There are many well-known traditional, highly respected producers in this area like, for example, Schloss Vollrads and Schloss Johannisberg. This region also boasts Germany's internationally famous research institute and winemaking college at Geisenheim. Many winemakers from all over the world make the pilgrimage to study here.

## ∽ RHEINPFALZ ∽

This area contains the 'Deutsche Weinstrasse' a popular tourist wine trail, that links all the small wine-producing villages of the Pfalz. It runs from Schweigen, just north of Wissembourg on the French border, to Bockenheim to the west of Mannheim. The wines from this region have a good balance between the acidity of the north (i.e. Mosel and Rheingau) and the alcohol of the south (i.e. Baden), although the yield is the highest of any region in Germany.

The vineyard holdings are larger and flatter than the Mosel, making it far more economic to produce wine. The area is protected by the Haardt mountains and those vineyards that are planted on gently sloping sites directly in the shadow of these mountains produce the best wines. The vineyard area has now been expanded into the flat land out of the mountain shadow over the last 20 years, and these produce wines of higher quantity but lower quality.

A wide variety of grape varieties are grown here, the most important being Riesling, Müller-Thurgau, Kerner, Morio Muskat, Weissburgunder, Grauburgunder and Spätburgunder. In the south of the region in the late 1960s many producers planted new crossings like Ortega, Optima, Huxelrebe and Bacchus, which produced high sugar levels and yields but they have never matched the quality of the classic varieties.

The south of the Rheinpfalz produces more quantity than quality and much of it ends up as Liebfraumilch.

## ∽ NAHE ∽

This is a small region of around 5,000 hectares (12,350 acres) of vineyards. It follows the river Nahe, a tributary of the Rhine, as it flows from Sobernheim past Bad Kreuznach to Bingen where it flows into the Rhine. These soft, aromatic wines are a cross between the acidic wines of the Rheingau and the fuller, more alcoholic wines of the

Rheinpfalz. All the classic grapes are grown, although hardly any red wine is made and many producers sell their grapes to four big co-operatives.

## ❧ RHEINHESSEN ❧

The Rheinhessen is a large area of around 20,000 hectares (49,420 acres), contained within a loop of the river Rhine during its course from Worms past Mainz to Bingen, and is bounded on its west side by the Nahe river. It is a relatively flat region where many of the vineyards are mechanized, and almost half the production goes into Liebfraumilch.

Apart from the classic varieties many new varieties are grown, like Bacchus and Ortega. The vineyards directly on the Rhine, known as the Rheinfront, are some of the best in the region, particularly Oppenheim and Guntersblum. The wines in general tend to be on the sweeter side, largely due to consumer demand. But sadly, since the wine scandals, locals are a little sceptical about high-quality sweet wines and so many producers are finding it difficult to sell their top wines. One of the best known wines from the region is Niersteiner, originally from the single village of Nierstein but now produced in a much larger region, thus losing much of its character.

*Harvesting in Berg Rottland vineyard in the Rheingau.*

### RECOMMENDED PRODUCERS

**Rheingau**
Geheimrat Aschrott
Staatsweingut Bergstrasse
Wegeler Deinhard
Staatsweingut Eltville
J. Fischer Erben
Schloss Groenesteyn
Landgräflich Hessisches
 Weingut
Hans Hulbert
Schloss Johannisberg
Graf von Kanitz
Georg Müller Stiftung
von Oetinger
Schloss Reinhartshausen
Balthasar Ress
Reuter & Sturm (Sekt)
Riedel
Klosterkellerei Sankt
 Hildegard
Schloss Schönborn
Langwerth von Simmern
Troitzsch
Schloss Vollrads
Dr R. Weil
Domdechant Werner'sches
 Weingut

**Rheinpfalz**
Acham-Magin
Von Bassermann-Jordan
F & G Bergdolt
Winzergenossenschaft Bad
 Durkheim
Josef Biffar
Reichsrat von Buhl
Dr Bürklin-Wolf
Dr Deinhard
Georg Siben Erben
Fuhrmann-Eymael
Georg Henninger IV
Dr Kern
Knipser-Johannishof
Koehler-Ruprecht

**Rheinpfalz – cont.**
Georg Mossbacher
Mossbacherof
Müller-Catoir
Weinkellerie
Nieder Kirchen
Okonomierat Rebholz
Karl Schaefer/Dr
 Fleischmann
Eduard Schuster
Wilhelm Spindler
Karl Werlheim
Dr Heinz Wertheim
Werlé

**Nahe**
Paul Anheuser
Hans Crusius
Nahe Winzerkellereien
Niederhausen
Graf von Plettenberg
Prinze zu Salm-
 Dalberg'sches
 Weingut
Villa Sachsen
Schmitt
Staatliche
Weinbaudomanen

**Rheinhessen**
Anton Balbach
Heinrich Braun
Gustav Gessert
Gunderloch-Usinger
Louis Guntrum
Heyl zu Herrnsheim
Kappellenhof
Carl Koch Erben
Dr Reinhard Muth
Rappenhof
Villa Sachsen
Schales
Gustav Adolf Schmitt
P. J. Valckenberg
Schloss Westerhaus

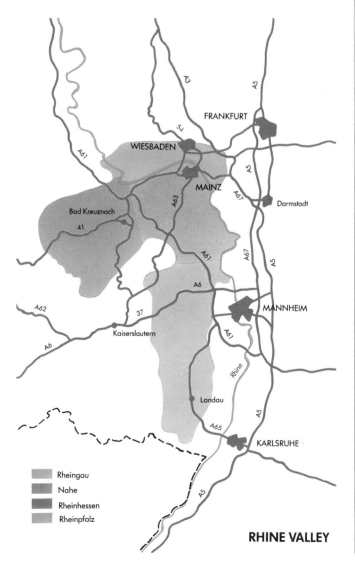

Rheingau
Nahe
Rheinhessen
Rheinpfalz

**RHINE VALLEY**

FRANKFURT
WIESBADEN
MAINZ
Darmstadt
Bad Kreuznach
MANNHEIM
Kaiserslautern
Landau
KARLSRUHE

# THE REST OF GERMANY

## ∾ AHR AND MITTELRHEIN ∾

Ahr and Mittelrhein are two of Germany's smallest and most northerly wine-producing regions, and very little of either region's wine is exported. In the Ahr the locals are very fond of their own wines, and in the Mittelrhein much is sold to the numerous tourists who visit the area.

The Ahr produces predominantly red and rosé wines from the Spätburgunder and the Portugieser grapes. These are able to flourish due to the shelter the vineyards get from the Hohe Eifel hills. The main grape of the Mittelrhein is the Riesling and, although the region does not have much of a reputation, it has the potential of producing very high quality wines.

## ∾ BADEN ∾

Baden is Germany's most southerly wine-producing area. It's warmer than most of the other regions and has one feature that residents of most other parts of Germany would die for – sunshine! It stretches from the foothills of the Black Forest in the north, right down to Basel in Switzerland and then east to the shores of Lake Constance (Bodensee). It's a sprawling, seemingly random collection of areas, producing very varying styles of wine from many different grape varieties. The only way one can hope to come to grips with it is to look at it as different areas, and not as a cohesive region.

The most northerly part is Badisches Frankenland, producing mostly dry wines of an identical style to those of neighbouring Franconia (see right). Then comes Badische Bergstrasse Kraichgau, stretching from Heidelberg down to Baden-Baden and mostly planted with Müller-Thurgau. South of Baden-Baden, comes the Ortenau, an area of volcanic, steeply sloping land, capable of producing some classic Germanic-style wines. Next comes the Breisgau, where again Müller-Thurgau is the most planted variety. The impressive volcanic peak of the Kaiserstuhl (seat of the king) produces dry wines which can be of very high quality. The most southerly of the main stretch of Baden is the Markgräflerland, an area producing very interesting wines which resemble more those of Alsace than other German wines. The grapes planted include Weissburgunder, Gewürztraminer and Gutedel. The last area of Baden is on the shores of Lake Constance, and produces light, fresh, easy-drinking whites and rosés, the former mostly made from Müller-Thurgau.

Over 90 per cent of Baden's production comes from a huge co-operative, the Zentralkellerei Badischer Winzer-

genossenschaften, normally abbreviated to ZBW. This is an impressive winery, stuffed to the roof with the latest technology – it looks like something out of a James Bond thriller. While huge quantities of wine are made here, all the smaller, more interesting or better quality vineyard sites and grape varieties are vinified separately. Many of these wines are then aged in oak barrels to give them further nuances.

## ∾ HESSISCHE BERGSTRASSE ∾

Situated to the east of the Rheingau, this is Germany's smallest wine-producing region and her wines are rarely to be found outside the region.

## ∾ FRANKEN (FRANCONIA) ∾

This north-easterly region of Bavaria is known for its beer and its wine, bottled in the distinctive squat flask-shaped bottles known as *bocksbeutel*. Silvaner and Müller-Thurgau are the most widely planted varieties although others like Ortega, Scheurebe and Bacchus are there too. Sadly Riesling only accounts for a tiny percentage of the vineyards. While other areas like the Rheingau are jampacked with vineyards, those in Franken are interspersed with fields and forests. The region has a continental climate and the winter frosts can severely reduce the yields.

The wines, many of which are made by co-operatives,

include some excellent examples of Silvaner, showing its earthy, vegetal, almost smokey flavour. Unfortunately, as has happened in many other parts of Germany, the boring Müller-Thurgau seems to be replacing much of the more characterful Silvaner.

## ∽ WÜRTTEMBERG ∽

The wine made in this area is rarely seen outside the region, simply because the locals drink it all. The best vineyards are those on the south-facing slopes between Heilbronn and Winnenden, not far from Stuttgart. Over half the vineyards are planted with red grape varieties, mainly the Trollinger grape, making fairly light-bodied red wines. Riesling is the most important white variety, and makes quite full-bodied wines here. Co-operatives make much of the region's wine and their members drink most of it!

**SEKT** This is Germany's well-known sparkling wine, consumed in huge quantities and often made from the thin acidic juice of unripe grapes. In the past much of it was made from grapes produced outside Germany. Over 25 million cases are produced annually, the majority of which is consumed in Germany.

Sekt is mainly made by the tank method of fermentation (see pages 8-14 on winemaking), less expensive than the *méthode champenoise,* and the majority of wines are medium-sweet. The exception to this are wines made by some smaller producers who use pure Riesling and make their wines using the *méthode champenoise,* known in German as *Flaschengärung.*

*ABOVE: Many producers still use wooden barrels for ageing their wines. LEFT: Schlossberg vineyards below the Festung Marienburg castle in Würzburg in the Franken region.*

# SPAIN

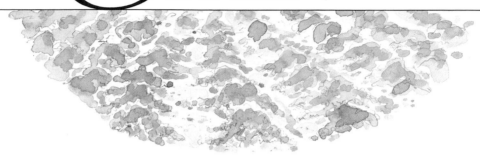

$\mathcal{S}$PAIN IS NO LONGER the producer of plonk it was 15 years ago. Then, with only a few exceptions, both the wines drunk locally and those exported tended to be mass-produced low-quality wines, often sold and transported in bulk tankers, cheap but not always very cheerful. Now the quality of the wines exported has gone up dramatically in Spain's bid to gain a foothold on the European quality ladder. Many of the changes can be attributed to Spain's entry to the EEC and extra grants, particularly for the co-operatives and the new centralized research centres. In addition, leading Spanish wine producers have made increased efforts to lead their

country into modern wine concepts, realizing that their colleagues had to pull their socks up if their wine industry was to survive.

Spain's not just about Rioja – there are a whole host of other exciting red wines on offer. They are often better value for money than their classic French counterparts and, because they do not yet enjoy international superstar status, more mature vintages are available than from Bordeaux (for example), often directly from the *bodegas* who traditionally sell their wine only when it is ready to drink. Some of Rioja's Reservas and Gran Reservas are the best value quality wines available today.

Spanish white wines have undergone a very welcome winemaking revolution: the grapes are picked earlier and the must is cold-fermented in temperature-controlled stainless-steel fermentation vats, essential in a country with such a hot climate. As a result the tired, dark yellow, oxidized wines of the past are beginning to disappear and refreshing crisp dry whites are taking their place. Gone are the appalling Spanish 'Sauternes' and 'Graves'; at long last the Spanish are beginning to realize the potential of their own regional wines.

Around 65 per cent of all Spanish wine is made in co-operatives, and things are beginning to change here too. Traditionally, growers were paid more for grapes with high sugar levels, which encouraged them to deliver overripe grapes to make wines with a high alcohol level. Now at the best co-operatives they are paid according to quality, and winemakers look out for a balance between sugar and acidity, rather than concentrating on making wines with a high alcohol level.

The grape varieties are changing too. Some of the more innovative producers are forsaking high-yielding varieties like the white Airén, the country's most widely planted grape, in favour of other more interesting varieties. Led by Miguel Torres in Catalonia, producers are beginning to

*Clay wine jars are still used as fermentation vessels in parts of Spain while other companies have now replaced them with more costly stainless steel vats.*

Rioja Alta
Rioja Baja
Rioja Alavesa
Navarra
Catalonia
Ribera del Duero
Valdepeñas
La Mancha
Valencia
Jerez
Montilla

see the potential of other non-indigenous grape varieties like Chardonnay, Gewürztraminer, Riesling, Sauvignon Blanc, Cabernet Sauvignon, Pinot Noir and Merlot. Some of the best results seem to come from blending the local and foreign varieties together.

Spain's other most famous vinous product is sherry, a unique wine from the south (see page 182).

## ﹌ DENOMINACION DE ORIGEN ﹌ – THE QUALITY CONTROL

This is Spain's equivalent of the French *Appellation Contrôlée* system and covers 60 per cent of Spain's wine production. Wines have to be made from permitted grape varieties and adhere to restricted yields, as well as passing tasting and analytical tests. To correspond with the French *vins de pays*, Spain has introduced *vinos de la tierra*, wines that name the region in which they are produced (at least 60 per cent of the grapes must come from the named region) on the label. All this is good news for the consumer who now has a better chance of determining which region's wines are to his or her liking. But, as in all countries, some of the best wines come from areas not yet officially recognized and granted a D.O.

To sum up, Spain is *exciting*. I'll go on experimenting with new wines from unheard-of regions because so much potential has been revealed in the past ten years that I'm *sure* there are plenty more enjoyable surprises in store.

# ℛIOJA & 𝒩AVARRA

ℛioja and Navarra nestle next to each other in northern Spain, and are two of the country's most important red-wine-producing regions. Rioja has established a well-deserved reputation for quality, and has been in existence as a 'serious' wine-producing region for well over a century. Navarra is younger in its reputation but has great potential.

## ☙ RIOJA ❧

Stop anyone in the street and ask them to name one Spanish wine: the chances are they'll say Rioja. For this was the Spanish success story of the 1970s and the wine that put Spain firmly in the consumer's mind as a quality wine producing country.

Dismissed by the traditional wine trade for many years, Rioja filled a niche, especially when Bordeaux prices started to rocket. More and more people became interested in good wine and looked for a cheaper substitute for claret. Rioja was the ideal choice and many old vintages were available at remarkably reasonable prices.

It's not just coincidence that Rioja became known as 'the poor man's Bordeaux'. Back at the end of the 19th century when phylloxera destroyed most of Europe's vineyards, wine-producers fled from Bordeaux and began making wine in the yet-to-be-affected Rioja region, just south of them over the Pyrenees. They brought with them their traditional winemaking techniques, and in particular the practice of ageing their wines in small 225-litre oak barrels. It's this process that gives Rioja its distinctive and attractive soft, creamy, vanilla-like aroma and flavour. The process has hardly changed today, although some new-wave producers like Olarra are making very successful wines using modern techniques.

Rioja at its best is sensational – mouth-filling, rich, vanilla-tinted fruit and, when mature, velvety rich. And wines like mature Reserva 904 and 890 (from La Rioja Alta) and Prado Enea (from Muga) are some of my all-time favourite red wines.

In Rioja there are three main areas of vineyards all clinging on to northern Spain's Ebro Valley, between Haro and Alfaro. At Haro the river Ocha (or Oja) joins the river Ebro, hence the name Rioja.

## ☙ THE MAIN GRAPE VARIETIES ❧

Rioja is blended, both from different grapes and from the three different regions within the area. The main red grapes grown are Tempranillo, Garnacha, Graciano and Mazuelo for red Riojas and Viura and Malvasia for whites.

## ☙ THE THREE REGIONS OF RIOJA ❧

### Rioja Alta

Situated in the north-west of the Ebro Valley, the eastern point of the Rioja Alta joins Alavesa and Baja at the massive town of Logroño, the wine-producing centre of the region, and most of its vineyards lie to the south of the river. The hilltop town of Haro, at the western end of the Alta, houses many of the top *bodegas*, including Muga, CVNE and La Riojas' Alta. With just under 40,000 acres (16,000 hectares), Alta is the biggest of Rioja's three regions. It encompasses a variety of soils, producing several different styles of wine,

*New oak barrels add a vanilla flavour and nuances to the wines of Rioja.*

*Pangos and Sierra de Cantabria near Laguardia in Rioja Alavesa.*

although the wines from this region are generally full bodied and capable of ageing well. Although normally blended with the wines from the other regions, certain *bodegas* make wines from pure Rioja Alta grapes.

### Rioja Alavesa

Alavesa also enjoys an Atlantic climate that cools the hot air, producing long, sunny summers and cold frosty winters. There are just under 20,000 acres (8,000 hectares) of vines grown on calcareous clay. Because of the varying soils and micro-climates, this large region produces both full-bodied and lighter style wines which are almost always blended. Some wines like Domecq Domaine and Cantino are made from pure Alavesa grapes.

### The Rioja Baja

The Rioja Baja is much hotter than the other two sub-regions and has a Mediterranean rather than Atlantic climate with long, very hot summers. This type of climate combined with the alluvial fertile soil produces jammy, alcoholic wines that have a baked aroma and flavour and are much less complex than wines from the other regions. They are ideal for beefing up the final Rioja blend.

## THE TRADITIONAL VERSUS THE MODERN

Two very different styles of winemaking exist in the Rioja region, both producing very different (and exciting) wines. On the one hand companies like Muga and CVNE continue the traditional Bordelais practice of ageing their wines in oak to give them a vanilla flavour and aroma, while others, like the high-tech Bodegas Olarra, age few of their wines, preferring to make a lighter, more fruity wine suitable for younger drinking. Apart from the official classification on the back label (see below), consumers have no way of knowing which wine is of which style. This is why it's worth remembering which *bodegas'* wines you like.

## WHITE WINES

In common with the rest of Europe, white winemaking techniques in Rioja have changed dramatically over the last ten years. Today the tendency in Rioja is to make cold-fermented, squeaky-clean white wines that are fresh and zippy and are designed to be drunk young. This style of wine, (Marqués de Cáceres is the best example) is not aged in oak. Some *bodegas* like Marqués de Murrieta still make delicious old-style white Riojas that are more like mature, sometimes maderized, full white Burgundies in style.

## CLASSIFICATION

To get some idea of the style of Rioja, look carefully at the bottle's back label. It will feature a map of Rioja with one of the following terms printed over it.

### Sin crianza

The wine has not been wood-aged so it will be a light fruity red, crisp rosé or zippy white.

### Crianza

These wines have spent at least one year in wood so therefore will have a mild oaky flavour and more weight than *sin crianza* wines.

### Reserva

*Reserva* wines must have been aged for a minimum of three years (two for whites), of which one year must be in oak barrels. *Reserva* wines are generally only made in the better harvests, and many can be kept for an extra few years, becoming softer and more complex with time.

### Gran Reserva

These are the top wines that are aged for a minimum of two years in barrel and two in bottle or vice versa. Rich and velvety, both *Reservas* and *Gran Reservas* are brilliant value for money.

## NAVARRA

Navarra is a very attractive region to visit with plenty of excellent *paradors* (Government-owned hotels) to stay in, like the one in the castle at Olite. Its rolling hills are full of vines and asparagus ferns waving in the wind. Or alternatively if you want some action and it appeals to you, you can follow Ernest Hemingway's example and watch a bullfight in Pamplona.

As an added bonus you can wash down plates of asparagus with one of the local wines, which are constantly improving in quality. Navarra houses Spain's leading vinification and vine research station, a fact that augurs well for Navarra's future. The red wines are made predominantly from the Garnacha grape, accounting for over 90 per cent of Navarra's wine and, while they share certain similarities with red Riojas, particularly when young, few age well. In the future, however, new plantings of Tempranillo and Cabernet Sauvignon may well produce longer lived reds from the region.

Throughout Spain, Navarra is known for its production of full-bodied rosé wines, again made from Garnacha. Improved winemaking facilities in the region's co-operatives have seen far better quality rosés appearing, full of clean, ripe, fresh fruit, rather than the tired old oxidized Garnacha wines which used to be the norm. In particular Chivite's Gran Feudo rosé has shown other sceptical producers what can be done when the grapes are handled correctly. Whites have also improved recently for the same reasons. Navarra has potential particularly if more growers plant the new grape varieties like Riesling, Chardonnay and Cabernet Sauvignon that have done so well in the experimental vineyards.

---
NAVARRA – RECOMMENDED PRODUCERS
---

| | |
|---|---|
| Bodegas Irache | Bodegas Villafranca de Navarra |
| Bodegas Julián Chivite | Cenaisa |
| Bodegas Ochoa | Señorio de Sarria |

---
RIOJA – RECOMMENDED PRODUCERS
---

| Producer | Top Brands |
|---|---|
| Bodegas Alavesas | Solar de Samaniego |
| Bodegas Berberana | Carta de Plata, Gran Reserva |
| Bodegas Beronia | Reserva |
| Bodegas Bilbainas | Vendimia Especial |
| Bodegas Campillo | Gran Reserva, Marqués de Villamagna |
| Bodegas Domecq | Domecq Domaine Reserva |
| Bodegas El Coto | El Coto, El Coto Imaz Reserva |
| Bodegas Lagunilla | Viña Herminia |
| Bodegas Lan | Gran Reserva |
| Bodegas Martinez Bujanda | Reserva, Gran Reserva |
| Bodegas Montecillo | Montecillo, Viña Cumbrero |
| Bodegas Muga | Prado Enea |
| Bodegas Olarra | Cerro Añón |
| Bodegas Riojanas | Monte Real, Viña Albina |
| Contino | Contino Rioja Reserva |
| CVNE | Imperial, Vina Real, Monopole |
| La Rioja Alta | Viña Alberdi, Viña Ardanza, Reserva 904 & 890 |
| Marqués de Cáceres | Rivarey, Reserva |
| Marqués de Murrieta | Castillo Ygay Reserva Especial |
| Marqués del Puerto | Reserva |
| Federico Paternina | Gran Reserva |
| Salceda | Viña Salceda |
| Vina Tondonia | Viña Tondonia, Viña Bosconia, Viña Cubillo |

*The Señorio de Sarria estate in Puente la Reina in Navarra.*

# THE REST OF SPAIN

While Rioja and Jerez (see the chapter on fortified wine) are two of the most interesting areas of Spain in qualitative terms, they are only fairly small in terms of Spain's total production. The biggest area is La Mancha, bigger than any other demarcated region in Europe and producing a third of all Spain's wines. In quality terms, however, it's not wildly exciting. Much more interesting are the wines from Ribera del Duero, Toro and Miguel Torres' wines from Penedés in Catalonia.

The rest of Spain splits up geographically into four main regions: Catalonia (still wines and Cava); The Provinces of Castilla-León; The Centre (La Mancha and Valdepeñas); The South-East (including Jumilla, Yecla and Valencia). There are several other minor wine-producing regions dotted about like Rias Baixas, Tierra de Barros, Ribeiro, Somontano, Valdeorras, El Bierzo, but their produce is currently of little interest.

## ∾ CATALONIA ∾

Catalonia lies to the west of the city of Barcelona and has a hot, arid climate, not ideal for producing top quality wines. But despite the climate, Catalonia produces some really exciting wines, many from non-Spanish grapes (like Chardonnay, Gewürztraminer, etc), and many of them, produced by the pioneering firm of Miguel Torres. The most important sub-region is Penedés, the home of the remarkable wines of Miguel Torres and most of Catalonia's best wines. Catalonia also produces Cava, the sparkling wine made by the *méthode champenoise*.

Most of the wine produced in Catalonia is white (thanks to Cava), although before the phylloxera disaster at the end of the 19th century, the majority was red.

It's impossible to name a typical grape of Catalonia, because each producer has their own favourite, and different grapes are better suited to the very varied geography of the region. But amongst those grown are:
**White:** Muscat, Moscatel de Grano Pequeno, Xarel-lo, Macabeo, Parellada, Chardonnay, Chenin Blanc, Gewürztraminer, Riesling.
**Red:** Garnacha, Monastrell, Cariñena, Ull de Llebre, Pinot Noir, Cabernet Sauvignon.

'Foreign' grapes (the last four whites, and the last two reds above) make the best wines, with producers like Torres and Jean León leading the way.

Torres, a company which started in 1870 is headed by father and son, both named Miguel Torres (senior and junior). It was Torres Senior who originally put the com-

pany on the map, but his son continued and expanded on this base, and it is now rated as one of the world's top winemakers. His experiments with different grapes and different sites are revolutionary, and he has even established the production of some outstanding wines in Chile.

They have experimental vineyards and even commercialize grapes like Gewürztraminer in Viña Esmeralda. Their winemaking is second to none in the region.

The other most notable Penedés still wine producer is Jean León, producing remarkable Chardonnay and Cabernet Sauvignon.

As anyone who has taken a holiday on the Costa del Sol will know, Catalonia is the home of Cava. But watch out – while most Cava is made in Catalonia it's not a geographic term – Cava can be produced from any of the officially recognised Cava areas which are spread all over Spain.

If you order a bottle of Champagne in Spain you'll most likely be given a bottle of Cava. And whilst the Champagne producers would disapprove of this (and I sympathize with them) Cava can be a great value glass of fizz, and the best *can* rival lesser Champagnes (and at a cheaper price), even if they are in a different style. One of the most interesting producers is Raimat, which produces an amazing sparkling Chardonnay – this can rival even a Grande Marque Champagne in quality, and at less than half the cost! There are just three grape varieties used for making Cava as it is normally encountered: Macabéo (the same as Viura in Rioja), Xarel-lo and Parellada.

## ∾ THE CENTRE – LA MANCHA AND VALDEPENAS ∾

La Mancha's production is 90 per cent white, made mainly from the Airén grape, and most of it very dreary indeed. There is just one producer of note, and even that company's wine does not strictly fall under the La Mancha DO, as it isn't made from approved grape varieties. The wine in question is the remarkable Marques de Grinon Cabernet Sauvignon, made with the help of Professor Emile Peynaud and Alexis Lichine, two of the wisest old men of Bordeaux. The same firm also make an excellent white in Rueda.

Valdepenes mostly produces very boring white wine from the Arién grape. But there are a few red wines worth seeking out because of their tremendous value for money. Although the best reds are made entirely from the Cencibel grape, some of the lesser quality red wines only contain as little as 20 per cent Cencibel, the other 80 per cent being made from white grapes.

## ∼ THE PROVINCES OF CASTILLA-LEON ∼

This area is to be found in the northern centre of Spain, about halfway between La Mancha and the northern coast of Spain. Although not large, it is responsible for some very high quality and good value wines. The four most interesting regions, of which the first three are DOs, are Ribera del Duero, Rueda, Toro and León.

### Toro

Toro's best wines are the red, and its top producer (by a long way) is Bodegas Farina, making full, complex, high quality reds with masses of fruity character. By law the wines must be made from at least 75 per cent Tinto de Toro, and a maximum 25 per cent Garnacha, but the best wines tend to be made entirely from Tinto de Toro. Toro's wines will last for decades and, at the moment, are one of Spain's great undiscovered secrets. Buy them now!

### Ribera del Duero

Ribera del Duero is the home of Spain's rarest and most sought-after red wine, Vega Sicilia. This big, rich, very concentrated wine only has a tiny production, and is of such quality that it rivals some of the top wines of Bordeaux.

This remote wine growing region nestles up at the highest altitudes possible for wine production (800 metres above sea level), and this is a major factor responsible for the very high quality of some of its wines. Most of the grapes are a local variation of the Tempranillo, known by various names including Tinto Fino, although there are increasing numbers of French grapes like Cabernet Sauvignon, Merlot and Malbec. In fact, although people think of Miguel Torres as Spain's pioneer in planting foreign grape varieties, Vega Sicilia has had Bordeaux grapes in its vineyard since the beginning of the 20th century.

Vega Sicilia makes three wines: Unico (the ultra-expensive one), and two wines known as Tinto Valbuena. The other big producer from this region is Bodega Ribera Duero, based at Peñafiel. Their top wines, Reserva and Protos, can be superb, although the quality is variable. Their humble Tinto, however, can be excellent value.

There are also two relatively new producers who make some very exciting red wines: Pérez Pascuas with Viña Pedrosa and Alejandro Fernandes with Vina Pesquera.

### Rueda

Rueda's main production used to be heavy, fortified, sherry-style wines, and there are still a few good examples. The emphasis has shifted to more acceptable whites which are designed to be consumed young. These are among the best in Spain, with character and fresh clean fruit.

Rueda's best whites are made mostly from the Verdejo grape, which produces very full-bodied wines with plenty of flavour. It is important to pick the grapes early otherwise they produce wine that is too alcoholic.

The top two producers are Marqués de Riscal and Marqués de Griñon, both of whom make very good red wines elsewhere (Rioja and La Mancha respectively).

### Leon

Not classified as a DO, León can produce good, gutsy reds, mostly from the Prieto Picudo grape, that can equal (and better) other DO wines.

## ∼ THE SOUTH-EAST ∼ (INCLUDING JUMILLA, YECLA AND VALENCIA)

These areas produce low-quality wines (mostly reds made from the Monastrell grape) with a stewed, jammy character which reflects the very hot, arid climate. With greater investment in modern winemaking technology there is the potential to produce wines of decent quality, demonstrated by Bodegas Bleda, producers of Castillo Jumilla.

---

### RECOMMENDED PRODUCERS

| Still Wines (Catalonia) | Brands/Good Wines |
|---|---|
| Ferrer | Viña Laranda |
| Jean Leon | Cabernet Sauvignon, Chardonnay |
| Marqués de Monistrol | Gran Reserva |
| Masia Bach | Viña Extrisima, Reserva |
| Mas Rabassa | Xarello & Macabéo |
| Raimat | Cabernet Sauvignon, Chardonnay |
| Miguel Torres | Whites: Viña Sol, Gran Viña Sol, Viña Esmarelda, Mimanda. Reds: Sangre de Toro, Gran Sangre de Toro Reserva, Viña Magdala, Coronas, Gran Coronas Reserva |

| Cava | Speciality Brands |
|---|---|
| Cavas Hill | – |
| Codorniu | Non Plus Ultra, Chardonnay |
| Conde de Caralt | Brut Nature |
| Castellblanch | Brut Zero |
| Freixenet | Cuvée DS, Brut Nature |
| Jean Perico | – |
| Marqués de Monistrol | Brut Nature |
| Mont Marcal | – |
| Parxet | Brut Nature |
| Raimat | Blanc de Blancs Cava Brut |
| Segura Viudas | Blanc de Blancs |

### The Provinces of Castilla-León

| Producer & Brands | Region |
|---|---|
| Alejandro Fernandes (Viña Pesquera) | Ribera del Duero |
| Bodegas Mauro | Ribera del Duero |
| Bodegas Ribera Duero | Ribera del Duero |
| Marqués de Griñon (white) | Rueda |
| Marqués de Riscal | Rueda |
| Perez Pascuas (Vina Pedrosa) | Ribera del Duero |
| Vega Siculia (Unico & Tinto Valbuena) | Ribera del Duero |

### The Centre – La Mancha and Valdepeñs

| Producer | Region |
|---|---|
| Bodegas Los Llanos | Valdepeñas |
| Bodegas Félix Solis | Valdepeñas |
| Marqués de Griñon (red) | La Mancha (but not DO) |
| Viña Albali | Valdepeñas |

# PORTUGAL

PORTUGAL HAS BEEN SLOWER than its Iberian neighbour, Spain, in telling the world about its great value wines. True, everyone has heard of the fortified wines, port and madeira (see page 178), but how many people know that, for instance, an Australian winemaker is making fabulous off-dry cold-fermented Muscat in the Setúbal peninsula?

One of Portugal's main problems is its attempt to arrive at a sane classification and official quality-control system. France has had its *Appellation Contrôlée* system for years, Italy's disastrous DOC system is well established (unfortunately), and Spain is making an intelligent (and mostly successful) attempt at improving quality through its DO system. Even the New World wine-producers, especially California, are coming to grips with this thorny problem. But Portugal faces a crisis with its entry into Europe's Common Market – it can't decide what to do. Portugal's traditional winemaking habits don't help the process – Garrafeira, for instance, can be a (normally red) wine from any region, chosen by the producer as being particularly good and then aged in casks for an indefinite period.

None of this helps you, the wine-drinker, one iota, so ignore any official or quasi-official classification until Portugal has got its legislative act together in a few years' time. In the meantime it's best to stick to the great wines from certain producers in specific areas, because they will be the ones producing the really exciting wines.

Portugal has three types of winemaker: first, the small growers, most of whom, with a few exceptions, don't produce anything exciting. Most are too small to make a sensible investment in vinification technology and know-how, and many sell their wines to co-operatives or larger companies. Second are the co-operatives, which can produce sound, everyday wines. Many, however, are sub-standard, with the odd exception. Finally, the larger private producers: these are the ones producing Portugal's most exciting

*Picking grapes in the Minho region where Vinho Verde is made. As the vines are trained so high farmers often grow other crops, such as cabbages below them.*

same grapes as port, they are generally grown on the less good vineyard sites. Recently one or two have been produced that have made the wine world sit up and take notice. In particular Grande Escolha, from Champalimaud's Quinta do Côtto, which is aged in new oak. It is a fabulous wine, rich and full, and will last for years. Quite different in style again is Barca Velha, made by Ferreira. They have also pioneered a *macération carbonique* wine which shows how light and fruity Douro reds can be if well handled. Both the large co-operatives in the region are also making sound reds but it's best to forget about the whites – they leave much to be desired.

### Vinho Verde

If you take the train from Oporto up the Douro Valley you'll arrive in Minho, Vinho Verde country, after an hour or so. The vines climb up high, twisting their way around trees and wires, overshadowing the cabbages and other vegetables that are planted beneath them. Vinho Verde means 'green wine'. This does not refer to the colour of the wine, nor to the fact that the grapes are picked when unripe, but to the lush mass of green that covers the region during the summer and at harvest time.

More red wine than white (surprisingly) is made in this region, although consumer demand has led many growers to replace black grape varieties with white and so the emphasis might well change. Much of the wine is made by co-operatives, to whom the many thousands of small growers bring their produce.

White Vinho Verde, as it is drunk in the region, is crisp and dry – the more medium ones have only been concocted for export markets. Historically the wines contained a slight spritz, the result of the natural malolactic fermentation taking place in the bottle, although today many of the commercial brands are lightly carbonated. Some of the best wines are those from single *quintas* (farms).

### Bairrada

The Bairrada region is south of Oporto, and over 90 per cent of the production is red wine. The wines, made from the local Baga grape, are heavy in tannin, a characteristic which becomes less apparent when they are drunk with

table wines. They have often invested more than the co-operatives and can produce exceptional quality at very low prices. An example of this type of company is José-Maria da Fonseca at Azeitão.

∽ PRINCIPAL REGIONS ∽

### Douro reds

These are the table wines produced high up in the Douro Valley where port is made. Made predominantly from the

*Picking grapes on the steep slopes of the river Douro, where both red table wine and port are made.*

the local food. One of the best producers is Caves St João who have many fascinating old vintages on offer, demonstrating Bairrada's ageing potential.

### Dão

Dão is east of the Bairrada region and is centred around the town of Viseu. Like Bairrada, over 90 per cent of the production is red and made predominantly from the Touriga Nacional, the quality port grape, which makes a dry, full bodied, fairly tannic red. The quality is not generally exciting, although there are a few producers like Grão Vasco making interesting wines.

### Alentejo

This is Portugal's largest wine-producing area, stretching from half way down Portugal almost to the country's south coast tourist area – the Algarve. It covers roughly a third of Portugal and was not traditionally a vine-producing region, although recent plantings suggest that it has the potential to become one of Portugal's most exciting wine regions. Peter Bright of João Pires, for example, has recently been making some really excellent experimental wines here, including a remarkable Chardonnay, as well as the mouthfillingly delicious red Tinto da Anfora, vinified in traditional large clay amphorae (hence the name). The reds are generally full-bodied and this is certainly an area to watch in the future.

### Carcavelos

Less than a thousand cases of wine are now made in this region lying between Lisbon and the west coast. A rich, sticky, nutty, amber coloured fortified wine is made at Quinta do Barão.

### Estremadura

This region is situated along the Atlantic coast north of Sintra. Both red and white wines are produced here, most of which are sold to co-operatives. One of the best co-operatives, also the name of one of Estremadura's sub-regions, is Arruda, which produces big, beefy red wines which are great value.

### Colares

This area is best known for its upgrafted, phylloxera-free vines grown in the sand-dunes that produce deep red wines, tannic and mouth-puckering when young but, after five to ten years, becoming softer and more complex. All the wine is made at the local co-operative.

### Setúbal

This region is well-known for the delicious Moscatel de Setúbal (see section on fortified wines), but it is also the home to two of Portugal's most exciting wine-producers – José-Maria da Fonseca (not to be confused with the port producer of the same name) and João Pires. The latter make the base wine for one of the world's best-selling table wines, the sparkling rosé Lancers, but their very talented Australian winemaker, Peter Bright, is also responsible for the delicious white João Pires Muscat Branco (light and fragrant), and the remarkable reds Quinta da Anfora and Quinta da Bacalhôa, as well as some very interesting experimental wines. Indeed, Quinta da Bacalhôa is not made from Portuguese grapes at all, but is a blend of Cabernet Sauvignon and Merlot aged in new oak. José-Maria da Fonseca, João Pires' sister company, is one of Portugal's oldest established companies and makes several outstanding wines, including the reds Periquita and Quinta da Camarate.

Peter Bright, with the financial backing of João Pires, has shown that Portugal can make superb wines, and that the many distinctly dodgy wines from Portugal could be improved enormously. If more producers follow his example (as has happened in Spain) Portugal will become a winemaking country to take very seriously. Such is Bright's wine-making kudos in Portugal that João Pires Muscat Branco is always one of the most expensive wines on a Portuguese restaurant's wine list.

---

### RECOMMENDED PRODUCERS

(For producers of port, madeira or Moscatel de Setúbal see separate lists on page 181 and page 186).

Arruda Co-operative
Cantanhede
Carvalho
Caves Aliança
Caves Sao João
Caves Velhas
Champalimaud (especially
  Quinta do Côtto and
  Grand Escolha)
Grão Vasco

João Pires (especially Quinta
  da Bacalhôa, Tinto da Anfora,
  Muscat Branco and
  Chardonnay)
José-Maria de Fonseca
  especially Periquita,
  Quinta da Camarate,
  Garrafeiras and
  Pasmados)
Ribeiro & Ferreira

# ITALY

ITALY PRODUCES AROUND A QUARTER of the entire world's wine production, a startling feat for a country of its size. It has a long tradition of wine-making stretching back over 2,500 years, when it is known that grapes were grown and wine was made. At that time the style of the wines produced would have been totally different to those of today – they would not have been bottled, for instance, but made and sold in amphorae. It seems fair to assume that the wines drunk during Roman orgies were a far cry from the majority of Italian wines we know (and sometimes love) today.

Sadly a lot of Italy's vast production is of the lowest possible quality – rubbish produced in bulk using outmoded techniques and equipment. It's enough to make Italy's

quality wine-producers cry! But meanwhile their less conscientious colleagues rub their hands in glee, secure in the knowledge that the punters will buy any old wine, as long as it says Frascati, Soave, Lambrusco, Chianti or Valpolicella on the label.

But things are changing, and Italy might once again become a wine-producing country to be taken seriously, although this is no thanks to the quality legislation dealing with wine. Some of the most exciting wine coming out of Italy today is classified as plain *vino da tavola*, the lowest quality grade, because it does not fit into the officially accepted categories.

### ∽ THE CLASSIFICATION ∾

Before the introduction of Italy's quality classification in 1963, the country's wine regions were in a real shambles, so the introduction of the Denominazione di Origine Controllata (DOC) seemed like a great step forward. But the problem was that too many were granted, some to regions producing wines of terrible quality, and so the DOC system lost its *raison d'être* almost instantly. There are more than 250 different DOC, but within each there are literally hundreds of styles of wine, and although they specify permitted grape varieties, they do not dictate styles of wine. This all makes it very difficult for the consumer to have any idea of what a specific wine will taste like. And despite the huge number of wines available with DOC status, collectively they only account for around 10 to 15 per cent of Italy's production.

*Vino da tavola*, Italy's table wine, covers a wide variety of styles from very inferior wines to some of Italy's best. The latter include wines like Tignanello and Sassicaia, made by producers who actually wish to remain outside the DOC because certain grape varieties are not allowed. The best example of this is the Cabernet Sauvignon (not

*A Tuscan landscape where poppies flourishing next to the vines show the lack of chemical pesticides used.*

LIGURIAN SEA

CORSICA
(FRANCE)

ADRIATIC SEA

TYRRHENIAN SEA

VALLE
D'AOSTA
Aosta

TRENTINO
ALTO ADIGE
Bolzano

FRIULI
VENEZIA
GIULIA

S33

Lake
Como
Lake
Maggiore

LOMBARDY

Trento

Piave

Bergamo

VENETO

TRIESTE

A9

A26

A4

MILAN

BRESCIA

A21

Vicenza

A4

Lake
Garda

A5

A4

A7

VERONA

PADUA

VENICE

TURIN

A5

Po

A1

Cremona

Adige

S309

Asti

Piacenza

PARMA

Po

A21

A21

PIEDMONT

A21

EMILIA-
ROMAGNA

A13

S309

A26

A7

MODENA

BOLOGNA

A6

A1

LIGURIA

GENOA

A12

A14

San Remo

A10

S1

Rimini

La Spezia

A1

FLORENCE

SAN MARINO

Pisa

Ancona

LEGHORN
(LIVORNO)

Tiber

THE
MARCHES

Siena

S1

TUSCANY

A14

Lake
Bolsena

Oristano

UMBRIA

Orvieto

ABRUZZI

LATIUM

Pescara

ROME

A25

A14

A2

S148

S213

MOLISE

A14

NAPLES

CAMPANIA

Foggia

S655

A16

A16

BARI

A3

Salerno

A14

A3

APULIA

S16

S18

BASILICATA

S379

Brindisi

A3

TARANTO

Lecce

S106

S16

Otranto

S18

CALABRIA

A3

SARDINIA

Sassari

S199

Olbia

S131

Tirso

S131

Oristano

Flumendosa

S131

A3

S106

Trapani

A29

PALERMO

Marsala

A29

A19

S113

A20

MESSINA

A19

A18

Reggio di Calabria

SICILY

A19

S115

S640

A19

CATANIA

S114

S115

Siracusa

The wines of North-West Italy

The wines of North-East Italy

The wines of West Central Italy

The wines of East Central Italy

The wines of Southern Italy

allowed in any DOCs in Tuscany, although permitted in several in Friuli and Süd Tirol), currently producing some of Italy's finest wines.

Clearly a classification system that accurately reflects quality needs to be put into practice in Italy as soon as possible. Encouragingly, the powers that be seem to be aware of this necessity, and recently a higher quality level was introduced, Denominazione di Origine Controllata e Garantita, which has so far only been awarded to six wines.

### ∽ GRAPE VARIETIES AND STYLES OF WINES ∽

Italy has hundreds of different styles of wines and grape varieties, the most important of which are discussed in the relevant chapters.

One of Italy's main problems has been huge over-production, but this goes back to the beginning of the century. After phylloxera (a louse that decimated many of Europe's vineyards) had spread throughout Italy, producers anxious to regain their losses with speed planted the highest cropping varieties they could get hold of, without considering the potential quality (or lack of it). Today, the best producers take more care in the vineyards, restricting their yields and planting the most suitable grape varieties for their particular soil and climate.

There has been much experimentation with 'foreign' noble grape varieties like Cabernet, Merlot and Chardonnay, with spectacular results. But many growers believe that, with modern winemaking techniques, some of their indigenous grape varieties such as Aglianico, Barbera, Montepulciano d'Abruzzo, Nebbiolo, Sangiovese and Tocai Friulano have the potential to make stunning wines.

| VINTAGE CHART | |
|---|---|
| The comments shown here apply only to the red wines. Most Italian whites should be drunk as young as possible. | |
| 1988 Very good | 1977 Terrible (apart from |
| 1987 Good | some Veronese wines |
| 1986 Good | and Chianti – some of |
| 1985 Very good | which were excellent) |
| 1984 Very poor | 1976 Good |
| 1983 Very good | 1975 Very good |
| 1982 Good – but better | 1974 Very good |
| than 1983 for Brunello | 1973 Average |
| 1981 Good (superb for | 1972 Variable – some good, |
| Chianti Ruffino, only | most poor |
| good for Classico) | 1971 Outstanding |
| 1980 Poor | 1970 Good |
| 1979 Good | 1969 Good |
| 1978 Outstanding | |

# NORTH-WEST ITALY

*T*his is one of Italy's most important red wine regions, and can be split into four main areas: Piedmont, Lombardy, Liguria and Valle d'Aosta. The big, full-bodied red wines of North-West Italy complement the fabulous local food available which includes lots of game, blue cheese and truffles.

### ∽ PIEDMONT (PIEMONTE) ∽

This is the most important of the four regions in fine wine terms. Its name means 'foothills', and these slopes are ideal for successful vinegrowing. Apart from Asti, Piedmont is not an important region for white wines, although some interesting oak-aged Pinot Bianco and Chardonnay wines are beginning to emerge from top producers like Pio Cesare and Gaja. In addition, there are some very exciting dry whites being made from grapes like Arneis and Favorita. Traditionally, however, it's the reds that are

responsible for the region's reputation.

There are three main grape varieties used in Piedmont, two red and one white:

#### Nebbiolo
This grape variety produces full-bodied, tarry wines with tough, cherry-stone-like fruit and quite a bit of tannin. Contrary to popular belief, the colour of genuine Nebbiolo wines is not inky-black, but can be anything from light red to reasonably deep red. It is the grape responsible for one of Italy's greatest classic wines, Barolo, one of the six DOCG wines. The best Nebbiolo are those that come from around the town of Alba. It takes several years (sometimes as many as 20) for the harsh tannin and acidity of Barolo to soften out and the fruit come through, although now some producers are starting to leave the wine in contact with the skins for shorter periods to reduce the tannin levels.

# NORTH EAST AND NORTH WEST ITALY

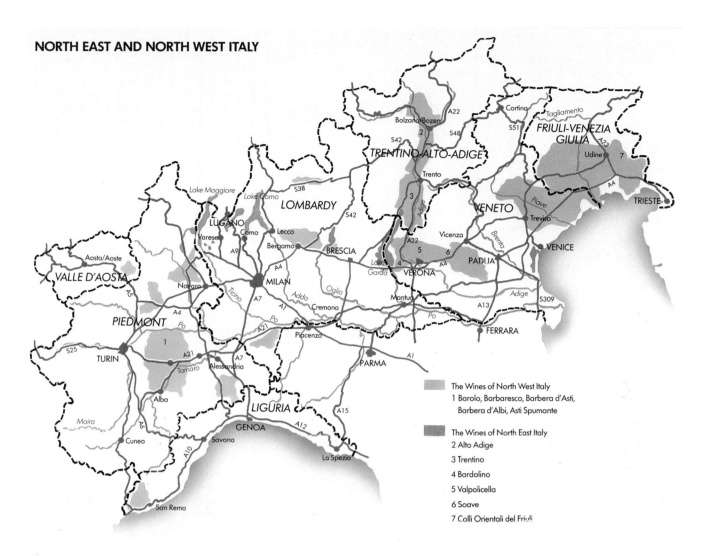

The Wines of North West Italy
1 Barolo, Barbaresco, Barbera d'Asti,
  Barbera d'Albi, Asti Spumante

The Wines of North East Italy
2 Alto Adige
3 Trentino
4 Bardolino
5 Valpolicella
6 Soave
7 Colli Orientali del Friuli

*Cantina Aldo Conterno in Monforte d'Alba in Piedmont.*

Nebbiolo is also responsible for Barbaresco, another DOCG wine, and named after the village of the same name. Made from pure Nebbiolo, Barbaresco tends to be less fierce than Barolo with slightly less tannin, so it can be enjoyed earlier. Some of the best wines come from Angelo Gaja.

Other wines made from Nebbiolo include the lighter Carema, Gattinara (smooth and fruity but tannic wines), Spanna (a delicious *vino da tavola*), and the light but fruity Roero and Nebbiolo d'Alba.

### Barbera

This is much more prolific than Nebbiolo in the region and is often a welcome change if you've been tasting Nebbiolo-based wines all day, because, although it is high in acidity, it is low in tannin and has a plummy fruity character. Some of that tannin can be replaced by ageing the wine in French barrels, a practice that is gaining popularity in the region. Among the best examples are those from Asti, Alba and Monferrato.

### Moscato

This is the Italian name for the aromatic Muscat grape that produces the well-known light, sweet, grapey sparkling wine, Asti Spumante. High in natural sugar with enough acidity to provide balance, this grape makes sparkling wines with low alcohol of around 7 per cent, making Asti a favourite aperitif wine. Huge amounts of this wine are made using a variation of the *charmat* method (see page 12). Moscato d'Asti is similar to Asti but less fizzy. Drier sparkling wines (which are known as *spumanti secchi*) are made around Turin using several grape varieties. These include Pinot Bianco and Pinot Grigio, Riesling and Chardonnay.

### ∽ LOMBARDY (LOMBARDIA) ∾

To the north-east of Piedmont is the plain of the Po valley, to the north of which the Swiss Alps rise up. The region's centre is the sprawling city of Milan. Apart from the regions of Oltrepò Pavese (south of the River Po), Valtellina (much further north, close to Switzerland) and Lugana (on the shores of Lake Garda), the biggest vineyard areas are to be found near Lago d'Iseo, to the north-east of Milan: Valcalepio and Franciacorta.

### ∽ OLTREPO PAVESE ∾

The best wines from this region are varietal reds such as Barbera, Bonarda and white from Cortese, Pinot Bianco, Pinot Grigio and Riesling. Much of Oltrepò Pavese's produce is sold to companies in Piedmont and is used to make sparkling wine.

### ∽ VALTELLINA ∾

Nebbiolo is grown in this region, with the most impressive wines coming from the superior vineyards of Grumello, Inferno, Sassella and Valgella. The vineyards are so steep that a glass of tannic Valtellina Superiore is necessary to help steady those suffering from vertigo! Sfursat, a bitter

*Vineyards near Barbaresco in Piedmont where the Nebbiolo grape flourishes.*

sweet red wine made from semi-dried grapes, comes from Valtellina.

Also look out for the red wines, Franciacorta Rosso and Valcalepio, both of which contain either Cabernet Franc or Cabernet Sauvignon, though most often the former.

### ∽ LUGANA ∾

Floral whites from the Trebbiano grape are made in this DOC on the shores of Lake Garda.

### ∽ LIGURIA ∾

A small attractive region of mountain slopes, Liguria's wines are a far cry from the quality possible in Piedmont or Lombardy. It is better known for its tourist industry than its wines. The locals and tourists generally drink most of the region's production.

### ∽ VALLE D'AOSTA ∾

Situated high in the mountain slopes, this region produces everyday drinking wines. The tourists generally help out the locals with any wine surplus to their requirements and very little is exported.

## RECOMMENDED WINES (DOC, VT & Brands)
### R=red; W=white; Ro=rosé; S=sparkling; E=everything

### Luguria

| | |
|---|---|
| R | Barbera di Lenero |
| W | Cinqueterre |
| W | Pigato di Albenga (or Ligure) |
| R, W | Riviera Ligure di Ponente |
| R | Rossese di Dolceacqua (or Dolceacqua) |
| R | Terizzo |

### Lombardy (Lombardia)
Non-Italian grape varieties grown: Merlot, Müller-Thurgau, Riesling, Cabernet.

| | |
|---|---|
| R | Barbera |
| R | Botticino |
| W | Clastidium |
| R, W | Colle del Calvario |
| R, W, Ro | Colli Morenici Mantovani del Garda |
| R, W, SW | Franciacorta |
| R | Groppello |
| SR | Lambrusco Mantovano |
| W, SW | Lugana |
| R | Maurizio Zanella |
| W | Moscato di Scanzo |
| R | Narbusto |
| E | Oltrepò Pavese |
| R | Riviera del Garda Bresciano |
| R | Ronco di Mompiano |
| R, W | San Colombano al Lambro (or San Colombano) |
| W | Tocai di San Martino della Battaglia |
| R, W | Valcalepio |
| R | Valtellina |
| R | Valtellina Superiore (including Grumello, Inferno, Sassella and Valgella) |

### Piedmont (Piemonte)
Non-Italian grape varieties grown: Cabernet Sauvignon, Chardonnay, Riesling, Müller-Thurgau.

| | |
|---|---|
| W | Arneis dei Roeri |
| R | Barbaresco |
| R | Barbera d'Alba (and d'Asti) |
| R | Barolo |
| R | Boca |
| R | Bramaterra |
| R | Bricco del Drago |
| R | Bricco Manzoni |
| R | Briona |
| R | Caramino |
| R | Carema |
| W, SW | Cortese di Gavi (or Gavi) |
| R | Dolcetto (plus d'Acqui, d'Alba, d'Asti, di Diano d'Alba, di Dogliani, delle Lange Monregalesi & di Ovada) |
| R | Fara |
| W | Favorita |
| SR | Freisa (plus d'Asti and di Chieri) |
| R | Gabiano |
| R | Gattinara (including Monsecco) |
| W | Gavi dei Gavi |
| R | Ghemme |
| R | Grignolino d'Asti |
| R | Lessona |
| W, SW | Moscato d'Asti (or Moscato d'Asti Spumante, including Asti & Asti Spumante) |
| R | Nebbiolo d'Alba (including Roero) |
| R | Rouchet |
| R | Spanna |

### Valle d'Aosta
Non Italian grape varieties grown: Pinot Noir, Müller-Thurgau, Gamay.

| | |
|---|---|
| R | Aymaville |
| R | Chambave Rouge |
| R | Crème du Vien de Nus |
| R | Donnaz |
| R | Enfer d'Arvier |
| R | Gamay della Valle d'Aosta |
| W | Maivoisie de Nus |
| W | Moscato di Chambave |
| W | Passito di Chambave |
| R | Petit Rouge |
| R | Sang des Salasses |
| R | Torrette |
| R | Vin des Chanoines |
| W | Vin du Conseil |

## RECOMMENDED PRODUCERS

### Liguria
Agricoltura di Cinqueterre
Cozzani
Eno Val d'Arroscia
Enzo Guiglielmi
Michele Guiglielmi
Parodi
Rolandi
Tognoni

### Lombardy
Barboglio de Giaocelli
Bellavista
Berlucchi
Ca' del Bosco
Castello di Grumello

Castello di Luzzano
Longhi-De Carli
Monte Rossa
Montorfano

### Piedmont
Elio Altare
Produttori di Barbaresco
Marches di Barolo
Cavallotto
Ceretto
Fratelli Cigliutti
Domenico Clerico
Aldo Conterno
Giacomo Conterno
Luigi Dessilani

Duca d'Asti
Angelo Gaja
Gancia
Gavi di Gavi
Bruno Giacosa
Franco-Fiorina
Fontanafredda
Martini
Bartolo Mascarello
Giuseppe Mascarello
Castello di Neive
Pasquero Secondo
Pio Cesare
Renato Ratti
Alfredo Roagna
Luciano Sandrone

Vallana
Vietti
Roberto Voerzio

### Valle d'Aosta
Clos Gerbore
Don Augusto Pramotton
Ezio Voyat
Filippo Garin
Instituto Agricole Régional Aoste
Gratien Montrosset
Aldo Perrier
La Sabia
Thomain

# North-East Italy

### ✎ TRENTINO-ALTO ADIGE ✎

**Alto Adige**

Situated in the craggy Dolomite mountains, this is a breathtakingly beautiful region to visit, with steep slopes covered in vines, often trained on high pergolas. The Etsch (also kown as the Adige) river has cut a narrow valley through the mountains, creating all sorts of micro-climates in the region. This area, Italy's most northerly, is also known as the Südtirol by the German-speaking natives. As a result of its proximity to Austria several Germanic varietals are grown here including Riesling, Sylvaner, Traminer (although this could be said to be a native) and even Müller-Thurgau, a grape that appears to make much more aromatic and interesting wines at such a height. Other white grapes include Moscato, Pinot Blanc and Chardonnay. The wines tend to be aromatic, although those made from the Chardonnay grape are lighter than their French counterparts.

Black grape varieties include the Vernatsch, which makes light reds like Lago de Caldaro, and Lagrein, which makes both rosés and heavy, earthy reds. Also found are grassy flavoured Cabernet Franc, Cabernet Sauvignon as well as some Pinot Noir and Merlot.

**Trentino**

This Italian-speaking region is flatter than the Alto Adige and produces large quantities of wine, which tend to be less exciting and of lower quality than the Südtirol wines. Similar grape varieties are planted with the addition of some indigenous ones and where producers restrict the yields, some good wines can be made. Sparkling wine is also made, some of it *méthode champenoise*.

### ✎ VENETO ✎

This is a large area, containing the attractive walled town of *Romeo and Juliet* fame, Verona. Most of the vineyards are in the south of the region, planted on the alluvial plains. Veneto is the home of three of Italy's best known wines: Soave, Bardolino and Valpolicella. Regrettably all three have suffered in quality because of their own popularity.

### ✎ FRIULI-VENEZIA GIULIA ✎

This is one of Italy's most exciting wine regions, boasting lots of noble grape varieties. The noble grapes planted here have been in place ever since the growers replanted after phylloxera. The largest area, Grave del Friuli, can produce all levels of wine, mainly varietals, whose quality depends entirely on the skill of the winemaker.

As in any other region it's often a better bet to look for the name of the grower, rather than the region, on the label. This will often give you a much more reliable indication of the quality of the wine.

Many of the top wines come from Colli Orientali del Friuli, a hilly region near the Yugoslavian border. This region makes both stylish single variety whites as well as good reds. Other good varietal reds come from the Collio Goriziano zone (or Collio) and Schioppettino. Top whites include Ronco della Acacie and Vintage Tunina, arguably Italy's greatest dry white.

### ✎ SOAVE ✎

Soave is made from the Trebbiano and Garganega grapes, both relatively bland, but the best single-vineyard examples where yields are restricted have a far greater concentration of fruit, and are crisp and zippy with a citrusy tang. The best wines are suffixed by Classico, coming from the hillier region.

### ✎ BARDOLINO ✎

This wine used to be more popular than it is today. Originally the grapes came from a town of the same name on Lake Garda, although today this light red wine comes from a much wider area. A Bardolino wine may also be rosé, and is sometimes slightly sparkling.

### ✎ VALPOLICELLA ✎

The best Valpolicella comes from the Classico area, a hilly region that produces some quality grapes, and it's a more full bodied red than Bardolino.

Recioto della Valpolicella is made from bunches of grapes that are picked and then left to dry. The raisin-like grapes can make either a sweet wine or a dry one, which is known as Amarone.

But there's more to this region than the famous three. Lots of producers are making excellent *vini da tavola*, often from grape varieties not permitted within DOC rules. There are now some interesting wines made from the Cabernet Sauvignon grape, some of which are DOC, including wines from Lison-Pramaggiore and Brentino (DOC Breganze).

## RECOMMENDED WINES (DOC, VT & Brands)
R=red; W=white; Ro=rosé; S=sparkling; E=everything

### Friuli-Venezia Giulia
Non-Italian grape varieties grown: Cabernet Franc, Cabernet Sauvignon, Merlot, Sauvignon Blanc, Traminer, Chardonnay, Pinot Nero, Malbec, Müller-Thurgau.

| | |
|---|---|
| R, W, Ro | Aquilea |
| R, W | Carso |
| R, W | Collio Goriziano (or Collio) |
| R, W | Colli Orientali del Friuli |
| R | Dragarska |
| R | Franconia |
| R, W | Grave del Friuli |
| R, W | Isonzo |
| R, W | Latisana |
| R | Montesclapade |
| W | Picolit |
| R | Schioppettino |
| W | Terre Alta |
| W | Vintage Tunina |
| R | Zuc di Volpe |

### Trentino-Alto Adige
Non-Italian grape varieties grown: Cabernet Franc, Cabernet Sauvignon, Merlot, Sauvignon Blanc, Traminer, Chardonnay, Pinot Noir, Malbec, Müller-Thurgau, Sylvaner, Riesling.

| | |
|---|---|
| R, W | Alto Adige (Südtiroler) |
| R, Ro | Caldaro or Lago di Caldaro (Kalterersee) |
| R | Castel San Michele |
| R | Casteller |
| R | Colli di Bolzano (Bozner Leiten) |
| W | de Vite |
| R, W | Foianeghe |
| W | Fontana d'Oro |
| W | Goldenmuskateller |
| R | Kolbenhofer |
| R | Maso Lodron |
| R | Meranese di Collina (Meraner Hügel) |
| R | Morlacco |
| R | Novaline Rubino |
| R | Pragiara |
| R | San Leonardo |

### Trentino-Alto Adige—continued

| | |
|---|---|
| R | Santa Maddalena (Sankt Magdalener) |
| R, W | Sorni |
| SW | Spumante (not DOC) |
| W | Terlano (Terlaner) |
| R | Teroldego Rotaliano |
| R, W | Trentino |
| R, W, Ro | Valdadige (Etschtaler) |
| W | Valle Isarco (Eisacktaler) |
| R | Vicariati |
| Ro | Vin dei Molini |

### Veneto
Non-Italian grape varieties grown: Cabernet Franc, Cabernet Sauvignon, Chardonnay, Merlot, Sauvignon Blanc, Pinot Noir, Pinot Blanc.

| | |
|---|---|
| R, Ro | Bardolino |
| W | Bianco di Custoza |
| R, W | Breganze |
| R, W | Capitel San Rocco |
| R | Capo del Monte |
| R | Castello di Roncade |
| R, W | Colli Berici |
| R, W | Colli Euganei |
| W, SW | Gambellara |
| R | La Pergole |
| R | La Sassine |
| W | Lessini Durello |
| R, W | Lison-Pramaggiore |
| R, W, SW | Montello e Colli Asolani |
| R, W | Piave |
| R | Quarto Vecchio |
| R | Raboso |
| W | Recioto Bianco di Campociesa |
| W | Recioto della Valpolicella & di Soave |
| W | Soave |
| W | Soave Classico |
| W | Torcolato |
| R | Valpantena |
| R | Valpolicella |
| R | Venegazzu della Casa |

*Picking Corvina grapes in Veneto to make Valpolicella.*

*Palu in the Valle di Cembra in the Trentino region, against the stunning backdrop of the Dolomite mountains.*

---

## RECOMMENDED PRODUCERS

**Friuli-Venezia Giulia**
Ca' Bolani
Cappelletti
Castelvecchio
Collavini
Comelli
Borgo Conventi
Giovanni Dri
Giacomelli
Girolamo Dorigo
Carlo Drufovka
Livio Felluga
Ronchi di Fornaz
Eno Friulia
Gradnik
Gravner
Jermann
Plozner

Abbazia di Rosazzo
Mario Schiopetto
Giuseppo Toti
Volpe Pasini
Puiatti
Radikon

**Trentino-Alto Adige**
Antinori (sparkling)
Barone de Cles
Ricardo Battitotti
Bollini
Conti Bossi Fedrigotti
Cavit
Foradori
Guerrieri Gonzaga
Joseph Hofstätter
Frescobaldi (sparkling)

Kuenburg
Lagariavini
Lageder
Letrari
Conti Martini
Niedermayr
Pojer and Sandri
Instituto San Michele
   all'Adige
Armando Simoncelli
Herbert Tiefenbrunner
de Tarczal
Walch
Zeni

**Veneto**
Allegrini
Anselmi

Bertani
Bolla
La Fattoria
Conte Loredan Gasparini
Guerrieri-Rizzardi
Paolo de Lorenzi
Maculan
Masi
Fattoria di Ogliano
Pieropan
Giuseppe Quintarelli
Santa Margherita
Santa Sofia
Santi
Fratelli Tedeschi
Torresella
Venegazzù
Zenato

# THE REST OF ITALY

## WEST CENTRAL:
### LATIUM (LAZIO), TUSCANY (TOSCANA) AND UMBRIA

The big exciting area in West Central Italy is Tuscany, once famous (or infamous) for Chianti. But now Tuscany is the home to some really remarkable unorthodox red and white wines, outside the DOC and DOCG regulations, using both Italian (mainly Sangiovese) and other (Cabernet Sauvignon and Chardonnay) grapes. This trend was started back in 1948, with the pioneering work of the Marchesi Incisa della Rocchetta who planted the vineyard that was to produce Sassicaia, a big, rich, classy wine made from 100 per cent Cabernet Sauvignon. Many other producers have followed suit (Antinori being one of the first with Tignanello with 20 per cent Cabernet), and there are now plenty to choose from (see table). Some of Tuscany's best modern style wines are made from 100 per cent Sangiovese. The unifying factor in all these new super wines is that they are all aged in small oak barrels. Unfortunately these wines are not cheap, but they *are* worth the money, and are some of Italy's finest wines. Tuscany is also home to the deservedly famous and long-lived Brunello di Montalcino, as well as the equally famous but sometimes overrated Vino Nobile di Montepulciano.

Umbria and Latium, known for Orvieto and Frascati (both fairly bland white wines), are not principally quality wine regions. There are of course exceptions, and Umbria's leading light is Lungarotti, a company producing some excellent and innovative wines. Also noteworthy are Bigi, Montoro, Ruggero Veneri and Adanti. Latium's only two outstanding wines are Fiorano and Torre Ercolana, the latter being produced only in minuscule quantities (less than 1,500 bottles a year!).

## EAST CENTRAL:
### ABRUZZI, EMILIA ROMAGNA AND MARCHE

Emilia-Romagna is the most important of these three regions, with some very exciting varietal wines, and others. It is the home of Lambrusco which, while not about to set the world on fire in qualitative terms, has been immensely successful, particularly in North America and Britain. Many consumers like its low alcohol, slightly fizzy character and find it less demanding than still wines.

The Marches is only known for Verdicchio, a dry, crisp white, which can be recommended from a good producer. But it has a couple of secret weapons up its sleeve with Rosso Cònero and Rosso Piceno, both very attractive red wines. Abruzzi has lagged behind on the quality front, but some of the Rossi (from the Montepulciano grape) being produced in large quantities show promise.

## SOUTH:
### APULIA (PUGLIA), BASILICATA, CALABRIA, CAMPANIA, MOLISE, SARDINIA (SARDEGNA), SICILY (SICILIA)

These seven regions, the most southerly in Italy, produce a vast quantity of wine, but much less than the north of any serious quality, with only a few exceptions the most notable being Sicily's Regaleali. The climate is too hot for anything really interesting to emerge, although Sardinia has shown that the adoption of cool fermentation techniques can produce wines that are at least light, clean and fresh. Perhaps if more modern techniques were introduced these areas could consequently produce better results and more satisfying wines.

*Vineyards in Tuscany, famous for producing Chianti. Today, however, many exciting non-DOC wines are emerging from this region.*

## RECOMMENDED WINES (DOC, VT & Brands)
R=red; W=white; Ro=rosé; S=sparkling; E=everything

### WEST CENTRAL
### Tuscany (Toscana)
Non-Italian grape varieties grown: Cabernet Sauvignon, Chardonnay, Merlot.

NB: Wines marked with an asterisk are Tuscany's new breed of oak-barrel-aged varietal wines, made by just one producer in each case – the name shown is the brand name.

| | | | |
|---|---|---|---|
| W | Bianco Vergine della Valdichiana | R | Morillone* |
| R | Borgo Amorosa* | R | Mormoreto* |
| R | Cepparello* | W, SW | Moscadello di Montalcino |
| R | Brunello di Montalcino | R | Palazzo Altesi* |
| R | Bruno di Rocca* | R | La Pergole Torte |
| R | Brusco dei Barbi* | R, W | Pomino |
| R | Cabreo Podere il Borgo* | R | Querciagrande* |
| | | R | Rosso di Montalcino |
| W | Cabreo Vigneto la Pietra* | R | Sammarco* |
| | | R | Sangioveto delle Torri* |
| R | Capanelle Rosso* | | |
| R | Carmignano | R | Sangioveto di Coltibuono* |
| R | Chianti (plus Classico) | | |
| | | R | Sassicaia* |
| W | Colline di Ama* | W | Sassolato* |
| R | Coltassala* | R | I Sodi di San Niccolo* |
| R | Concerto* | | |
| R | La Corte* | R | Solaia* |
| W | Le Crete* | R | Solatio Basilicata* |
| R, W | Elba | R | Tavernelle* |
| R | Flaccianello della Pieve* | R | Tignanello* |
| | | W | Torricella* |
| W | Fontanelle* | R | Vigorello* |
| R | Ghialie della Furba* | W | Villa di Capezzana* |
| R | Grattamacco* | R | Vinattieri Rosso* |
| R | Grifi* | W, SW | Vernaccia di San Gimignano |
| R | Grosso Sanese* | | |
| R, W, Ro | Maremma | W | Villa Antinori Bianco |
| R, W | Monte Antico | | |
| R, W | Montecarlo | W | Vin Santo |
| R | Morellino di Scansano | R | Vino Nobile di Montepulciano |

### EAST CENTRAL
### Emilia Romagna
Non-Italian grape varieties grown: Cabernet Franc, Cabernet Sauvignon, Merlot, Chardonnay, Pinot Blanc, Sauvignon, Riesling, Pinot Noir, Müller-Thurgau.

| | |
|---|---|
| W | Albana di Romagna |
| R | Barbarossa di Bertinoro |
| W, SW | Bianco di Scandiano |
| R, W, SW | Colli Bolognesi |
| R, W, SR, SW | Colli di Parma |
| R, SR | Colli Piacentini |
| SR, SW, SRo | Lambrusco (including L. Grasparossa di Castelvetro, L. Reggiano, L. Salamino di Santa Croce & L. di Sorbara) |
| R | Ronco Casone, R. dei Ciliegi and R. della Ginestre |
| R | Rosso Armentano |
| R | Sangiovese di Romagna |
| W, SW | Trebbiano di Romagna |

### SOUTH
### Apulia (Puglia)
Non-Italian grape varieties grown: Malbec, Cabernet Franc, Pinot Blanc, Chardonnay

| | | | |
|---|---|---|---|
| R | Aleatico di Puglia | R, Ro | Orta Vova |
| R, Ro | Alezio | W | Ostuni (Bianco Di Ostuni) |
| R, Ro | Brindisi | | |
| R, W, Ro | Cacc'e Mitte di Lucera | R | Ostuni Ottavianello |
| R | Castel del Monte | R | Portulano |
| R, Ro | Copertino | R | Primitivo di Manduria |
| R, W, Ro | Donna Marzia | | |
| R, W | Favonio | Ro | Rosa del Golfo |
| R | Il Falcone | R | Rosso Barletta |
| R, W, Ro | Leverano | R | Rosso Canosa |
| W, SW | Locorotondo | R | Rosso di Cerignola |
| W, SW | Martina or Martina Franca | R, W, Ro | Salento |
| | | R, Ro | Salice Salentino |
| R, Ro | Matino | R, Ro | Squinzano |
| W | Moscato di Trani | R | Torre Alemanna |
| R | Nardò | R | Torre Quarto |

*The Selvapiana Estate in Tuscany where Chianti is produced.*

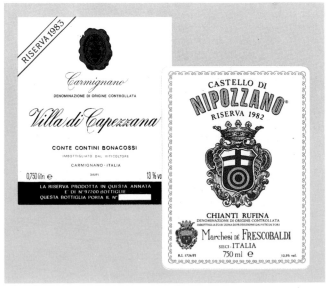

*V*iews over the south east of Siena in Tuscany.

## RECOMMENDED PRODUCERS

**Tuscany (Toscana)**
Altesino
Amorosa
Avignonesi
Badia a Coltibuono
Barone Ricasoli
Biondi-Santi
Boscarelli
Capannelle
Castelgiocondo
Castellare di Castellina
Castello dei Rampolla
Castello di Cacchiano
Castello di Ama
Castello di Fonterutoli
Castello di Rampolla
Castello di Querceto
Castello di Volpaia

Castello Vicchiomaggio
Fassati
Fontodi
Fratelli Bologna
  Buonsignori
Isole e Olena
Lisini
Marchesi Antinori
Marchese Frescobaldi
Marchesi Incisa della
  Rocchetta
Melini
Monte Vertine
Podere Il Palazzino
Podere Capaccia
Poggio Antico
Ruffino
San Felice

San Paolo in Rosso
Tenuta Caparzo
Tenuta Il Poggione
Vechie Terre di Montefili
Villa Banfi
Villa Cafaggio
Villa Cilnia
Villa di Capezzana
Vinattieri

**Emilia Romagna**
Baldi
Bruno Negroni
Cesare Raggi
Fattoria Paradiso
Luzzano
Moro
Spalletti

Terre Rosse
Vallania
Vallunga

**Apulia (Puglia)**
Felice Botta
Calò
Baron Bacile di Castiglione
Cirillo-Farrusi
Tenuta di Mitrano
Riforma Fondiaria
Rivera
Simonini
Strippoli
Taurino
Vinicola Amanda
Vinicola Miali
Conti Zecca

# AUSTRALIA

NTIL THE LAST FEW YEARS most of the world (with the notable exception of Australia) thought that Australian wines were to be laid down and forgotten about (for ever!). Australians had a reputation for downing gallons of home-produced lager (tinnies) in bars, and for producing quantities of dubious wines with imitative names like 'Burgundy' or 'Chablis'.

But many non-Antipodeans would be surprised to learn that Australia has been producing wines seriously for over a century (firms like Brown Brothers were established in the 19th century), and in fact the first vines were planted in Australia in the late 18th century.

But the dreadful reputation of Australian wines was established by the androgynous, characterless and quite frankly appalling wines (these were the rule, not the exception) made until the early 1960s. It was only from this date on that Australian winemakers started to take wine seriously and, with the odd exception like Penfold's Grange Hermitage, it has only been in the 1980s that the rest of the world has really found out about them.

The revolution in quality terms has been immense. Australia now boasts some of the world's most talented and knowledgeable winemakers, trained at their own wine school at Roseworthy in South Australia and they are producing every style of wine imaginable. All the latest winemaking technology is to be found in Australia and has produced sensational results, especially for white wine production where it is essential to have temperature-controlled fermentation. The Australians are also extremely knowledgeable as to the effects different types of oak can have on the wine, and are refining their wood ageing process all the time.

And the Australians, true to form, are not hide-bound and tied to outmoded traditions, unlike many European winemakers. They are constantly experimenting with planting different grape varieties in different climatic areas, and take notice of the results.

## ∾ CLIMATE AND GEOGRAPHY ∾

Australia is a very large country, boasting just about every geographical and climatic variation, so the winemakers have a larger choice of options than one perhaps imagines – many people's image of Australia is just that it is all blisteringly hot. However, some of the southern regions are actually cooler than the classic French wine regions. The grapes that produce the best wines are those grown in the more temperate climates and as a result the best vineyards are in the cooler southern part of the continent, and normally in the coastal regions.

Australia is made up of seven states: Western Australia, South Australia, New South Wales, Victoria, Tasmania, Northern Territory and Queensland. The latter two states are too northerly for serious winemaking, so are not mentioned here.

*The old still house at the Seppeltsfield winery. This is one of the original wineries of the Barossa Valley in South Australia.*

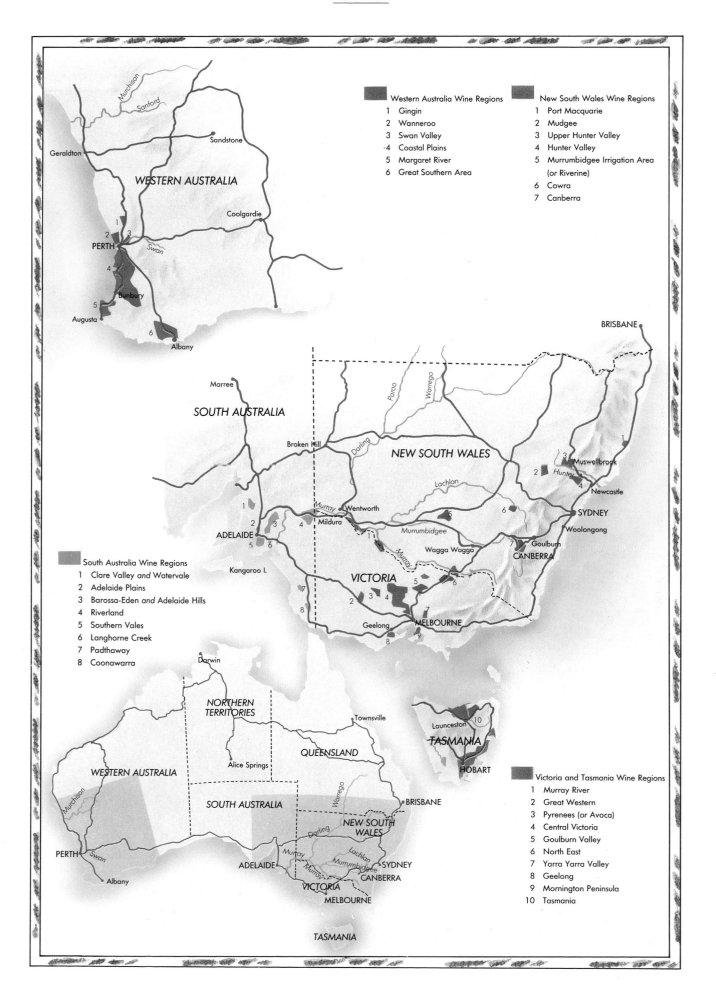

Western Australia Wine Regions
1  Gingin
2  Wanneroo
3  Swan Valley
4  Coastal Plains
5  Margaret River
6  Great Southern Area

New South Wales Wine Regions
1  Port Macquarie
2  Mudgee
3  Upper Hunter Valley
4  Hunter Valley
5  Murrumbidgee Irrigation Area (or Riverine)
6  Cowra
7  Canberra

South Australia Wine Regions
1  Clare Valley and Watervale
2  Adelaide Plains
3  Barossa-Eden and Adelaide Hills
4  Riverland
5  Southern Vales
6  Langhorne Creek
7  Padthaway
8  Coonawarra

Victoria and Tasmania Wine Regions
1  Murray River
2  Great Western
3  Pyrenees (or Avoca)
4  Central Victoria
5  Goulburn Valley
6  North East
7  Yarra Yarra Valley
8  Geelong
9  Mornington Peninsula
10 Tasmania

∽ STYLES OF WINE & GRAPE VARIETIES ∽

Almost all Australia's best wines are named after the grape they are made from, so they are known as 'varietals'. And the wines that have won the hearts of wine-drinkers worldwide in the 1980s are the whites, especially the Chardonnays. Australian Chardonnays from top producers have beaten traditional white Burgundies hands down in tastings. But there are also some classic reds made from Cabernet Sauvignon and Shiraz (the French Syrah), a grape that does well in some parts of Australia. Shiraz is the grape of the famous Grange Hermitage from Penfolds.

Sometimes people group Australian and Californian wines together, saying they are the same style. Indeed ten years ago, this was often the case. Both countries were going for an upfront fruit approach. But now the Australians have realized that there is more to great wines than full ripe fruit and have refined their wines, making them much more complex.

The following grape varieties tend to produce the best quality wines currently made in Australia, but many other varieties are grown. **Dry white:** Chardonnay, Gewürztraminer, Muscat, Sémillon, Chenin Blanc, Rhine Riesling, Sauvignon Blanc. **Sweet white:** Muscat, Orange Muscat, Riesling. **Red:** Cabernet Sauvignon, Merlot, Malbec, Shiraz (also known as Hermitage), Pinot Noir.

# SOUTH AUSTRALIA

South Australia produces more wine than any other Australian state, and is responsible for over 50 per cent (more than 24,000,000 cases a year) of all the wine produced in Australia. Although much of this is bulk wine, produced in the Riverland area, there are plenty of smaller producers (and some which are not so small) producing really exciting good quality wines. These include Berri Estates, Hardy's, Henschke, Kaiser Stuhl, Krondorf, Lindemans, Leo Buring, Orlando, Penfolds, Petaluma, Pewsey Vale, Pirramimma, Rosemount, Seaview, Seppelt, Wolff Blass, Wynns and Yalumba. And the range of wines available for South Australia is astonishing, with all of these

producers producing a multitude of medal-winning wines.

∽ GEOGRAPHY ∽

The wines of South Australia, which covers the central southern part of Australia, are mostly produced within about 120 kilometres of Adelaide, with the exception of Padthaway/Keppoch and Coonawarra which are about 200 and 300 kilometres respectively to the south-east.

The winegrowing areas range from the enormous (Riverland), to medium sized (Barossa-Eden, Adelaide

*The ultra modern Penfolds winery in the Barossa Valley.*

Hills and Southern Vales-Langhorne Creek), to small (Adelaide Plains, Clare Valley and Watervale, Coonawarra and Padthaway/Keppoch). And it tends to be the smaller ones that produce the best wines.

## Riverland

This produces vast quantities of cheap, well-made, everyday wine, from several varieties, although Muscat and Shiraz are among the most popular. Water from the Murray river is used to irrigate the area.

## The Adelaide Plains

This region produces what is arguably Australia's most famous wine, Max Schubert's Grange Hermitage from Penfolds. But although this wine still includes grapes from the original Shiraz vineyard in Adelaide now, as is common practice in most of Australia, top-quality grapes are bought in from Barossa, Clare, Langhorne Creek and McLaren Vale and then blended.

## Barossa

The Barossa is responsible for over 25 per cent of Australia's grape production and as a result there is a huge variety of different styles of wines from this region. As well as producing masses of fortified wine (although the demand for these wines is starting to slow down) good Shiraz wines are made. Now both Cabernet and Pinot Noir (a grape that is being increasingly planted in Australia) are planted as well as more Sémillon, Chardonnay and Riesling, the best examples of the latter now coming from the cooler vineyard sites in the hills. Many regions think of Barossa as the main source of cheap table wines, and mould their style on the current trends in the Barossa. And because Barossa's quality is constantly improving this is having a positive knock-on effect on other regions within Australia.

## Adelaide Hills

In the Adelaide Hills Brian Croser, one of Australia's great winemakers, is causing shock waves throughout the wine world with his Petaluma wines, made from grapes from Coonawarra and Clare as well as his *méthode champenoise*

wines from the Piccadilly vineyards. Once you've tasted this stylish fizz it comes as no surprise to learn that the Champagne company Bollinger has a share in it.

## Southern Vales and Langhorne Creek

While the Southern Vales and Langhorne Creek region (including McLaren Vale) are one of Australia's traditional winemaking regions, new styles of wines are being developed here. This is the region that's the home to top winemakers like Geoff Merrill and Greg Trott (of Wirra Wirra) as well as the older companies like Pirramimma and Hardys. The rich, meaty Shiraz wines that characterized this region in the past are being replaced by more elegant reds and stylish whites made from Sauvignon Blanc and Sémillon.

## Clare Valley and Watervale

Clare Valley and Watervale produce some of the best zippy Rhine Rieslings, crisp, herbaceous Sauvignon Blancs from Barry and Quelltaler, the latter also making a rich, ripe, oaky Chardonnay. Red wines fare less well and tend to be tough and unyielding, but recent plantings of Merlot are helping to soften the wines. Some producers have started making *maceration carbonique*-style light reds that come as a shock to the tough Australian palate but please wine-drinkers more accustomed to European-style wines.

## Padthaway/Keppoch

Padthaway (also known as Keppoch) lies to the north of Coonawarra and the acres of machine-harvested grapes are largely controlled by Hardy's, Seppelt and Lindeman's, all of whom are known for their Chardonnays. But it's worth looking for the Sémillon wines from this region which can be very good.

## Coonawarra

Coonawarra produces very good wines both from the large companies like Lindemans and Mildara and from the smaller ones like Bowen Estate. Here the Cabernet Sauvignon and Shiraz reign supreme making rich, berry-flavoured reds.

*Grapes are often harvested at night to avoid the extremes of the daytime temperatures.*

## CLIMATE

The climate of South Australia varies from the unbearably hot (not suitable for quality wine-production) to cooler, more temperate regions (Coonawarra and Padthaway/Keppoch) which tend to produce the most elegant wines.

## STYLES OF WINES

In common with most of Australia's wine-producing regions virtually every style of wine is produced here, from dry white to ultra-sweet white, to red. You can find luscious Padthaway/Keppoch Rhine Riesling Beerenauslese from Hardy's, elegant but buttery Show Reserve Chardonnay from Rosemount in Coonawarra, massive and powerful Cabernet Sauvignon-Shiraz from Wolff Blass and long-lasting Grange Hermitage from Penfolds.

Wine of every quality level is produced as well: the Riverland area is responsible for huge quantities of indifferent bulk wine, whereas Padthaway/Keppoch, Coonwarra and Barossa produce some of Australia's finest wines.

| IMPORTANT WINE REGIONS | |
| --- | --- |
| Adelaide Plains | Padthaway |
| Barossa-Eden & Adelaide Hills | Riverland |
| Clare Valley and Watervale | Southern Vales-Langhorne Creek (including McLaren Vale) |
| Coonawarra | |

## RECOMMENDED PRODUCERS

| Winery | Area | Winery | Area |
| --- | --- | --- | --- |
| Jim Barry | Clare Valley and Watervale | Maxwell | Southern Vales-Langhorne Creek |
| Barossa Valley Estates | Barossa-Eden & Adelaide Hills | Geoff Merrill | Southern Vales-Langhorne Creek |
| Berri Estates | Riverland | Mildara | Coonawarra |
| Bowen Estate | Coonawarra | Mountadam | Barossa |
| Brands Laira | Coonawarra | Norman's (inc Chais Clarendon) | Southern Vales-Langhorne Creek |
| Château Reynella | Southern Vales-Langhorne Creek | Orlando | Barossa-Eden & Adelaide Hills |
| Coriole | Southern Vales-Langhorne Creek | Penfolds | Barossa-Eden & Adelaide Hills |
| D'Arenberg | Southern Vales-Langhorne Creek | Petaluma | Barossa-Eden & Adelaide Hills |
| Elderton | Barossa | Pewsey Vale | Barossa-Eden & Adelaide Hills |
| Richard Hamilton | Southern Vales-Langhorne Creek | Pirramimma | Southern Vales-Langhorne Creek |
| Thomas Hardy | Riverland + Padthaway | Quelltaler | Clare Valley and Watervale |
| Henschke | Barossa-Eden & Adelaide Hills | Redman | Coonawarra |
| Hill-Smith | Barossa-Eden & Adelaide Hills | Renmano | Riverland |
| Hollick | Coonawarra | Rosemount | Coonawarra |
| Kaiser Stuhl | Barossa-Eden & Adelaide Hills | Roseworthy College | Adelaide Plains |
| Katnook | Coonawarra | Rouge Homme | Coonawarra |
| Kay Brothers | Southern Vales-Langhorne Creek | Saltram | Barossa-Eden & Adelaide Hills |
| Kidman | Coonawarra | Seaview | Southern Vales-Langhorne Creek |
| Tim Knappstein | Clare Valley and Watervale | Seppelt | Padthaway |
| Krondorf | Barossa-Eden & Adelaide Hills | S. Smith & Son | Barossa-Eden & Adelaide Hills |
| Leasingham | Southern Vales-Langhorne Creek | Watervale | Clare Valley and Watervale |
| Leconfield | Coonawarra | Wolff Blass | Barossa-Eden & Adelaide Hills |
| Peter Lehmann | Barossa | Wirra Wirra | Southern Vales-Langhorne Creek |
| Lindemans | Clare Valley and Watervale + Padthaway | Wynns | Coonawarra + Padthaway |
| Leo Buring | Barossa-Eden & Adelaide Hills | Yalumba | Barossa-Eden & Adelaide Hills |
| Marienberg | Southern Vales-Langhorne Creek | Yaldara | Barossa-Eden & Adelaide Hills |

*Vineyards stretch for miles across the Barossa Valley in South Australia.*

# VICTORIA AND TASMANIA

Victoria is Australia's smallest state, and produces only a seventh of the quantity of wine produced by South Australia and New South Wales. But it's no dwarf in quality terms and boasts several well-established wine companies like Brown Brothers (established 1889 and now run by the fourth and fifth generations of the family), Château Tahbilk (est. 1860) and Morris Wines (est. 1859). And some of the more recently established wineries have an interesting story like Taltarni, founded by the sons of Château Lafite-Rothschild's technical director in 1972.

Tasmania is still a very small producer, having been established only recently, but there appears to be great potential for quality wines and it's just beginning to be considered as a serious wine-producing area. It has the benefit of a temperate climate and, being cooled by the sea, does not experience the intense heat of the mainland areas.

*Grapes about to be pressed at Brown Brothers in Milawa, Victoria.*

## IMPORTANT WINE REGIONS

| | |
|---|---|
| Central Victoria | Murray River |
| Geelong | North East |
| Goulburn Valley | Pyrenees (or Avoca) |
| Great Western | Tasmania |
| Mornington Peninsula | Yarra Yarra Valley |

## RECOMMENDED WINERIES

| Winery | Area |
|---|---|
| Baileys | North East |
| Balgownie | Central Victoria |
| Bannockburn | Geelong |
| Brown Brothers | North East |
| Château Remy | Pyrenees |
| Château Tahbilk | Goulburn Valley |
| Château Yarrinya | Yarra Yarra Valley |
| Coldstream Hills | Yarra Yarra Valley |
| Craiglee | Central Victoria |
| Delatite | Victoria |
| Dromana | Mornington Peninsula |
| Elgee Park | Mornington Peninsula |
| Heathcote | Central Victoria |
| Heemskerk | Tasmania |
| Henke | Victoria |
| Hickinbotham | Geelong |
| Flynn & Williams | Central Victoria |
| Idyll | Geelong |
| Jasper Hill | Central Victoria |
| Knight's Wines | Central Victoria |
| Lindemans | North East |
| Main Ridge | Mornington Peninsula |
| Merricks | Mornington Peninsula |
| Merricks Estate | Mornington Peninsula |
| Montara | Great Western |
| Mount Chalamber | Great Western |
| Mount Mary | Yarra Yarra Valley |
| Pipers Brook | Tasmania |
| Seppelt | Great Western |
| Taltarni | Pyrenees |
| Tisdall | Victoria |
| Virgin Hills | Central Victoria |
| Wantirna | Yarra Yarra Valley |
| Yarra Yering | Yarra Yarra Valley |
| Yeringberg | Yarra Yarra Valley |

## ❧ CLIMATE ❧

Victoria's climate ranges from the very hot inland conditions in the north to milder, more temperate climates nearer the coast. Naturally this produces a wide range of wines. One of Victoria's greatest assets is its versatility.

## ❧ STYLES OF WINE & GRAPE VARIETIES ❧

The north-east produces vast quantities of sweet fortified wines made from the Muscat and Muscadelle (tokay) grapes. Both Brown Brothers and Orlando have flaunted popular opinion by planting some of their vineyards in the foothills of the Australian alps, and are producing wines from several noble grape varieties. Many, however, would put this success down to winemaking, rather than the climate.

The central vineyards produce a startling variety of wines from many of the well-respected names, like Seppelts who produce a delicious sparkling wine using the three Champagne grapes, Pinot Noir, Pinot Meunier and Chardonnay. Excellent full-bodied reds are made in this region, epitomized by Taltarni in the Pyrenees, Château Tahbilk in the Goulburn Valley and the John Walker's Walkershire Cabernet and Shiraz blend.

The southern coastal climate wines are typified by the excellent wines of the Yarra Valley, only seen abroad fairly recently, which show great promise, as do the wines from the Mornington Peninsula.

The best wines are made from the following grapes: *Dry white:* Chardonnay, Gewürztraminer, Muscat, Sémillon, Chenin Blanc, Riesling, Sauvignon Blanc. *Sweet white:* Muscat, Orange Muscat, Riesling. *Red:* Cabernet Sauvignon, Merlot, Malbec, Shiraz, Pinot Noir.

# New South Wales

New South Wales is home to many of Australia's smaller top white wine producers. Names like Peterson's, Rosemount, Wollundry and Rothbury instantly conjure up recollections of some really exciting buttery Chardonnays I have drunk.

The main vineyard areas are smaller and more spread out than most of the other states, and produce a vast range of different styles. The best vineyards tend to be on the hills rather than the flat, and on the western slopes of the Great Western range are the vineyards of Bathurst-Orange, Cowra, Mudgee and Tumbarumba.

The Hunter Valley (particularly the Lower Hunter Valley) is the state's flagship quality region and is found on the eastern slopes, where the climate is much wetter. It used to be famous for its enormously big, typically hot climate Shiraz wines which were not very attractive and must have helped perpetuate the thinking that Australian wines should be laid down and forgotten about. But the region now produces really great Chardonnays, classy Shirazes and, more than anywhere else in Australia, magnificent dry but rich Sémillons. As wineries have been in existence in this region since the 1830s, the Hunter Valley was traditionally thought of as producing Australia's finest wines. Having said that, the planting of all the vineyard areas much further south (and the fact that today a wine-grower would probably not consider planting anywhere as far north as the Hunter) now mean that these wines have many convincing rivals from other regions.

The tiny Port Macquarie region has been neglected for decades but is worth a mention because of John Cassegrain. He established a winery in Port Macquerie in 1980 and the results so far are impressive, to say the least. It should be interesting to follow developments here.

The Murrumbidgee Irrigation Area (not the most romantic name in the world!) produces a very large quantity of cheap everyday wine of varying qualities, the best of

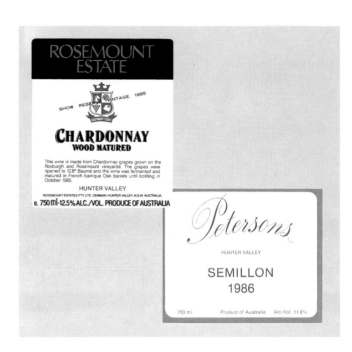

The main grapes are the same as the rest of Australia (see page 146), although there are also plantings of some more obscure varieties like Trebbiano and Verdelho.

| IMPORTANT WINE REGIONS | |
|---|---|
| Canberra | Mudgee |
| Cowra | Murrumbidgee Irrigation |
| Hunter Valley | Port Macquarie |

| RECOMMENDED WINERIES | |
|---|---|
| *Winery* | *Area* |
| Allandale | Hunter Valley |
| Amberton | Mudgee |
| Arrowfield | Hunter Valley |
| Botobolar | Mudgee |
| Brokenwood | Hunter Valley |
| Cassegrain | Port Macquarie |
| Château Francois | Hunter Valley |
| Craigmoor | Mudgee |
| De Bortoli | Murrumbidgee Irrigation Area |
| Hungerford Hill | Hunter Valley |
| Hunter Estate | Hunter Valley |
| Huntington Estate | Mudgee |
| Lake's Folly | Hunter Valley |
| Lindeman's | Hunter Valley |
| McWilliam's | Murrumbidgee Irrigation Area |
| Miramar | Mudgee |
| Montrose | Mudgee |
| Peterson's | Hunter Valley |
| Richmond Grove | Hunter Valley |
| Robson | Hunter Valley |
| Rosemount | Hunter Valley |
| Rothbury Estate | Hunter Valley |
| Tulloch | Hunter Valley |
| Tyrrell's | Hunter Valley |
| Wollundry | Hunter Valley |
| Wyndham Estate | Hunter Valley |

which comes from McWilliams and Wynns. While the region is looked down on somewhat by producers in other regions, when Chardonnay is in short supply they don't appear to mind buying in grapes from the Murrumbidgee Irrigation Area.

The most exciting quality wine from this region is de Bortoli's amazing Botrytis Sémillon. This very concentrated late harvest wine can rival some of the best Sauternes! And a few other producers have made some stunning late harvest Botrytis-infected Rhine Rieslings.

∽ CLIMATE ∽

The climate is more like southern France and northern Italy, without any really hot continental areas such as those found in inland Victoria. The Murrumbidgee Irrigation Area has its own micro-climate, and the introduction of irrigation has transformed a previously barren area into a lush area of vegetation.

*Rosemount Winery, one of the top wineries in the Upper Hunter Valley.*

# WESTERN AUSTRALIA

Although Western Australia is Australia's newest and most exciting state in terms of quality wines, the northern wine-growing area of the Swan River was established as long ago as 1829 by botanist Thomas Waters, one of the first colonists. He planted 40 acres of vines in the middle of what is now a suburb of Perth, and called the vineyard Olive Farm. And until only 20 years ago the nearby Swan River was the main quality wine-producing area of this isolated state. Two other important wineries which followed Waters' example in the 19th century were Sandalford and Houghton, both of which are still producing superb wines.

The area causing the real excitement today, however, is the Margaret River, about 150 miles south of Perth on the coast. The first vines were planted here by Dr Tom Cullity (founder of Vasse Felix) in 1967, following advice from the government agronomist Dr John Gladstones. Dr Gladstones' opinion was that the climatic conditions of Margaret River were remarkably similar to those of France's greatest table wine districts. This opinion has turned out to be remarkably accurate, and Margaret River soon became full of doctors planting vineyards! After Dr Cullity, Dr Kevin and Mrs Di Cullen founded Cullens Willyabrup, Dr Bill Pannell Moss Wood, and David and Sandy Hohnen Cape Mentelle. Since then a number of other wineries have sprung up, and the overall quality is outstanding.

There's a local saying that if you ever fall ill in Margaret River there's no need to go to a hospital, just find the nearest vineyard!

Although Western Australia's best vineyards are the Margaret and Swan Rivers there are other, larger, wine producing areas, although most of these do not produce anything of great interest. The only other region which appears to have potential is the cooler area around Mount Barker in the Great Southern Area, where Plantagenet and Forest Hill are already producing interesting wines.

*ABOVE: Cullens Willyabrup vineyards in the Margaret River area, with sheep grazing in the foreground.*
*LEFT: Most Australian wineries age their wines in new oak barrels, mainly from France.*

## ∾ CLIMATE AND GEOGRAPHY ∾

The two best quality vineyard areas of the Swan River and Margaret River have very different climatic conditions, with the Swan River being situated almost 200 miles to the north of Margaret River, meaning that former is inevitably much hotter. In spite of this, the Swan River is often clouded over, and every day around noon a wind known as The Fremantle Doctor sweeps in from the sea to cool the vineyards.

Margaret River, called after the small town of the same name, enjoys the cool European climate so accurately forecast by Dr Gladstones, and is ideal for growing classic French grape varieties.

## ∾ STYLES OF WINE & GRAPE VARIETIES ∾

The wines that have really made Western Australia famous outside Perth are the dry whites, and in particular the fabulous rich, buttery but elegant Chardonnays from Margaret River. But the Chardonnays from the Swan River should not be overlooked: they can be very nearly as good, with producers like Houghton and Sandalford producing exceptional whites as well as reds.

The reds from Western Australia, and in particular from Margaret River and the Swan River, tend to be more elegant and refined, less jammy than other Australian reds, and are capable of exhibiting more finesse.

The principal grape varieties grown in Western Australia are the same as those grown throughout Australia (see page 146), although there are some interesting smaller plantings of unusual grapes like Verdelho, Zinfandel, Touriga, Tinta Cão and Cabernet Franc.

### IMPORTANT WINE REGIONS

| | |
|---|---|
| Coastal Plain | Margaret River |
| Gingin | Swan Valley |
| Great Southern Area | Wanneroo |

### RECOMMENDED WINERIES

| Winery | Area |
|---|---|
| Alkoomi | Great Southern Area |
| Ashbrook | Margaret River |
| Capel Vale | Coastal Plain |
| Cape Clairault | Margaret River |
| Cape Mentelle | Margaret River |
| Château Xanadu | Margaret River |
| Cullens Willyabrup | Margaret River |
| Evans & Tate | Swan River + Margaret River |
| Forest Hill | Great Southern Area |
| Freycinet Estate | Margaret River |
| Gillespie | Margaret River |
| Happs | Margaret River |
| Houghton | Swan River + Great Southern Area |
| Jane Brook | Swan River |
| Leeuwin | Margaret River |
| Moss Wood | Margaret River |
| Olive Farm | Perth Suburbs |
| Peel Estate | Coastal Plain |
| Plantagenet | Great Southern Area |
| Redgate | Margaret River |
| Sandalford | Swan River + Margaret River |
| Vasse Felix | Margaret River |
| Westfield | Swan River |

*Evans and Tate vineyards in Swan Valley.*

# NEW ZEALAND

ntil very recently New Zealand was only known by foreigners for its lamb and its kiwi fruit. But recently New Zealand's white wines, and in particular the outstanding crisp, superbly vinified Sauvignon Blancs, have made an enormous impact on wine lovers the world over. Kiwi Sauvignon Blanc can rival the top French wines Sancerre and Pouilly-Fumé, and has been known to beat them in many a blind tasting.

Although vines were planted as long ago as 1819 at Kerikeri in the Bay of Islands, it is not certain whether or not wine was made from them. What is sure, though, is that James Busby, the founder of Australia's wine industry, arrived in New Zealand in 1832 and immediately planted a vineyard which soon produced wine. This was located at his home in Waitangi, also in the Bay of Islands, and so he was also the founder of New Zealand's wine industry.

After Busby a few other fledgling vignerons of various nationalities attempted to keep things ticking over, but were eventually defeated by phylloxera, oidium (one a louse, the other a mildew) and last, but not least, the very strong Temperance movement. By 1900 there was virtually no wine being produced in New Zealand, and it was only after the government enlisted the services of an oenologist from Dalmatia, Romeo Bragato, to find a cure for phylloxera that the industry started to revive. Bragato thought that the climatic conditions for wine production were excellent and heavily influenced the wine industry at that time, even though it was very small. But even with interesting plantings of Cabernet Sauvignon, Pinot Noir, Malbec, Shiraz and Chardonnay being recorded in 1902, the wine industry had to struggle against enormous forces like the law on total Prohibition, passed in 1919, and imports of cheap

*The Te Mata Coleraine vineyard based at Hawkes Bay on the North Island.*

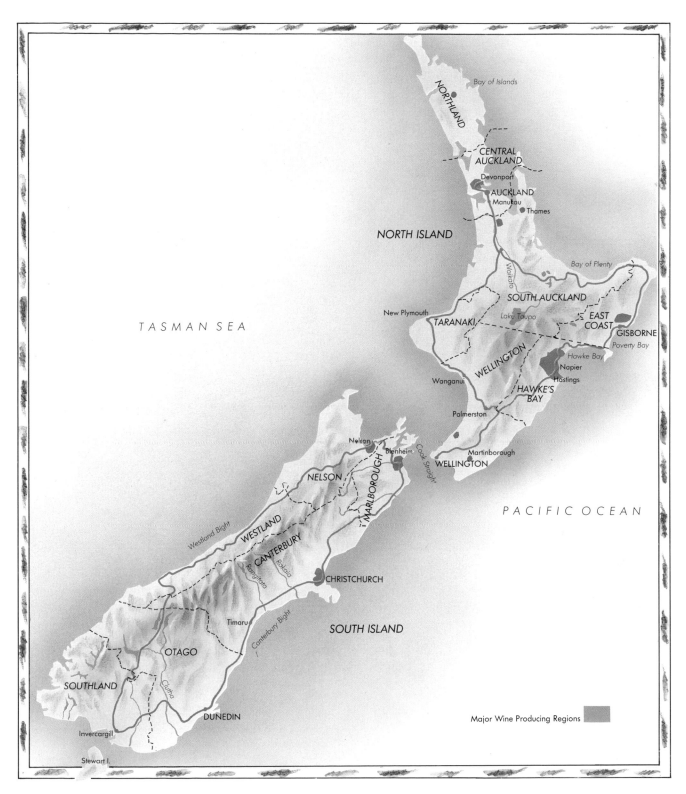

Major Wine Producing Regions

foreign wine. But New Zealand servicemen returning home thirsty after the First World War saved the wine industry, demanding the right to drink their nation's wine.

For most of this century New Zealand has produced only indifferent, very ordinary wines, most made from that dull grape the Müller-Thurgau, New Zealand's equivalent to the dreaded Liebfraumilch. But that's changing radically – in recent years the government has given grants to growers to uproot vineyards because of over-production of cheap, low-quality wine and many producers have

replaced their Müller-Thurgau with the increasingly popular noble grape varieties. This process, however, will take a long time to finally filter through to the consumer, and there is still a huge production of medium sweet Müller-Thurgau wines, all made using the standard German practice of adding Süssreserve. But luckily the majority of these indifferent wines are consumed locally.

The 1980s marked the renaissance of New Zealand's industry, with the emergence of top quality crisp herbaceous Sauvignon Blancs, fresh, steely Chardonnays and

oaky Sémillon wines. In addition there are some delicious dessert wines coming out of New Zealand, like Redwood Valley Late Harvest Rhine Riesling or Matua's sensational Late Harvest Gewürztraminer.

There are even some interesting reds, like Cabernet Sauvignon, Cabernet/Merlot and Pinot Noir just beginning to emerge. The best New Zealand winemaking today is of a very high standard, taking advantage of all the new technology, as well as using traditional maturing methods such as wood ageing. The old spectre of dull, boring wines is thankfully beginning to disappear.

Today over 85 per cent of New Zealand's wine production comes from just two huge companies, Montana and Corbans, both of whom produce quality wines. In addition a handful of smaller wineries have been established over the last few years, following the lead of Cloudy Bay.

## ∾ CLIMATE AND GEOGRAPHY ∾

New Zealand is divided into two islands, the North and the South. The wine industry was founded on the North Island and most quality producers are based there, many with their headquarters around the Auckland area. The South Island is the home to some important producers, too, notably Cooks (owned by Corbans), one of New Zealand's

first wine exporters.

The North Island's climate is slightly warmer, and quite a bit wetter than the South Island, but both islands are more temperate then either California's or Australia's winegrowing regions. This very important factor enables New Zealand to produce wine from European grape varieties that is more elegant, and has more potential, than either Australia or California. The whites have already proved their worth, and it remains to be seen if the reds will follow suit.

Although most of the North Island's producers are based around Auckland many of them buy grapes from the important vineyard areas of Hawkes Bay and Gisborne on the east coast. This will generally appear on the label, saying Producer X's Hawkes Bay (or Gisborne) Grape Variety (normally Chardonnay or Sauvignon). Even some of the South Island producers make wines from grapes grown in the North Island.

But the South Island, with its cooler climate and lower rainfall, is potentially *the* up and coming production area, with the region of Marlborough already well established. Some people think, judging by the *méthode champenoise* wines New Zealand has started to produce, that the South Island vineyards have the capability of producing New Zealand's answer to Champagne.

1987

NELSON

SAUVIGNON BLANC
WOOD AGED

*Redwood Valley Estate*

GROWN AND PRODUCED BY HERMANN AND AGNES SEIFRIED
UPPER MOUTERE, NELSON, NEW ZEALAND.
PRODUCE OF NEW ZEALAND

12% Vol.                                          750ml

BROOKFIELDS
CABERNET
MERLOT
HAWKES BAY

Alc. by Vol. 12.3%      1987      Contents 750 ml.
VINTED AND BOTTLED IN NEW ZEALAND BY
BROOKFIELDS VINEYARDS (1977) LTD, NAPIER.

ABOVE: *Vineyards of the Brancott Estate on South Island owned by Montana.*
BELOW: *Large stainless steel vats at Cooks Winery.*

## RECOMMENDED PRODUCERS

### North Island

| Winery | Based at |
| --- | --- |
| Babich | Auckland |
| Brookfield | Hawkes Bay |
| Collard Brothers | Auckland |
| Coopers Creek | Auckland |
| Corbans | Auckland |
| Delegat's | Auckland |
| De Redcliffe | Mangatawhiri Valley |
| Dry River | Martinborough |
| Glenvale | Hawkes Bay |
| Goldwater | Waiheke Island, Nr Auckland |
| Kumeu River | Auckland |
| Lincoln | Auckland |
| Matawhero | Gisborne |
| Matua Valley | Auckland |
| Mission | Hawkes Bay |
| Montana | Gisbourne |
| Morton Estate | Bay of Plenty |
| Ngatarawa | Hawkes Bay |
| Nobilo's | Auckland |
| Penfolds | Auckland |
| Selak | Auckland |
| St Nesbit | South Auckland |
| Te Mata | Hawkes Bay |
| Totara | Thames |
| Vidal | Hawkes Bay |
| Villa Maria | Auckland |

### South Island

| Winery | Based at |
| --- | --- |
| Cloudy Bay | Blenheim |
| Cooks | Te Kauwhata |
| Hunter's | Blenheim |
| Montana | Blenheim |
| Redwood Valley | Nelson |
| Stoneleigh | Marlborough |
| St Helena | Christchurch |
| Te Whare Ra | Blenheim |

# AMERICA

ENTION AMERICAN WINE and most people automatically think of California – the sunshine state that has made such inroads into the international wine scene over the last 10 to 15 years. But although California has a large wine production and is excellent at publicizing its wines, most of North America's states produce wines of some sort or another. Apart from California, other exciting states include Oregon, Washington and New York State, all of which are producing excellent, top quality wines.

North America's history of winemaking dates back to 1521, when invading Spaniards planted the first vines. The country's winemakers have had some fairly major obstacles thrown in their way over the course of the last century, including phylloxera and prohibition, but they have survived and are now prospering. It's really only in the last 20 years that the rest of the world has come to know and love American wines.

The United States of America's main wine-producing regions are: California; the North West (Oregon, Washington and Idaho) and the North East (New York State, Pennsylvania, West Virginia, Virginia and Maryland).

Canada also has two very small wine-producing regions, one in British Columbia and one at Niagara in Ontario, but as yet there is little to get excited about with Canada's wines.

*The colourful sign that greets you when you enter the Napa Valley in California.*

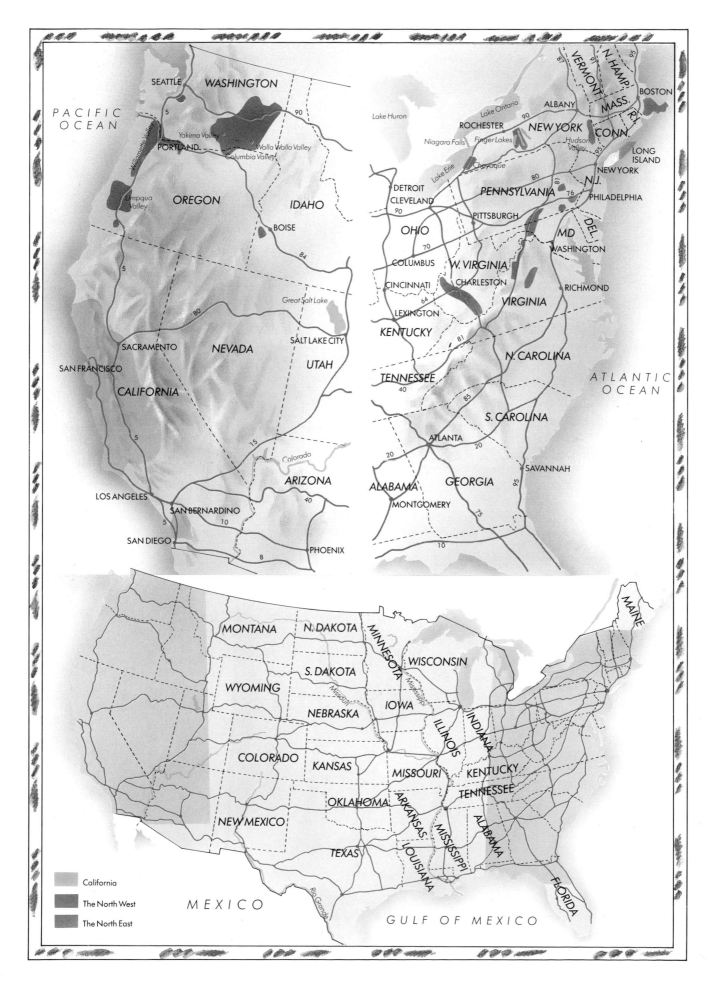

## ∾ THE MAIN GRAPE VARIETIES ∾

The indigenous varieties of North America are not *Vitis vinifera* (see the section on grape varieties) but a less 'noble' species, *Vitis labrusca*. This type of grape has a totally different taste. Many waves of immigrants had planted European varieties that were then wiped out by the phylloxera insect in the 19th century. Fortunately the native *V. labrusca* vines were immune to the disease so, after phylloxera had ravaged Europe, *V. vinifera* vines were grafted on to them. American rootstocks were in great demand from producers around the world, who followed the American lead.

The following includes the important grape varieties found in North America, though other varieties are grown. All those marked with an asterisk are more fully described in the section entitled *The Grape Trail* (see pages 15-24).

### Red grapes

**Alicante Bouschet**   This is a strange-tasting grape – you either love it or you hate it. It is a *teinture* (tincture) grape, in other words one with black flesh and juice which makes very deep coloured inky black wine.

**Barbera**   It seems strange to find an Italian grape in California, but the Barbera's natural acidity makes it very welcome for blending with grapes with lower acidity.

**Cabernet Franc***   Hardly planted at all but, along with Malbec, is blended with Cabernet Sauvignon in California's everlasting attempt to out-Bordeaux Bordeaux.

**Cabernet Sauvignon***   In California this takes on intense berry aroma, with minty eucalyptus overtones. It can make very rich, intense wine with a high alcohol content, although in cooler areas it can have more elegance. Heitz Martha's Vineyard, Mondavi Reserve or Grgich Cellars Cabernet Sauvignon are outstanding examples.

**Gamay Beaujolais**   Known throughout the rest of the wine world as the Pinot Noir*. Real Gamay* (as grown in Beaujolais) is not found in North America.

**Grenache***   See grape varieties, page 22.

**Mataro**   This is the Mourvèdre as found in the Rhône Valley and southern France.

**Merlot***   Not that widely planted (at least not when compared to Cabernet Sauvignon), it produces velvety smooth wines.

**Mission**   Planted by the Franciscan monks, this grape does not produce wine of any note.

**Pinot Noir***   This is probably the least successful grape variety in terms of taste, particularly in California. But Oregon's Pinot Noirs so far are stunning.

**Zinfandel**   Zinfandel is a phenomenon that, as far as I am aware, is peculiar to California, although there is a very small amount that has been imported into Australia. The Californians tend to look down on it because it is so widely planted and prefer to talk about and drink more noble grape varieties like Cabernet Sauvignon. It is an impressive grape variety because of its ability to produce innumerable different styles of wine and therefore it is often difficult to identify when tasted blind. It can produce both light Beaujolais-style wines through to extremely heavy, rich, tarry wines not dissimilar to those made from

*The tasting room of Le Reve Winery in Long Island, a firm favourite with the visiting tourists.*

the Syrah grape. In addition, more recently, it has been producing what the Caifornians call white Zinfandels but to you and me are in fact pink (or 'blush') wines which are slightly sweet. It's quite a difficult grape variety to describe – many people have described it as 'foxy', but as I've never smelt a fox I cannot comment on the accuracy or otherwise of that statement. When made in the full-bodied style it has a ripe plummy, musky, almost brambley fruit aroma which can become jammy when grown in very hot regions of the Central Valley of California.

### White grapes

**Chenin Blanc***   In California, this grape tends to have less acidity than it does in France because it gets more sunshine, but even so the grape's natural acidity makes it popular. Few fine Californian wines are made from this grape although it accounts for around 20 per cent of plantings. Much of it goes into 'jug' wines (cheap blended wines) although it is rarely named on the label.

**Emerald Riesling**   Used for much jug wine from the Central Valley, this is a cross between Muscadelle and Riesling and combines aroma with acidity and large yields.

**French Colombard**   This grape accounts for almost 40 per cent of the vines planted and, together with Chenin Blanc, is responsible for much of the jug wine of the region. It can produce either dry or off-dry wines, although few of them are of outstanding quality.

**Gewürztraminer***   The Californian examples rarely seem to exhibit the same spicy lusciousness shown by the top Alsace wines.

**Pinot Blanc***   When aged in oak this grape can show more style than many of the Alsace examples.

**Sauvignon Blanc***   While the early 'Fumé Blancs' (the common American term for this grape's wine) were green, grassy and wood aged, there is now a move afoot, led by certain producers like Mondavi, to soften the gooseberry-like fruit and produce a more elegant, complex wine.

**Sémillon***   This flourishes in California, and makes excellent wood-aged dry whites as well as botrytized sweet wines.

**White Riesling**   The best wines made with this grape (also known as the Johannisberg Riesling) are deliciously sweet late-harvest varieties.

# CALIFORNIA

California's wine history goes back further than many non-Americans might imagine – wines have been produced here since the late 18th century when Spanish missionaries planted vines in San Diego, but the industry proper was founded by the builder of California's first log house, George Calvert Young, who planted the first vines in Napa in 1838. By the 1850s his vineyard was producing 900 litres (200 gallons) of wine a year and 22,700 litres (500 gallons) by 1860. In the mid-19th century a number of vineyards were founded, including those owned by Frank E. Kellogg (1846), Colonel Joseph B. Chiles (1858), Judge J. H. McCord (Oak Grove), the Thomson Brothers (1852) and John M. Platchett (1853). By 1870 this was America's leading wine-producing state.

The Californian wine industry has survived the two scourges of phylloxera and prohibition better than most other states, the first by regrafting on resistant rootstocks and the second by sheer persistence. Wine was produced during prohibition, hiding behind the term 'sacramental' wine, supposedly produced for the church. Unfortunately prohibition meant that many of the better grape varieties

*Harvested grapes at Fetzer's Valley Oaks Winery.*

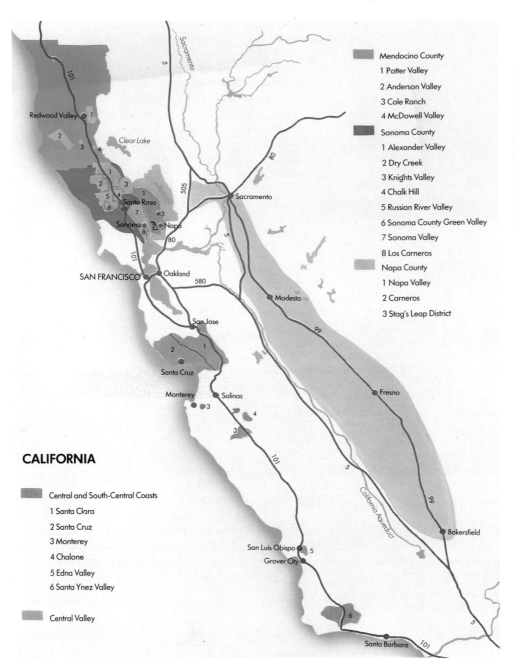

**CALIFORNIA**

Central and South-Central Coasts
1 Santa Clara
2 Santa Cruz
3 Monterey
4 Chalone
5 Edna Valley
6 Santa Ynez Valley

Central Valley

Mendocino County
1 Potter Valley
2 Anderson Valley
3 Cole Ranch
4 McDowell Valley

Sonoma County
1 Alexander Valley
2 Dry Creek
3 Knights Valley
4 Chalk Hill
5 Russian River Valley
6 Sonoma County Green Valley
7 Sonoma Valley
8 Los Carneros

Napa County
1 Napa Valley
2 Carneros
3 Stag's Leap District

*Robert Mondavi's Winery in the Napa Valley, where some of California's finest wines are produced.*

were uprooted and replaced with inferior ones. It took a good 40 years after prohibition was repealed in 1933 to replant the vineyards with quality varieties.

What makes California wines (and Australian) wines so 'user-friendly' today is the way the producers have marketed the 'varietal' concept of only using one type of grape in a wine and stating this firmly and clearly on the label. Many producers say that the person responsible for starting this habit was the wine shipper and writer Frank Schoonmaker who, in 1939, declined to patronize growers who continued to exploit the French terms like Chablis and Champagne, instead urging them to use the name of the grape variety.

Today huge amounts of wine are produced in California, but the vast majority of it is jug wine from the hot Central Valley. Many of the smaller 'boutique wineries' (they are even called that when they are enormous) were developed in the 1960s and now produce California's top wines.

With their own leading wine college at the University of California, Davis, Californian winemakers are among some of the most highly trained and skilled in the world and their example has led many of Europe's top winmakers to study there too. Among the invaluable research at Davis is a temperature scale dividing California's winegrowing regions into five climatic zones, as well as recommending which grape varieties can be best grown in each. The theory is that this combination would provide the ideal text book wines, and this is exactly what happened for a few years. Well-made quality wines were being produced, all with blockbusting fruit, bursting at the seams with the varietal characteristics.

Once the 'wow' of the wine world had calmed down (these wines particularly shocked the French by romping home in blind tastings), criticisms like blowsy, overblown, lacking complexity, too alcoholic, too much like ripe berry juice' began to be heard. Californian wines were in danger

of becoming too samey. Slowly, a few growers decided to throw their textbooks away and make wines with real 'soul', with some character and readily identifiable as being different to their neighbours' wines. They began by choosing slightly cooler vineyard sites, picking the grapes earlier and giving their wine less time in oak. As a result a whole host of first-class wines have started appearing, much more elegant and complex, more in line with the style of top European wines.

These growers (who include luminaries like Robert Mondavi), coupled together with a few with no formal training, have produced some of California's finest wines, ones that have broken out of the mould and are excitingly different.

The Californians have not been slow to combine their winemaking technology with very keen observations of their European counterparts. The quality of wine from California, while high already, seems set to really get under way as we prepare to enter the next century.

### Barrel-ageing

Californian winemakers major on barrel-ageing. Mondavi is known throughout the world for his eye-opening oak-ageing tasting seminar where he shows examples of the same wine after it has been matured in a variety of different wooden barrels. They are very keen on noting the difference the degree of 'toasting' makes, that is the amount the inside of the barrel has been charred. The top wines tend to be those matured in the more costly French barrels, which gives a more subtle nuance of oak to the wine.

The key to choosing Californian wines, as with any other wines, is to stick with the producers whose style you like. One grower's Cabernet, for instance, can be entirely different in style to his neighbour's from just down the road.

### ∽ CLIMATE AND GEOGRAPHY ∽

The closest California has come to any classification system is the introduction of 'Approved Viticultural Areas of the United States' (AVAs), of which there are currently around 100. However, the most important in quality terms are in the comparatively small North Coast area to the north of San Francisco (encompassing Mendocino, Sonoma and Napa) and the Central Coast, between San Francisco and San Luis Obispo. The Central Valley actually produces the most wine, largely jug wine of varying qualities from huge wineries like Gallo.

*The impressive Greystone Cellars; part of the Greystone Winery of the Christian Brothers in the Napa Valley.*

## ∽ THE NORTH COAST AREA ∽

### Mendocino County

The cooler region of the Anderson Valley is thought to be one of the most suitable vine-growing regions in Medocino. At least the Champagne house Louis Roederer certainly thinks so as they have made a massive investment of over 15 million dollars in Chardonnay and Pinot Noir vineyards and a winery to make their *méthode champenoise* wine. Although some areas are too hot for quality grapes, other vineyards areas are cooler because of their proximity to the coast, rating as the coolest regions (I and II) on the Davis scale. Fetzer in Redwood Valley make some impressive Cabernets, as do Edmeades Vineyards and Parducci Wine Cellars.

### THE AVAs OF MENDOCINO COUNTY

| | |
|---|---|
| Anderson Valley | Mendocino |
| Cole Ranch | Mendocino County |
| McDowell Valley | Potter Valley |

### Sonoma County

There are people (biased producers included) who feel that Sonoma has even more potential for producing great wines than Napa. Certainly the top wines currently coming out of this county are very impressive, and a quick glance at the list of names makes my mouth water. Sonoma has been somewhat overlooked in the past, possibly because of its large production of everyday wine. But since the rise of quality wines from wineries like Simi, the world has started to take more notice. One of the earlier wineries to produce top quality wine and achieve world-wide fame was Château St Jean, with its stunning white wines. Sonoma has a wide variation of climates and therefore produces many styles of wine. Some of the Cabernet-based blends I have tasted at Chalk Hill are among the best American wines I've come across and there's even an impressive *méthode champenoise* wine made at Iron Horse.

### THE AVAs OF SONOMA COUNTY

| | |
|---|---|
| Alexander Valley | Russian River Valley |
| Chalk Hill | Sonoma Coast |
| Dry Creek | Sonoma County Green |
| Knights Valley | Valley |
| Los Carneros | Sonoma Mountain |
| Northern Sonoma | Sonoma Valley |

### RECOMMENDED PRODUCERS

| | | |
|---|---|---|
| Adler Fels | Glen Ellen | Lytton Springs |
| Alexander Valley | Hacienda | Mark West |
| Clos du Bois | Hanzell | Matanzas Creek |
| Chalk Hill | Iron Horse | Pedroncelli |
| Château St-Jean | Jordan | Sam Sebastiani |
| Dion | Kenwood | Simi |
| Dry Creek | Kistler | Sonoma-Cutrer |
| Geyser Peak | Laurel Glen | Torres |
| | | William Wheeler |

*The modern Franzia Winery at Ripon, Central Valley.*

### Napa Valley

Driving along the highway through California's Napa Valley is like reading a Californian wine list, as the huge name plates of wineries rush by on either side of the road in rapid succession. The actual vineyards and wineries may be some distance away. The region stretches north to the town of Calistoga and south to Carneros. As a result there are a wide range of wines produced thanks to the different micro-climates. While Carneros, cooled by the bay breezes, is a Region I (on the Davis scale), Calistoga is hotter and is in Region III. The majority of vineyards are planted along the relatively narrow valley floor.

### THE AVAs OF THE NAPA VALLEY

| | |
|---|---|
| Carneros | Napa Valley |
| Howell Mountain | Stag's Leap District |
| Napa County | |

### RECOMMENDED PRODUCERS

| | | |
|---|---|---|
| Acacia | Domaine Chandon | Round Hill |
| Beaulieu | sparkling) | Rutherford Hill |
| Blue Heron | Far Niente | Schug |
| lake | Freemark Abbey | Saintsbury |
| Burgess | Grgich Hills | Schramsberg |
| Carneros Creek | Heitz | (sparkling) |
| Caymus | Mayacamas | Stag's Leap |
| Clos du Val | Mondavi | Sterling |
| Conn Creek | Montelena | Philip Togni |
| Cuvaison | Monticello | Trefethen |
| Diamond Creek | Phelps | ZD |

Napa, more than any other American wine-producing region, has been responsible for broadcasting the quality of America's wines abroad and there is no other Californian more directly involved in this process than the remarkable, tireless Robert Mondavi. This great man of wine has travelled the world, spreading the gospel of Californian wine and, back at home, producing some remarkable wines. He was the first to instigate a Cali-

fornian-French venture, when he launched Opus One in collaboration with the late Baron Philippe de Rothschild. His example has encouraged other top French winemakers to become involved in California, including Moët & Chandon (Domaine Chandon), Christian Moueix (Dominus) and Peter Sichel of Château Palmer.

### The Central and South-Central Coasts
The most important wine-producing regions in these two areas include Monterey, Chalone, Santa Clara, Santa Cruz, Edna Valley, and Santa Ynez Valley. There are some huge wine operations here, especially in the Central Coast region with the massive Paul Masson operation. There are also some exciting smaller wineries here, and the best wines include Ridge's sensational Cabernet, Calera's Pinot Noir, and Chalone's and Jekel's whites. The South-Central Coast's best wines include Edna Valley Vineyard's Pinot Noir, Firestone's delicious Pinot Noir and Chardonnay, and Zaca Mesa's fabulous Chardonnay.

### The Central Valley
This enormous area produces mainly jug wine in huge volumes, but there are a couple of interesting producers with very unusual wines. Angelo Papagni produces a remarkable massive, spicy red Alicante Bouschet that is unique in every respect, and Quady makes a delicious and distinguished sweet Muscat called Essensia.

### Other California regions

*The barrel room at Robert Mondavi's Winery in the Napa Valley.*

| RECOMMENDED PRODUCERS | | |
|---|---|---|
| Almaden | Felton-Empire | Mount Eden |
| Calera | Firestone | Vineyards |
| Callaway | Jekel | Angelo Papagni |
| Chalone | Kendall-Jackson | Quady |
| Concannon | Masson | Sanford |
| David Bruce | Mirassou | Wente |
| Edna Valley | Monterey | Zaca Mesa |
| Vineyard | | |

# THE PACIFIC NORTH-WEST

## ∽ OREGON ∽

One of the wine world's most exciting newcomers is Oregon. To give an idea of its potential, it's the only area in the world outside Burgundy to have succesfully produced top class Pinot Noir. In fact Joseph Drouhin, one of Burgundy's top producers, is so impressed by its potential that he has recently purchased a 40 hectare (100 acre) site and will be producing wine there.

Grapes have been grown in Oregon since 1859, but it has taken the best part of 130 years for the rest of the world to find out about its wines. It was as recently as the 1960s, when there was an exodus of winemakers from California, that many of today's wineries were established.

Oregon is sometimes grouped with Californian wines simply as 'American' wine, but the two states have very little in common, apart from sharing a border. Oregon has a much cooler climate than California, potentially better for quality wine production, although the climate is very varied. The feature most strongly influencing climate in Oregon is the Cascade Mountains, forming a natural barrier between the coastal region and the hot inland area, and also sheltering the western part of the latter.

The main growing region is the Willamette River valley, to the south of Portland, and between the Cascade Mountains and the much smaller Coastal Mountains of the Pacific coast. Here the climate is temperate, allowing the grapes to ripen slowly without producing too much alcohol. This is one of the main factors the growers cite as contributing to their success in producing complex and interesting wines, subscribing to the theory (also held in France's quality wine-producing areas) that grapes which ripen too early in the growing season will never match the complexity and finesse produced by those which have to struggle through to a late maturity.

## ∽ GRAPE VARIETIES AND STYLES OF WINE ∽

Although the region has a history of grape growing, it used to be poor quality *Vitis labrusca* grapes rather than the *V. vinifera* that were grown. Fortunately, some growers ignored the advice of University of California, Davis, who recommended that this region was suitable only for *V. labrusca* grapes. Instead, they planted Pinot Noir, Gewürztraminer, Pinot Gris, Chardonnay, Sauvignon Blanc and Riesling and have not looked back. It's Pinot

*New vineyards in the Willamette Valley, Oregon, planted by Robert Drouhin from Burgundy.*

*The irrigation of a circular vineyard at the Mercer Ranch Vineyards, in the Horse Heaven Hills, Washington.*

Noir that really put Oregon on the quality wine map, beating many a top red Burgundy in blind tastings. The most famous of these was in 1979 in Paris, where a 1975 Pinot from David Lett's Eyric Vineyard came second in a tasting of top red Burgundies. As one of the world's most difficult to grow varieties, this is no mean feat. While the Californians have trouble producing any really fine Pinot Noir, Oregon produces really impressive wines, full and earthy with the nuance of strawberries. Unlike California wines, which are often too high in alcohol and low in acidity, Oregon wines have the acidity necessary for a great wine. In Oregon, unlike most other new wine-producing areas, the two superstar grape varieties of the wine world, Chardonnay and Cabernet Sauvignon, fare less well, the latter rarely ripening properly. There is no doubt that this will be a state to watch out for in the future.

---

### THE AVAs OF OREGON

| Columbia Valley | Umpqua Valley | Willamette Valley |
|---|---|---|

---

### RECOMMENDED PRODUCERS

| Alpine | Eyrie | Rex Hill |
|---|---|---|
| Amity | Elk Cove | Tualatin |
| Benoit | Knudsen Erath | Tyee Wine Cellars |

---

## ❧ WASHINGTON ❧

Most of Washington's vines are grown inland, to the east of the massive Cascade Mountains in the Columbia Basin in what is a naturally semi-desert region. This is in total contrast to the temperate, coastal climate of Oregon. But man has been at work, harnessing the waters of the Columbia River to create extensive irrigation zones, and this is where the vines are grown.

Again, in contrast to Oregon, Washington has around 4,856 hectares (12,000 acres) of vineyards, compared to the former's meagre 1,200 hectares (3,000 acres), and the good news is that it is predominantly planted with *V. vinifera* grapes. Unlike California, where any land suitable for planting vineyards is at a premium, Washington's land is still relatively cheap and so there is the potential for far more quality vineyards. The main areas within the Colombian Basin, are the Walla Walla Valley and the Yakima Valley. With Columbia Valley, these two make up Washington's only three AVAs.

Grapes being grown in Washington include Chardonnay (when short of this grape, it is not unheard of for Napa wineries to buy it in from Washington), Cabernet Sauvignon, Pinot Noir, Sauvignon Blanc, Riesling (including some late harvest wines) and Chenin Blanc. The climatic condition of hot sunny days and fairly cold nights mean that the grapes are high in both sugar and acid, two factors rarely found together, but ideal for quality wine production. This factor, combined with the fact that noble grape varieties are being grown, indicates a rosy future for Washington's wines.

---

### RECOMMENDED PRODUCERS

| Arbor Crest | Preston | Salishan |
|---|---|---|
| Chinook | Quilceda | Snoqualmie |
| Columbia | Creek | |

---

## ❧ IDAHO ❧

The smallest of the northwest vineyards, Idaho has a continental climate of hot summers and very cold winters. As a result the vines (that have to brave the very low temperatures in winter) produce wines with good acidity and alcohol levels. The vineyards are at much higher altitudes than other neighbouring north west vineyards, and on sites in the Snake Valley River vineyards flourish at 2,000 feet. Although few wines have yet hit the export market, those Chardonnays and Cabernet Sauvignon wines I have tasted augur well for the future of Idaho's wines.

# THE NORTH EAST AND MEXICO

W hile many American states not mentioned in this book produce wine, they tend to use *V. labrusca* varieties and the wines are not up to the quality today's wine-lovers have grown to expect.

### ∾ NEW YORK STATE ∾

This is the leading wine force in the eastern states, particularly since the wide planting of *V. vinifera* that replaced some of the inferior *V. labrusca* in the 1970s, although there is still plenty of the latter planted. Although it has a continental climate with very cold winters, the State's abundance of large lakes like Erie mean a gentler microclimate prevails. The five principal wine regions in New York State are as follows, although they are split up into smaller AVAs.

The *Finger Lakes* area is known more by tourists for its scenery than for its wines and the *Chayaque* district sits in the western corner, near Ontario and next to Lake Erie. Then there are *Niagara County, Hudson Valley*, not far from Manhattan, and the east of *Long Island*.

It's estimated that over half of the State's grape produce (mainly the Concord, *V. labrusca* grape) is made into jam! Varietals are slowly catching on, and the Chardonnays in particular have received wide acclaim. The best wines often come from the smaller growers.

### ∾ MEXICO ∾

Wine has been made in Mexico since 1521, although many people assume its only nationally produced beverage is a spirit distilled from cactus juice, tequila. Today over 60,000 hectares (148,200 acres) are planted with vines although the bulk of the production is distilled. There are eight states growing vines and very slowly more quality *V. vinifera* grapes like Chenin Blanc and French Colombard are being planted, although they are still in the minority.

*ABOVE RIGHT: French oak barrels at Lenz Winery, Cutchague, Long Island.*
*RIGHT: The scenic vineyards on the west side of Lake Keuka, Hammondsport in the Finger Lakes area of New York.*

# SOUTH AMERICA

When anyone mentions American wine, people automatically tend to think of California. South America's best two wine-producing nations are Chile and Argentina. Both make superb wines, with Chile definitely having the edge on quality. The range of wine made is vast, with just about every conceivable grape variety being grown.

## ∽ CHILE ∽

One of the first indications Europeans had that Chile was capable of producing stunning wines was when Miguel Torres, of Spain's Penedés wine region's fame, invested in vineyards there and started producing some really excellent wines. However, the wine industry in Chile is not new, as vines were planted there in 1851 using imported European grape varieties, including all the classics: Cabernet Sauvignon, Merlot, Chardonnay, Sémillon and Sauvignon Blanc.

Chile is protected on all sides by natural barriers: the Andes to the east, the Pacific Ocean to the west, and the Atacama desert to the north. There are two main areas of production, the Central Valley which includes Maipo Valley, probably Chile's best known wine-producing area, famous for its red wine. The other main region is Secano, an area whose greatest potential lies in its production of classic white grape varieties.

Vines in Chile have a much longer life span than they do in Europe because the area is phylloxera-free. Instead of having to replant every 30 to 40 years, vines last over 100 years. They are planted in the volcanic soil in the valley floor of the Andes.

Using the classic varieties has meant that the wines of Chile are easy to sell in the 'varietal' conscious world.

**SOUTH AMERICA**

Secano
Maipo Valley

| RECOMMENDED PRODUCERS | |
| --- | --- |
| Concha Y Toro | Miguel Torrés |
| Cousño Macul | Los Vascos |
| Linderos | Viña Santa Helena |

## ∽ ARGENTINA ∽

Surprisingly Argentina is the fifth largest wine producing country in the world, but much of it never gets past the borders. The few wines that I have tasted have been impressive and range from Chardonnays and Sémillons to Cabernet Sauvignons (red *and* white) and Merlot. It will be interesting to see what comes out of Argentina over the next few years as there is obviously considerable potential here.

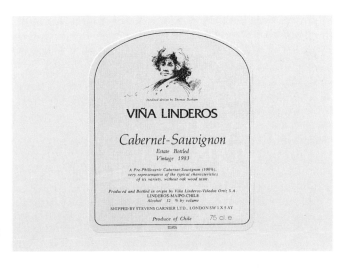

VIÑA LINDEROS

*Cabernet-Sauvignon*
Estate Bottled
Vintage 1983

A Pre-Phylloxeric Cabernet-Sauvignon (100%),
very representative of the typical characteristics
of its variety, without oak wood taste.

Produced and Bottled in origin by Viña Linderos-Viñedos Ortiz S.A.
LINDEROS-MAIPO-CHILE
Alcohol 12 % by volume

SHIPPED BY STEVENS GARNIER LTD., LONDON SW 1 X 9 AY

Produce of Chile        75 cl e

# OTHER WINE REGIONS

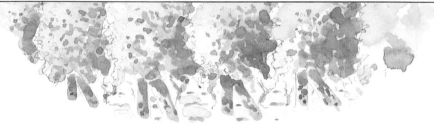

## EASTERN EUROPE

### ∾ BULGARIA ∾

Bulgaria is Eastern Europe's most exciting wine producer and the last decade has seen a dramatic increase in exports of her wines. While Bulgaria ranks as only the fourteenth largest wine producer in the world, it is the fourth largest exporter, behind only Italy, France and Spain. Great Britain is the largest importer of Bulgarian wine in bottle (buying over 1,500,000 cases in 1988) while West Germany takes the most in bulk.

The Bulgarians have been spot-on with giving the market what it wanted, and massive government subsidies have enabled them to undercut virtually every other wine of equivalent quality on the export markets. By opting for the varietal route they have ensured widespread interest in their wines.

The carrot that led the consumer to Bulgarian wines was their full-bodied but smooth Cabernet Sauvignon, full of varietal character and less than half the price of claret. Other varietals are quickly following Cabernet's success: soft, seductive Merlots, rich ripe Chadonnays, both oaked and un-oaked, clean, racy Rieslings and crisp, relatively full-bodied Sauvignon Blancs.

#### Geography and the wine regions
Most (55 per cent) of Bulgaria's wine is white, produced mainly in the east of the country, and the red wines come from vineyards in the north and the south.

There are five main regions of production: the Northern region, best known for its production of Cabernet Sauvignon; the Southern region, where Sakar Mountain Cabernet Sauvignon comes from; the Eastern region, well

*Vineyards overlooking the town of Tokaj on the river Tisza in Hungary.*

known for its production of Chardonnay, Riesling and Sauvignon; the South-Western region (the least important in terms of production), where Melnik is made, a red wine made from local indigenous grapes, and the Sub-Balkan region which produces some impressive sparkling wines.

### ∼ ROMANIA ∼

In theory Romania should have the potential to produce some fine wines, not dissimilar in style to Bulgaria's. But little Romanian wine seems to hit the export market. Noble grape varieties, as well as many unpronounceable indigenous ones, are planted in the vineyards, which cover almost the entire country.

### ∼ HUNGARY ∼

Bull's Blood and Tokay Aszú share the distinction of being Hungary's most famous wines. The former is a mass-production branded wine produced at Eger and, while perfectly palatable and having a history going back to 1552, it is not destined to set the fine wine world alight.

Tokay Aszú, on the other hand, is a legend in its own lifetime and comes from one of Hungary's smallest wine-producing areas. Tokay produces several wines apart from the famous, magnificently sweet, botrytis-infected version, including dry and medium sweet non-botrytized wines. The best wines are stored in remarkable labyrinthine tunnels hollowed out of the rock, where the bottles become covered with cobweb-like mould. The sweetness of Tokay is measured in puttonyos, with one putton being the driest. A putton is the wooden container in which the botrytized grapes are placed, and the ultra-sweet juice which runs off is used for sweetening the base wine for Tokay.

### ∼ YUGOSLAVIA ∼

The only Yugoslavian wine to have made any impression on the export market is Laski Riesling, a medium dry blend, not dissimilar to Liebfraumilch. But the country grows hundreds of other grape varieties, and has the potential to produce much more exciting wines than the world has so far witnessed.

### ∼ RUSSIA ∼

Although Russia is the third largest wine-producing country in the world, its wine is rarely found outside the country as it is largely drunk by the Russians. The huge quantity produced, however, is not quality-orientated and the few wines I have tasted are not impressive. The most palatable appear to be the sparkling wines.

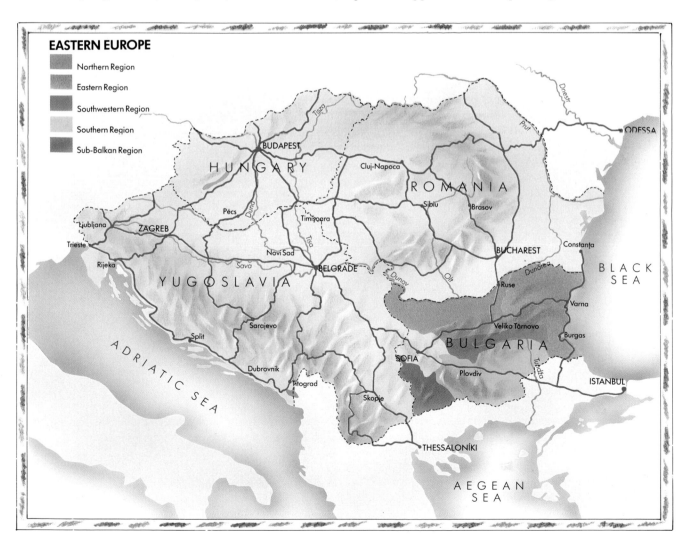

**EASTERN EUROPE**

- Northern Region
- Eastern Region
- Southwestern Region
- Southern Region
- Sub-Balkan Region

# SOUTH AFRICA

South Africa has a long history of winemaking, certainly dating back to 1659 when Jan van Riebeeck wrote about the making of the very first Cape wine. About 26 years later the now famous estate of Groot Constantia was founded by Simon van der Stel, determined to improve the (in his opinion) very poor standard of South Africa's wines. At one time during the 19th century, Britain was importing huge quantities of South African wine until a treaty was agreed with the French that dramatically reduced the amount. And even in the last few decades South African 'sherry' was very popular in Britain.

Today very little of South Africa's wine is exported due to the current social difficulties that the country faces. However, whatever one's political leanings, it cannot be disputed that South Africa makes some very fine wines and so it deserves a place in any serious and comprehensive wine study.

South Africa boasts a number of dedicated and dynamic winemakers who are frighteningly knowledgeable on any subject connected with vinification and viticulture. The best wines are stunning and world-class, although in volume terms most of the production is designed for local quaffing and is hardly exciting. Now the leading wine producers are moving away from the New World style of wine and striving for more elegance.

## GEOGRAPHY

South Africa's principal wine-producing areas are the Coastal and Breede River Valley Regions, located in the bottom south-west corner of the country and spreading out inland from Cape Town, although there are some vineyard areas further inland, approximately 900 kilometres north east of Cape Town, Pretoria called Orange River Valley, Douglas and Andalusia.

The main areas of the Coastal Region are Stellenbosch and Paarl, and those of the Breede River Valley Region are Worcester and Robertson. As well as vines, these areas are full of all sorts of other fruits like apricots, peaches and apples and, in Malmesbury, wheat fields, with more citrus fruits to the north around Clanwilliam. The area to the east of Cape Town, Little Karoo, is well known for its production of sweet sticky fortified wines. Hamilton Russell, however, has opened up the wine-producing areas and is producing wines of exceptional quality in his vineyards in the southeast at Hermanus in the Walker Bay ward (a ward is a smaller designated area within a district) of the Overberg district.

## GRAPE VARIETIES

### White wines

The main white grape variety is Chenin Blanc, accounting for over 30 per cent of all wine grapes grown in South Africa. Known also as Steen, this is the workhorse grape, used for making tens of thousands of gallons of dry to off-dry glugging whites, the best of which are made using cold fermentation. These wines are fresh, clean, zippy and relatively high in acidity. Chenin is also used to make sweet botrytis wines, the best of which is Nederberg's world famous Paarl Edelkeur.

Muscat d'Alexandrie, known locally as Hanepoot, is widely grown, making both fortified and non fortified white dessert wines. It's very aromatic and makes sticky, raisiny wines of both good and indifferent quality. Contrary to the popular belief, Hanepoot does not mean 'honeypot', but is thought to be a corruption of the Dutch word Hanekloot, meaning cock's testicle, which apparently is the same shape as the berries! Some innovative producers are now successfully making drier wines with Muscat d'Alexandrie.

Sauvignon Blanc is South Africa's most exciting white variety, especially when oak aged. Particularly impressive are the new Sauvignon Blanc plantings in Buitenverwachting and Klein Constantia, the former of which means 'beyond all expectations' – it seems to be living up to its name, at least in terms of the quality of the Sauvignon Blanc wines produced there. Because of the current popularity in South Africa for sparkling wines certain co-operatives are now making carbonated dry Sauvignon Blanc wines.

*Stellenbosch, one of the main areas of the Coastal Region.*

*Vineyards of the Delaire Estate, situated near Stellenbosch. The Simonsberg mountains can be seen in the background. Stellenbosch has the greatest concentration of South Africa's fine wine estates.*

**Chardonnay** Like many other countries, South Africa has latched on to Chardonnay and its winemakers are using it to make varietal wines, as well as some *méthode champenoise* wines where it is often mixed with Pinot Noir. There are also a few pure Chardonnay *méthode champenoises*. However, it still accounts for only a small percentage of vineyards planted.

### Red wines

**Pinotage** This is South Africa's very own grape variety, invented in 1925 by a Professor Perold who crossed Pinot Noir and Cinsault, a grape which Cape growers know also as Hermitage. The name is a mixture of parts of the words *Pin*ot and Hermi*tage*. It can produce both full-bodied dry reds and much sweeter wines with a heavy, baked aroma. It can also produce very tannic, plummy wines although the best are those where the vine's yield has been limited.

**Cabernet Sauvignon** This is either sold as a varietal or blended in with Merlot to make the Cape's version of the Bordeaux blends. Many South African Cabernets exhibit a browner colour (indicating low acidity or high pH levels) than Cabernets from elsewhere, and they can have a rather burnt aroma. Many of the best examples come from Stellenbosch, where the Simonsberg wines are richer than those from Heldelberg which tend to be lighter and more elegant.

**Syrah** Known locally as Shiraz, this gutsy red is used for many heavy smoky varietals and is also blended with Cabernet Sauvignon.

---

## RECOMMENDED PRODUCERS

There are five major wholesaler-producers:

*Gilbeys* including the Alphen, Bertrams ranges.
*Stellenbosch Farmers Winery* Nederburg and Zonnebloem ranges.
*Oude Meester Group* (Bergkelder) Fleur du Cap, Stellenryck, J.C. Le Roux ranges.
*Douglas Green of Paarl.*
*Union Wine* Bellingham and Culemborg.

*Private producers (including estates)*

| | | Co-Operatives |
|---|---|---|
| Allesverloren | Lemberg | Aan de Doorns |
| Altydgedacht | Lievland | Badsberg |
| Backsberg | Meerlust | Bolandse |
| Blaauwklippen | Middelvlei | Botha |
| Bon Courage | Neil Ellis Vineyard | Bottelary |
| Le Bonheur | selection | Du Toits Kloof |
| Boplaas | L'Ormarins | Nuy |
| Boschendal | Overgaauw | Robertson |
| Buitenverwachting | Rustenberg | Roodezandt |
| Clos Cabrière | Rust-en-Vrede | Rooiberg |
| Delaire | Simonsig | Simonsvlei |
| Delheim | Twee | Vlottenburg |
| Fairview | Jongegezellen | Vredendal |
| Groot Constantia | Uitkyk | Welmoed |
| Hamilton-Russell | Van Loveren | |
| Hartenberg | Villiera | |
| Jacobsdal | Vriesenhof | |
| Kanonkop | Welgemeend | |
| Klein Constantia | de Wetshof | |

---

# North Africa and the Mediterranean

North Africa and the Mediterranean certainly are not among the world's top-quality wine-producing areas – they have a very hot climate, normally too hot for successful wine production, and today the predominant religion (with the obvious exception of Israel) is Islam which does not allow alcohol.

But the Mediterranean was one of the earliest producers of wine in the world, pre-dating the now classic Europe by many centuries. Back when the eastern Mediterranean was well established as a wine-producer European wine would not have been called even 'New World' (as the Americas and the Antipodes are now known) – it wouldn't have been considered at all.

North Africa has been a wine-producer since Roman times, but production declined because of the still dominant Islamic religion. Starting in the 19th century, however, winemaking became re-established when Tunisia, Morocco and Algeria became French colonies. The immigrants inevitably wanted home comforts and one of the most important of these for the French was (and still is) wine. Naturally enough they planted vineyards to make their own colony-produced wine. As the vineyards became established they exported their wines in bulk (as well as in bottle) to their native France, where Burgundy producers bought them in huge quantities to blend in with their own weaker vintages. Lovers of old-style Burgundy are often unwitting aficionados of North African wine!

## ∾ NORTH AFRICA ∾

The vineyards of North Africa are mostly located along the Mediterranean and Atlantic coasts, and their most important production is beefy red and inelegant rosé.

### Algeria
Nothing of any great style is made here and little sign of the French colonialism of the past can be seen in the Algerian wines today. The reds are considerably better than the whites, and are full-bodied, rough but just about drinkable. One of the best reds is from Mascara.

### Morocco
Morocco is more suited to vine-growing than the other North African countries due to the cooling influence of the Atlantic. Some of the best wines are the dry, full-bodied rosés, like Rosé de Guerrouane, and the odd bottle of Cabernet Sauvignon can be found which is not unpleasant.

*The steep Moroccan Hill Vineyard in Morocco. Olive trees can also be seen growing here in the foreground.*

## Tunisia

Tunisia has a classification system based on the French *appellation contrôlée*, including AC, VDQS as well as Vins Supérieurs and Vins de Consommation Courante. As well as red and white wines, (the former are the better) a lot of sweet liqueur Muscats are made.

∽   THE MEDITERRANEAN   ∽

## Turkey

As anyone who has travelled to Turkey (now a popular holiday destination) knows, the local wines are nothing to write home about. It's best to stick to a good Turkish beer like Efes.

## Greece

In the days of Ancient Greece, this country used to produce some of the finest wines in the world, although I admit to not having tasted them – I'm relying on the testimony of worthies of the time like Homer and Plato. But in the 20th century Greece has been known only by the infamous wines Retsina and Demestica. The many other wines that are produced have tended to be flabby, oxidized and generally totally revolting. But there are some innovative producers appearing in Greece producing good, clean, fresh wines with character and one of the most interesting I have tasted is a very tasty white called Gentilini which is aged in new oak barrels and produced on one of the smaller islands.

*Vineyard terracing on the Greek island of Samos, where very sweet syrupy dessert wines and good dry table wines are produced.*

## Lebanon

Serge Hochar of Château Musar in Lebanon's Bekaa Valley has put Lebanon on the wine-producing map. He is making some excellent wine in this war-torn country whenever he can – often, after picking the grapes, he has been unable to get them to his winery because of crossing troop lines. Château Musar is a big, spicy, full-bodied red wine (although a white has occasionally been made) which stands up astonishingly well when put against more classic wines in blind tastings. It is made from a blend of Cabernet Sauvignon, Syrah and Cinsault, and has the capability to age very successfully. There are a few other wine-

makers but they are of little note – Hochar must be admired for his incredible perseverance and dedication in such adverse circumstances.

## Cyprus

No quality wines were produced here until recently, and Cyprus's wine industry was based almost totally on the dreadful 'Cyprus sherry'. But things are now changing and the wine industry has noted the needs of the new modern drinker who requires something fresher and lighter. New, better equipped wineries are beginning to appear, so perhaps in the future we can look forward to some more enjoyable wines from Cyprus. *V. vinifera* grapes are planted, and so the potential for reasonable quality is there.

## Israel

The best of the few wines I have tasted from this country come from vineyards high up in the Golan Heights, where the grapes are not so much at the mercy of the scorching sun. The Yarden Sauvignon Blanc is crisp and grassy, on a par with many a Sancerre, while the Gamla Cabernet Sauvignon is rich and full of ripe blackcurrant-tasting fruit.

## Egypt

Egypt certainly produces wines, but they are nothing to shout about. The only halfway decent wine I tasted in Egypt was the red Cleopatra, but given the choice I'd rather have lager or fresh fruit juice which is available in abundance.

75 CL. WINE     PRODUCE OF LEBANON

1980

MARQUE     DEPOSÉE

*Château Musar*
★
GASTON HOCHAR
PROPRIÉTAIRE VITICULTEUR
IMPORTED BY: CHÂTEAU MUSAR (UK) LIMITED · LONDON
MISE EN BOUTEILLES AU CHÂTEAU          GHAZIR - LIBAN

# OTHER EUROPEAN AREAS

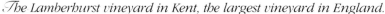

## ❧ ENGLAND ❧

Many people who actually live in Britain are surprised that anyone makes wine in this country – after all, the British *are* notorious for their love of discussing their normally atrocious climate. But surprisingly there is a long history of winemaking in Britain dating back to the Romans, who ordered their troops who were hanging about with nothing better to do to plant some vines. This tradition of planting vines in the country you colonize has been perpetuated by many nations – the French (North Africa), the Portuguese (Madeira and South America), the Spanish (South America), the British (Australia and New Zealand), following the example of those early civilizations.

It's very important not to confuse English and British wine. If it's wine made from grapes grown in English vineyards (the real thing) you want it's the former you should buy. Avoid British wine like the plague. It is cheap imported grape concentrate (like that found in home winemaking kits), brought in from countries like Cyprus and diluted in Britain with British water – it's not in the slightest bit British.

English wine-producers are a hardy lot, coping with inclement weather and adverse finances. Most make wine as a hobby and the number of English vineyards making a profit is only just out of single figures. The majority supplement their income with other farming activities, private incomes or other business activities.

The vast majority of vineyards planted in England (there is just one in Wales) are in the euphemistically termed 'sunny' south of England. In the south-east they are planted on the same chalk seam that crosses under the English Channel to become the chalk hills of Champagne.

In the 20th century's early days of English wine production, growers mainly planted high-yielding Germanic varieties like Müller-Thurgau. But, as elsewhere in the world, Müller-Thurgau did not produce anything of interest, and growers today use a bewildering number of different varieties, most of which are white, Germanic-type grapes. The best generally produce lower yields and are made from varieties with distinctive, often spicy characteristics, like Scheurebe, Seyval Blanc, Reichensteiner and Madeleine Angevine. There are even some adventurous winemakers (Bernard Theobald, for example) making reasonably successful Pinot Noir, a difficult variety at the best of times. The best English wine today is white, light, slightly off-dry and should be drunk when it is still fresh and young.

England suffers from the stigma that Europe's Common

*The Lamberhurst vineyard in Kent, the largest vineyard in England.*

---

176

---

Market refuses to classify her wines as anything higher than Table Wine, even though the best are better than many French *appellation contrôlée* wines. If this situation was to change there might be more incentive for people to make wine other than just as a hobby.

| RECOMMENDED PRODUCERS | | |
|---|---|---|
| Adgestone | Chilford Hundred | New Hall |
| Ascot | Chilsdown | Penshurst |
| Astley | Chiltern Valley | Pilton Manor |
| Barton Manor | Ditchling | Pulham |
| Beaulieu | Elmham Park | Rock Lodge |
| Berwick Glebe | Felsted | St George's |
| Biddenden | Hambledon | Staplecombe |
| Breaky Bottom | Ightham | Tenterden |
| Bruisyard | Joyous Garde | Three Choirs |
| Carr Taylor | Kents Green | Westbury |
| Cavendish | Lamberhurst | Wootton |
| Manor | Loddswell | Wraxall |
| Chalkhill | Moorlynch | Yearlstone |

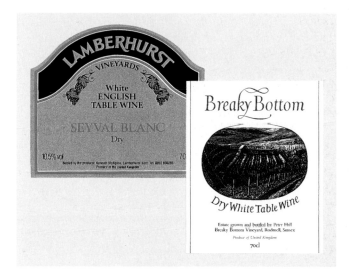

## ∽ AUSTRIA ∾

The wine produced in Austria so far this century has not set the world alight. It was normally similar to the lesser German wines, with a few exceptions from small growers making high quality wines in the Beerenauslese style (see page 114). Most of the wine, however, was overproduced and indifferent. But in 1985 the Austrian wine scandal broke in the world's press when it was discovered that a small number of fraudulent growers had been illegally adding diethylene glycol to their wines to sweeten them. Sales plummeted overnight and any Austrian wine (even the majority that had not been 'doctored') became unsaleable. The Austrian wine industry was forced to mend its ways overnight, and gradually started to take radical steps to improve matters. Lower-yielding higher quality varieties like Chardonnay have been planted, and some growers have even invested in small oak barrels for barrel-ageing. Over the next five years it will be very interesting to see what comes out of Austria – it has the opportunity of becoming a wine producer which is worth taking seriously.

## ∽ SWITZERLAND ∾

The Swiss are noted for many things – ski-ing, fondues, numbered bank accounts, tidiness, Zürich gnomes and Lake Geneva are among them. Wine does not feature in this list, although Switzerland produces a lot of it, most of which is consumed by the Swiss and the tourists. The wines, which are mostly white although there is some red, are light and pleasant, but nothing stunning is produced. The most widely planted grape variety is the white Chasselas which produces a more attractive wine than in France, where it is only used for very ordinary table wines.

*Vineyards above Sion, in Valais in Switzerland. This is the most intensively cultivated of Switzerland's cantons as well as being the oldest and most famous*

# FORTIFIED WINES

ORTIFIED WINES don't have castellated walls – they have alcohol added at some stage during their making. This results in a wine which is much higher in alcohol than table wine, with between 15 to 20 per cent by volume, as opposed to the normal 10 to 14 per cent for table wine. Most of them are sweet, with the exceptions of some sherry and madeira.

Apart from port and sherry, the two best known fortified wines, there is madeira, Moscatel de Setúbal, Muscat de Beaumes de Venise, Muscat de Rivesaltes, Muscat de Frontignan, Ratafia de Champagne, Pineau des Charentes, malaga, and the fabulous liqueur Muscats from Australia.

## ≈ PORT ≈

### The Douro Valley

This is one of my favourite wine-producing areas in the world. The now-lethargic river Douro is its centre, and the steep, terraced vineyards slope upwards from its banks. The atmosphere is calm and silent, the air crystal-clear and there isn't a tourist in sight. The vineyards are occasionally interrupted by the old port lodges, often whitewashed and many with the name of the quinta picked out in different coloured tiles on their roofs. For most of the year they are tranquil, but at harvest time they burst into frenzied and noisy activity. Not only is the region hauntingly beautiful, the product is delicious too.

### History

There are many legends as to how port, as we know it today, was invented, although the following is one of the most popular. During the 17th century Britain was at war with France and William of Orange banned the imports of all French wines. Portuguese wines took their place and, in

order to stabilize the wine during its long sea journey, judicious amounts of brandy were added. The British palate, used to the flavour of claret rather than the harsh, tannic flavour of the Douro red wines were delighted with the sweet and fortifying result.

### Winemaking – the old and the new

Brandy is no longer added during shipment. Instead grape spirit is added during the fermentation, when the required alcohol level is achieved (generally around 7 per cent, although this differs from year to year). Back at the pressing stage, many companies still 'tread' their grapes in the traditional way in large, open concrete shallow vats known as *lagares*. Others combine this method with a method known as autovinification, a process whereby the natural carbonic gas given off during fermentation pushes the fermenting juice over the 'cap' of skins, ensuring maximum colour and fruit extraction. After fermentation, which takes place up in the Douro near the vineyards, the port is transported down the twisting valley to Oporto by huge road tankers. Before the river Douro was dammed the wine was taken down the valley in barrels aboard traditional flat-bottomed sailing boats known as *barco rabelos*. After its lengthy journey, the port is aged in 'lodges' in Vila Nova de Gaia, on the left bank of the Douro facing the city of Oporto, although since 1986 this has not been mandatory. The amount of time it is aged and the size of the barrels depends on the style of port being made.

### Grape varieties and vineyards

All the vineyards in the steep granite and schist vineyards of the Douro Valley are classified from A down to F, with A as the best classification and grapes from these vineyards achieving the highest price.

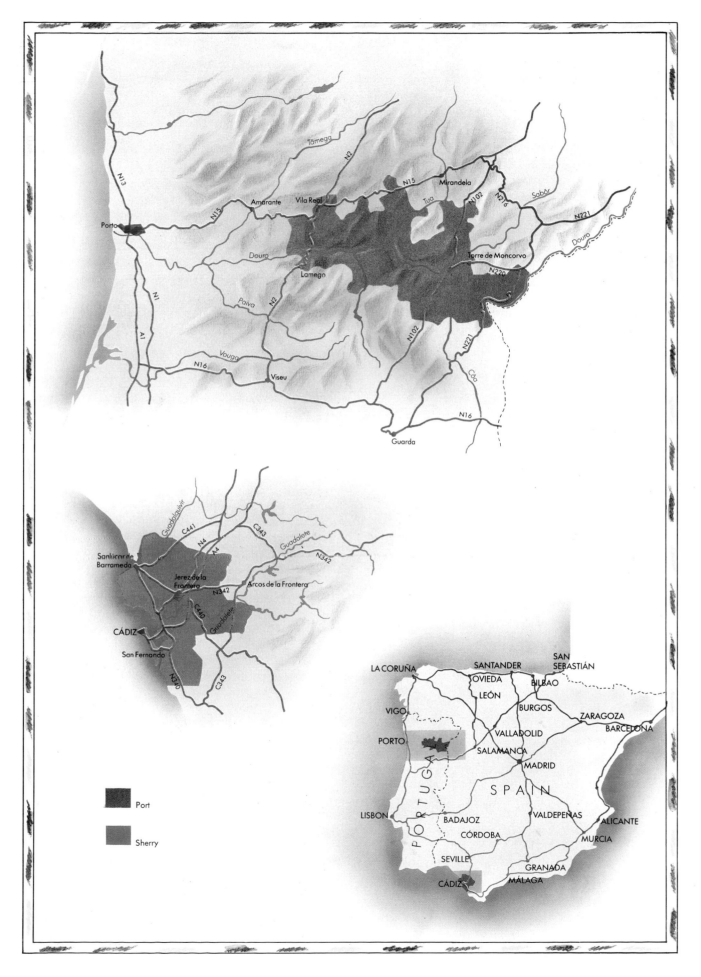

Tâmega
N2
N15
Mirandela
Amarante
Vila Real
N102
N16
Sabôr
N13
N15
Porto
N221
Douro
Torre de Moncorvo
Lamego
N220
Paiva
N2
N1
N102
N221
A1
Vouga
Côa
N16
Viseu
N16
Guarda

Guadalquivir
C441
C343
N4
Guadalete
Sanlúcar de
Barrameda
A4
N342
Jerez de la
Frontera
Arcos de la Frontera
N342
CÁDIZ
C440
Guadalete
San Fernando
N340
C343

LA CORUÑA
SANTANDER
SAN
SEBASTIÁN
OVIEDA
BILBAO
LEÓN
VIGO
BURGOS
ZARAGOZA
BARCELONA
VALLADOLID
PORTO
SALAMANCA
MADRID
P O R T U G A L
S P A I N
LISBON
BADAJOZ
VALDEPEÑAS
ALICANTE
CÓRDOBA
MURCIA
SEVILLE
GRANADA
CÁDIZ
MÁLAGA

Port

Sherry

*The old and new terraces in the Rio Torto Valley are separated by a track used by the pickers.*

There are 48 permitted grape varieties, white grapes as well as black. Those rated as the best are Touriga Nacional, Touriga Francesa, Tinta Barroca, Tinta Cão, Tinta Francisca and Tintoa Roriz.

### Different styles of port

Port is far more versatile than many people think. In France it's drunk as an aperitif, and in Portugal sometimes right through the meal.

There are many different styles of port available to the consumer, so many that even the retailers who sell port are often not clear about how they differ. The following itemizes the different types, describing the styles and telling you which need to be decanted.

**White Port**   This tastes like a more powerful version of dry white vermouth. It's great as an aperitif, and can be served either on its own, on the rocks or with tonic. It's also good with an entrée, its flavour cutting through the oiliness of pâtés, terrines and mousses, and in Portugal it's often added to clear consommés.

**Ruby Port**   Ruby port is at the bottom of the port quality scale, and is a blend of various different vintages matured in large wooden barrels. The older, better quality, rubies are known as Fine Old Ruby Ports. Once open ruby port will keep fresh from six to nine months and it can be drunk as an aperitif, with gamey dishes or cheese. It can also be drunk after a meal if you want something lighter than vintage port.

**Tawny Port**   This is the same colour as its name indicates, having a browny-orange hue. This colour can be because either white grapes have been added, or the wine has been matured for years in small wooden casks – being transferred from one cask to another, oxidation turns the wine a chestnut colour. Most tawny port is the blend of several vintages but you can find dated tawnies, like 'ten year old' and 'twenty year old', indicating the age of the youngest wine in the blend. Dated tawnies have a rich, nutty flavour of ripe cherries and make ideal aperitifs or cheese wines. They are nothing like as heavy as vintage port and don't need decanting.

**Vintage Character Port**   This is a term which may well disappear in the next few years because it is misleading, playing on the word 'vintage'. The quality varies from the cheapest ruby ports to a style of wine not dissimilar to vintage port but without the quality. It can be drunk at any time during a meal because it is relatively light and need not be decanted. Once open, the bottle can be kept for many weeks.

**Late-Bottled Vintage (LBV) Port**   This is like a mini-vintage port and shows the year of the harvest on the label. They are often made in years deemed not quite exceptional enough to be 'declared' as vintage port years and are aged in cask, so do not need to be decanted. The style is heavier than vintage character and they are normally drunk after a meal. They can be kept for several months after the cork has been drawn and can be outstanding value.

**Crusted or Crusting Port**   These are in a similar style to vintage port but are not from a specific year. Like vintage port they will throw a deposit in the bottle so it's essential to decant them. Crusted ports can age well in the bottle and are a similar weight to or heavier than LBV Ports. They are not so often seen today and can be good value, but they will not keep once opened.

**Vintage Port**   Unlike most other wines (but like Champagne), vintage port is not made every year. It's only when the shippers think the quality of a particular vintage is good enough that they will 'declare' a vintage, and even

*Treading grapes for port can be great fun! The treaders from Levandeira Farm whose wine is bought by Taylors, certainly think so.*

that does not happen until two years after the vintage. On average vintage port is only declared three or four times a decade. Bottled before the wine is two years old (unlike tawny port), vintage port develops in the bottle and throws a sediment so it must be decanted. This is the most full-bodied and powerful style of port, which takes at least 15 years to mature. Because it's made from the best quality grapes, and only in outstanding years, it is the most expensive port around. Vintage port deteriorates quite rapidly after being decanted – that's the reason the decanter keeps circulating round the table and that port always gets the blame for hangovers!

**Single Quinta Vintage Port**   Most port is a blend of wines from many different vineyards. But single quinta vintage ports come from a single estate (or *quinta*) and are the product of just one year. These tend to be made in vintages when a vintage is not declared, and are often great value. Recent vintages include 1978, 1974, 1972 and 1969, and these wines need to be decanted and drunk at one sitting.

### Decanting port

First you need presence of mind – don't just rush out and buy a bottle the same day you intend to drink it. The bottle needs to have been standing up for a few days before being opened (but don't keep it for longer periods standing up – the cork will dry out). Gently withdraw the cork, remembering that port corks are longer than most, so you'll need a really good corkscrew like a 'Screwpull'. Have a candle (or a torch) ready and place it so that when you hold the bottle horizontally the light will shine through from underneath. Take the decanter in your left hand and the bottle in your right (the other way round if you are left-handed), and start tilting the bottle gently. It's important to keep the label (or white paint splash) on the top, as the bottle will have been stored this way up for its entire life and the sediment will have settled on the opposite side. Pour the wine slowly into the decanter and when, with the aid of the torch or candle, you see the dark sediment reaching the bottle's shoulder it's time to stop. A small amount of port will remain in the bottle together

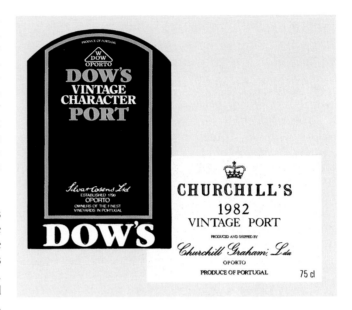

with the sediment and if you want you can pour that through muslin or a clean coffee filter into a glass and have an extra glass yourself. Although the purists would disagree, this technique can also be used for decanting a shaken-up bottle of port – I find it makes little difference and it's preferable to sieving vintage port with your teeth!

---

### DECLARED VINTAGES

All vintages are good by their very nature – a vintage port is only declared if the shipper considers the quality is above average. However, it's up to the individual shipper to determine what he thinks of the quality, so in many vintages not all the shippers will declare a vintage.

1985  Very good – declared by most shippers
1983  Very good – declared by about half the important shippers
1982  Good to very good – declared by about half the important shippers
1980  Quite light – declared by most shippers
1977  Exceptional – declared by virtually every shipper
1975  Quite light – declared by most shippers
1970  Very good – declared by most shippers
1967  Good – only major shipper to declare was Cockburn
1966  Very good – declared by most shippers
1963  Exceptional – declared by virtually every shipper
1960  Very good – declared by most shippers
1958  Good – declared by a few shippers
1955  Exceptional – declared by most shippers
1950  Very good – declared by most shippers
1945  Exceptional – declared by most shippers

---

### RECOMMENDED PRODUCERS AND SHIPPERS

| | | |
|---|---|---|
| Càlem | Graham | Ramos Pinto |
| Churchill | Guimaraens | Rebello Valente |
| Cockburn | Martinez | Royal Oporto |
| Croft | Niepoort | Sandeman |
| Delaforce | Offley Forrester | Santos Junior |
| Dow | Poças | Smith |
| Ferreira | Quarles Harris | Woodhouse |
| Fonseca | Quinta do Côtto | Taylor |
| Gould Campbell | Quinta do Noval | Warre |

*The famous barcos rabelos moored at Vila Nova de Gaia on the river Douro. Before the river was dammed the wine was taken down the valley aboard these.*

## ∽ SHERRY ∽

Sherry is one of the most misused terms in the world. While the name for this fortified wine is actually derived from the name of the region in southern Spain where it originated, Jerez, sherry does not enjoy the same protection of its name that some other wines like Champagne have established. All sorts of other 'mock' sherries exist including Cyprus, South African and so called 'British' Sherry, the latter being a product that is made from imported grape concentrate and diluted with water in Britain. And even real sherry, from its region of origination, is normally a poor shadow of the real thing, with enormous quantities of mediocre wine being produced. But all these pretenders to the sherry throne are a far cry from the real McCoy, the wonderful authentic sherries that are one of the world's best value top-quality wines. To have an idea of what sherry can be like at its magnificent best, find a bottle or two of the rare Almacenista sherries, principally exported by the firm of Emilio Lustau. These are sherries bottled from a single cask which has been bought from a small producer. They are the best quality sherries available as well as the most individual sherries that money can buy – and even so, compared to other regions of the world's top wines they are remarkably inexpensive.

### History
Sherry's fame was founded in Britain when Sir Francis Drake returned from 'singeing the King of Spain's beard' (destroying the Spanish fleet in their port by setting fire to the ships) with a ship full of barrels of sherry. But sherry is thought to go back in history far beyond that, to the Moors who invented the alembic still with which they manufactured the spirit to add to their wine.

### Vineyards and grape varieties
The sherry-producing vineyards are located around the port of Cádiz, in the north-west corner of the province with the same name. The largest and best known of the sub-regions is Jerez de la Frontera, surrounding the town of Jerez. Sanlúcar de Barrameda and Puerto de Santa Maria are the next best known. Most sherries, however, are blended wines from the different regions.

Many of the region's vineyards share the same type of soil, known as *albariza*, white in colour on the surface and rich in lime. Albariza is favoured for the best sherry vineyards because of its ability to retain water, an extremely important factor in an area prone to drought.

Sherry's main grape variety is Palomino (responsible for 93 per cent of the wine produced), thought to have originated in the region of Andalucia. The Palomino grape produces the ideal base wine from which to make sherry, a fairly light and uninteresting wine before it is fortified, and one low in acidity. Although this grape is grown elsewhere, sherry is by far the most successful wine it produces and it flourishes in the region's lime-rich soil. The only other sherry grapes are Pedro Ximénez (sometimes used on its own to make a very dark sweet wine) and Moscatel Fino.

*The Sandeman Vineyard in Jerez de la Frontera; although more famous for its port, this firm also produces good sherries.*

### The production of sherry
Because of the southerly location of Jerez, the harvest begins early in September. Traditionally harvesting and pressing was done by hand and foot, but machines are now taking over, to a lesser extent in the vineyards, but predominantly in the pressing process. Mechanical presses are now in common use throughout the region. The heat during the vintage is intense, and many of the larger companies have invested in temperature-controlled fermentation vats, although the smaller companies still ferment their wines in barrel.

After fermentation the wine is transferred into sherry 'butts' – 500 litre (110 gallon) oak casks which are sent to Scotland for maturing whisky when they have been used. These are then filled four fifths full, so that the wine can oxidize – an essential part of the process.

*Wooden casks of sherry, maturing in the cellars of Antonio Barbadillo in Sanlúcar.*

RECOMMENDED
PRODUCERS

Barbadillo
Bobadilla
Luis Caballero
Croft
Delgado Zuleta
Pedro Domecq
Diez Mérito
 (Don Zoilo)
Garvey
Gonzalez Byass
Harveys
Hidalgo
Emilio Lustau (esp. for
 Almacenista)
Osborne
Sandeman
Valdespino
Williams & Humbert

**Flor – the special sherry ingredient** Top class fino sherries owe their existence to the development of *flor* (meaning 'flower'), an off-white 'skin' which is a type of yeast that appears on the surface of the wine in the barrel. The yeast occurs naturally, and recently it has been established that it is present only on Palomino grapes grown in certain vineyard areas and fortified in a certain way. The eventual style of the sherry is largely determined by whether or not a butt develops *flor*. In the past it was a total mystery when and if this would happen at all, although the reasons are now known.

One of the winemaker's jobs, and one that is unique in sherry, is to classify the wines depending on which develop *flor*, and how they progress. Those that have none or little are fortified immediately, and the others carefully watched and reclassified to decide their eventual destiny. A complex system of coding is used, marked by chalk on the barrels, and there is even a code for embryo sherry that has turned to vinegar!

Unlike port, sherries do not carry a vintage. Instead, they are blended using the solera system. Essentially this consists of a number of barrels of sherry of different ages. When bottling is required a proportion of wine is drawn from the oldest barrel. This is then topped up by the same quantity from the next oldest barrel, which itself is topped up from the third oldest barrel, and so on. The *flor* in the older barrels is kept alive by the constant influx of younger wines, and the youngest barrel in the chain is topped up with very young, newly made sherry. Traditionally it was said that the barrels were stacked on top of each other, with the youngest wine at the top. However, this is not the case and generally the wines are syphoned off and moved wherever required.

*Near Jerez, a donkey aids in the digging of horizontal furrows between the vines, in order to catch any winter rain.*

*Pouring a 40 year old Manzanilla Pasada sherry prior to tasting in one of the bodegas of Antonio Barbadillo in Sanlúcar. Barbadillo is the leading Manzanilla shipper.*

### The different styles of sherry

**Fino**  This is the driest style of sherry, wines that are pale in colour and extremely dry. Those from the delightful fishing village of Sanlúcar de Barameda are known as Manzanillas and are said to have a salty taste due to the strong Atlantic winds that prevail in this area. This sounds unlikely until you taste them, and then you can see the resemblance. Fino sherries have been covered in *flor* when in barrel, hence their extreme dryness. Manzanilla Pasada is a fino that has been left to age longer than most fino sherries and so develops slightly more richness and colour.

**Palo Cortado**  These are wines originally classified as fino which have developed more body as they age, combining the bone-dry tanginess of fino with a rich nuttiness which can give the impression that they are slightly off-dry. These wines tend to happen rather than be deliberately created and vary enormously in style between different *bodegas*.

**Amontillado**  These are fino wines left to mature for much longer in cask than normal until the *flor* dies, normally after about six years. During the maturation period they develop a deep golden, orangey colour, the sharp edges of the acidity are softened and the fruit becomes richer. True amontillado sherries should be dry and it's only commercial exported versions that are medium sweet.

**Oloroso**  These sherries do not develop *flor*, being heavily fortified before being left to mature in barrel where they slowly oxidize. Golden-brown in colour, they have a richness reminiscent of caramelized brown sugar but are still totally dry. Most commercial olorosos are sweetened before sale, although much of the apparent sweetness from a real oloroso will come from the richness of the wine itself.

**Cream**  This is not an authentic type of sherry at all, and was developed exclusively for the export markets of the world, in particular Britain. It's a mass-produced sickly sweet drink and, although it does come from the region, the locals would not recognize it. However, there are some delicious, intensely sweet, rare wines produced from the Pedro Ximenez and Moscatel grapes which are authentic.

## OTHER FORTIFIED WINES

### Madeira

Madeira comes from the Portuguese island of the same name, lying in the Atlantic ocean to the west of Morocco. The terrain is spectacular with its steep, terraced vineyards and its lush carpet of verdant vegetation produced by the warm, wet climate.

The island became part of Portugal as long ago as 1418, and has been producing wine for over 500 years.

Madeira's wine is produced in four styles, ranging from light and very dry to lusciously rich and sweet: Sercial, Verdelho, Bual, and Malmsey. All of which are delicious, depending on how much sweetness you want. There are various terms for the age of a madeira: Reserve (5+ years old), Special Reserve (10+ years old), Extra Reserve (15+ years old) and Vintage (single year, 22+ years old).

Making Madeira involves one process which is unique in winemaking – baking the wine. Once the fermentation is finished the wine is placed in warm rooms called *estufas* (like ovens), where the temperature is slowly increased to 45°C (113°F), baking the wine. This process was invented in the 17th century when it was discovered that madeira wine being exported in the holds of ships was warmed to a high temperature during the journey, and that this actually improved the flavour! Madeira also uses the solera system (as in sherry) and a vintage madeira is very rare.

| RECOMMENDED PRODUCERS | |
|---|---|
| Blandy | Power Drury |
| Cossart Gordon | Rutherford & Miles |
| Leacock | |

## Málaga & Montilla

Apart from sherry, malaga is probably Spain's best known (though seldom seen) fortified wine. The region is part of Spain's tourist trap, Costa del Sol, about 120 kilometres (74 miles) north-east of Gibraltar. This delicious sweet, raisiny wine is not nearly as popular now as it was over 100 years ago, before phylloxera struck the region in 1876, but what that means is that today's wine-drinkers are getting a bargain! Málaga ranges in style from fairly light, smooth wines to very heavy, dark liquids.

| RECOMMENDED PRODUCERS – MALAGA | |
|---|---|
| Scholtz Hermanos | Larios |

Almost due north, inland of Málaga, is Montilla, and although many of its wines are not fortified, because the grapes achieve very high sugar levels due to the intense heat of the region, their style is similar, although not as refined, as that of sherry. Montilla can be a good value alternative to sherry.

| RECOMMENDED PRODUCERS – MONTILLA | |
|---|---|
| Alvear | Gracia Hermanos |
| Carbonell | |

## Moscatel de Setúbal

Moscatel de Setúbal is produced in Portugal's Setúbal Peninsula, and the vast majority of the production is made by just one company, José-Maria da Fonseca, although some is also made by the sister company, João Pires. Moscatel de Setúbal is a deep-coloured, rich, raisiny wine which comes in two basic styles – the traditional, very

*A typical Malmsey Vineyard on the north side of Madeira at São Vincente, where the sweet Malmsey style of Madeira is produced. The small twig windbrakers which can be seen are used to keep the salty sea spray from the grapes.*

*Tiled rooftops at Beaumes de Venise where the sticky sweet fortified Muscat de Beaumes de Venise wine comes from.*

raisiny, punchy version, and the modern, smoother, more velvety but equally delicious version. This very alcoholic nectar, often known simply as Setúbal, can age very well and 20-year-old blends can quite often be found for relatively little money.

### French fortified Muscats

The three main wines in this category all come from the southern part of France. Muscat de Beaumes de Venise has become fashionable relatively recently. It is a quality wine from the Southern Rhône, gloriously sticky and is delicious with strawberries, raspberries and essential with Christmas pudding. Muscat de Rivesaltes and Muscat de Frontignan come from further west in Languedoc-Roussillon. Both are very sweet and raisiny but lack the finesse of a good Beaumes de Venise.

### Pineau des Charentes

This is a lightly sweet wine fortified with inferior brandy produced in the Charentes area north of Bordeaux, famous for its Cognac. I think it a very unpleasant, coarse drink, although it is very popular in France.

### Australian Liqueur Muscats

The production of these wines is a tradition in Australia. They range in quality from the gruesome to the awesomely delicious. The best ones (Brown Brothers' Victorian Muscat is a good example) are intensely sweet and raisiny, with a very deep brown colour. These are highly recommended.

# QUESTION TIME

*T*his quick reference section answers some of the more commonly asked questions about wine. Each answer is a quick précis of what you'll find in the relevant sections in the book.

### ∾ 1. GRAPES ∾

**Q.** What is a noble grape variety?

**A.** Noble grapes are those rated as the best quality *vitis vinifera* grapes (see section on grape varieties). They include grapes like the favourites Chardonnay and Cabernet Sauvignon.

**Q.** What's the difference between Muscat and Muscadet?

**A.** Muscat is a very aromatic grape that generally makes sweet or off-dry wines, whereas Muscadet is a grape grown in France's Loire Valley, which makes a crisp dry white wine of the same name.

**Q.** What is a varietal wine?

**A.** One made from a single grape variety.

**Q.** What are botrytized grapes or grapes affected with noble rot?

**A.** These are grapes that, to the untrained eye, appear totally rotten and useless. Left on the vines long after normal grapes have been harvested, they become infected with a rot known as *Botrytis cinerea*. The grapes shrivel up and the natural sugar present in the grape becomes very concentrated. These are the grapes that make the great sweet wines of the world like French Sauternes and German Beerenauslese.

**Q.** What colour is the flesh of noble black grapes?

**A.** White. It is the skin that gives a wine its colour.

**Q.** What's the difference between Pouilly-Fumé and Pouilly-Fuissé?

**A.** The former is made from the Sauvignon Blanc grape grown in the Loire; the latter is a burgundy, from the Mâconnais, made from the Chardonnay grape.

### ∾ 2. TASTING TERMS ∾

**Q.** What is a corked wine?

**A.** A wine with a musty smell and a dank, fusty taste. It results from an infection in the cork and has nothing to do with bits of cork floating in the wine.

**Q.** What does 'letting a wine breathe' mean?

**A.** Taking the cork out of the bottle. However, this allows only the top centimetre or so to breathe, so the practice is something of a fallacy. If you want to let it breathe properly pour out half a glassful and swirl it around or decant it.

**Q.** What is a wine's aftertaste?

**A.** The lingering taste left in your mouth after you've swallowed the wine.

**Q.** What is tannin?

**A.** Tannin is a bitter substance, found in the grape's skin, pips and stalks. It also comes from oak barrels used for ageing wines. Tannin is essential if a wine is to age.

**Q.** What does the term 'drying out' mean?

**A.** This is used to describe wines past their best, when the fruit is disappearing rapidly.

**Q.** What do people mean when they say a wine is 'oaky'?

**A.** This means the wine has an aroma and flavour of oak, derived from the barrels in which it is aged. The newer the barrels the stronger the flavour.

**Q.** What is a blind tasting?

**A.** One where the identity of the wines is kept secret.

### ∾ 3. WINE MAKING ∾

**Q.** What is organic wine?

**A.** There is no official definition, but is taken to mean grapes grown without the use of chemical fertilizers or treatments (with the exception of spraying with Bordeaux mixture, a copper sulphate solution).

**Q.** Why is sulphur used in winemaking?

**A.** Sulphur prevents the growth of bacteria and yeasts as well as stopping oxidation during winemaking.

**Q.** Should I send back a bottle with crystals that look like sugar granules in the bottom?

**A.** No, these are tartrate crystals and do not affect the taste of the wine. They form if a wine has suddenly been subjected to extremely low temperatures.

**Q.** What is a fortified wine?

**A.** One to which alcohol (grape spirit) has been added to increase the strength. These include port, sherry and many dessert wines.

## ☙ 4. THE LABEL ☙

Q. How can I tell the alcohol level of a wine?

A. This is generally noted in the bottom corner of the label and is expressed in per cent alcohol by volume. Standard table wine is around 10 per cent, whereas fortified wines are over 15 per cent.

Q. Are vintage wines better than non vintage wines?

A. Not necessarily. Many table wines are designed to be drunk young and do not carry a vintage, nor does some of the best Champagne.

Q. Are the words 'Blanc de Blancs' on the label a sign of quality?

A. No, they simply mean that the wine is white and is made entirely from white grapes.

Q. What do the words 'Blanc de Noirs' mean?

A. White wine made from black grapes.

Q. What's the difference between Trocken and Trockenbeerenauslese?

A. Trocken is a dry German wine, and Trockenbeerenauslese a very sweet one, made from botrytized grapes.

## ☙ 5. GENERAL ☙

Q. How do you decant wine or port?

A. Try to ensure that the bottle has been standing up for a few days before being opened (but don't keep it for longer periods standing up – the cork will dry out). Gently withdraw the cork. Have a candle (or a torch) ready and place it so that when you hold the bottle the light will shine through from underneath. Take the decanter in your left hand and the bottle in your right, and start tilting the bottle gently. It's important to keep the label (or white paint splash) on the top, as the bottle will have been stored this way up for its entire life and the sediment will have settled on the opposite side. Pour the wine slowly into the decanter and when, with the aid of the torch or candle, you see the sediment reaching the bottle's shoulder it's time to stop.

Q. Is there anything you can do if an old wine has been shaken up?

A. Yes, if the sediment is in suspension you can filter it either through fine muslin or through a coffee filter.

Q. Does the size of the glass matter?

A. No, it really depends on how much you want to drink, although a larger glass will help release more of the wine's aroma.

Q. How many glasses do you get to a standard 75 cl bottle?

A. Six average-sized wine glasses. In a restaurant or at a party you can generally count on half a bottle a head.

Q. If a cork breaks does that mean the wine will be bad?

A. No, not necessarily. It can mean the wine has been badly stored, that it was not a good quality cork to start with, or that it was an old cork that had decayed.

*Decanting claret.*

# INDEX

**The publishers would like to thank the following for kind permission to reproduce their photographs:**
Anthony Blake Photo Library: 66, 71, 75, 85 bottom, 97, 99 top, 124, 180 left. Michael Boys Syndication: 44 top, 109, 174. Mike Busselle's Photo Library: 46, 52-3, 73, 87, 92 top, 110, 127. Cephas Picture Library/Nigel Blythe: 8 top, 12, 13 top, 52 left, 56, 119, 121 top, 121 bottom; Mick Rock: 2-3, 4-5, 6, 7, 8 bottom right, 9 top, 10 top and bottom, 11 top, 11 bottom, 13 bottom, 31, 34, 50-1, 58-9, 77 top, 78, 81, 88, 91 top and bottom, 92 bottom, 93, 94 top, 95, 96, 98, 99 bottom, 101, 102, 104-5, 106, 125, 126, 129, 135, 136, 139, 140, 142, 143, 158, 160, 161, 162-3, 163 bottom, 164-5, 165 top, 166, 167, 168 top and bottom, 177, 180 right, 181, 182-3, 184, 185, 187; Rodney Prynne: 173. Patrick Eager: 10 bottom right, 11 centre, 33, 48-9, 61, 63, 68-9, 76-7, 85 top, 88, 94 bottom, 103, 146, 147, 148, 149, 151, 152, 153, 154, 156-7, 157 bottom , 176. Susan Griggs Agency/Gert von Bassewitz: 141; Richard Laird: 9 bottom; Adam Woolfit: 112, 172; Ian Yeomans: 131. Robert Harding Picture Library: 41, 122, 175, 186; David Lomax: 115; Patrick Matthews: 132; Earl Young: 114. The Hutchison Library/Ann Usborne: 144. The Octopus Group Picture Library/Chris Linton: 14, 38; Colin Maler: 65, 67; Duncan McNicol: 43 bottom, 45 top; James Murphy: 42, 43 top, 44 bottom, 45 bottom; Charlie Stebbings: 189. D. C. Williamson, London: 170. Elizabeth Whiting and Associates: 40 top and bottom. Stuart Windsor: 82. Jon Wyand: 8 bottom left, 10 bottom left, 117 top and bottom, 183 bottom.

## Acknowledgements

Maps: Chris Forsey and Irwin Technical
Illustrations: Anne Ormerod and Nicky Kemball
Special Photography (pages 30, 32, 36 and 37): James Murphy